SCOTLAND'S
COMMON RIDINGS

SCOTLAND'S

COMMON RIDINGS

KENNETH R. BOGLE

TEMPUS

Front cover: The Hawick Acting Father, 2002.
(Derek Lunn Photography: www.dereklunn.com)

Frontispiece: The spirit of the Common Riding.
Hawick Cornet Greg McLeod arrives at the
Moor racecourse in 2003. *(Alastair Watson)*

First published 2004

Tempus Publishing Ltd
The Mill, Brimscombe Port
Stroud, Gloucestershire GL5 2QG
www.tempus-publishing.com

British Library Cataloguing in Publication Data.
A catalogue record for this book is available from the British Library.

ISBN 0 7524 2992 2

Typesetting and origination by Tempus Publishing.
Printed and bound in Great Britain.

Contents

Acknowledgements

This book is an updated and revised version of a Ph.D thesis that I wrote as a part-time student at the University of Edinburgh between 1990 and 1997. I am greatly indebted to my supervisors Professor Tony Goodman, Department of History, and Mr John Simpson, Department of Scottish History, who supported my proposal for postgraduate study and who were unfailingly helpful and knowledgeable. It is entirely a coincidence that both men subsequently retired from academic life. I would also like to thank Professor Michael Lynch, Department of Scottish History, for his help in reviewing some of the chapters.

I acknowledge the support of the Carnegie Trust for the Universities in Scotland, without whom the original thesis and subsequent book would not have been written.

The thesis and book were written whilst working with the Department of Education, Lothian Regional Council, and latterly with the Department of Education, The City of Edinburgh Council. I would like to thank many work colleagues for their help and encouragement, and for covering my many absences, both official and furtive. I owe particular thanks to Stuart Campbell, Graham Munn (and his pipes), Dr Bruce Wallace, George Reid, Jackie Henrie, Wendy Laird, Pat Wilson, David Walker, Len Grannum and the late Bill Duncan.

Like all researchers, I am indebted to the staffs of various libraries, museums and archive centres, who answered my enquiries with politeness and professional expertise. In particular, the staff of Wilton Lodge Park Museum, Hawick; Hawick Town Hall; Scottish Borders Library Service; Edinburgh University Library; The National Library of Scotland; The City of Edinburgh Library Service; and the National Archives of Scotland. Special thanks to Hugh Mackay, formerly of Hawick public library, now enjoying retired life.

One of the great pleasures of writing a book of this kind was meeting people whose knowledge of their local riding was, and always will be, vastly superior to my own. In particular, my friend and former teacher Ian Landles, who truly earns the title of 'Mr Hawick', gave me many helpful comments and was unsparing in his encouragement and time. I am also grateful to the late Frank Scott for securing me an elusive ticket to the Hawick Colour Bussing. Walter Elliot and Jack Harper of Selkirk provided very useful comments and advice. I am grateful to my parents, Jim and Grace Bogle, who have seen many Common Ridings between them, and also to my family and friends for their interest and support.

I am, of course, extremely grateful to Tempus Publishing, who agreed to take on the Scottish ridings from far-away Stroud. Extra-special thanks are due to Wendy Tse and Emily Pearce, who guided me through the publishing process with proficiency and great skill.

This book is adorned with some marvellous illustrations, most of which have never appeared in printed form before now. I am very grateful to a number of people who helped me obtain these and who kindly gave me permission to reproduce them in this book: Ian Landles (again); Sheila Noble of Edinburgh University Library; Dorothy Grierson of Pringle of Scotland; the Trustees of the National Library of Scotland; Alastair Watson of the *Southern Reporter*; Michael Mee of the *Hawick News*; and Ian Watson and Peter Kemp of *The Herald*, who kindly supplied the final image in the book. Special thanks are due to Riddell Graham and Amanda Goller of the Scottish Borders Tourist Board; Ian W. Mitchell, who gave me access to the magnificent Clapperton Photographic Collection in Selkirk; Zilla Oddy of Scottish Borders Museum Service, who skilfully co-ordinated my requests across several different centres; and Derek Lunn of Hawick, who cheerfully responded to my last-minute demands with efficiency and good humour. Derek also kindly supplied the striking cover photograph. Thanks guys to all of you! The author and publishers have made every effort to contact the holders of copyright material and we apologise in advance if we have inadvertently infringed copyright.

Two final things. What follows is my own work, interpretations and, in some places, opinions. Any mistakes are mine and the good people mentioned here are entirely blameless. I apologise now for my own fallibility. Lastly, my biggest debt of all is to my wife and friend Alison. Without her encouragement, love and support, this book would not have been written. I dedicate my work to her as a small token of my gratitude.

The Scottish ridings are unique and wonderful things, which mean a great deal to lots of people. I hope that I have done them justice.

Dr Kenneth R. Bogle
Edinburgh 2004

Introduction

Every year, thousands of people in towns and villages across the lowlands and the Borders of Scotland take part in a series of community festivals called the Common Ridings or the Riding of the Marches. These festivals are loosely based on the old custom of a ceremonial procession, often on horseback, around the boundaries or 'marches' of the town lands, the purpose of which was to define the area and check any encroachment on it by neighbouring landowners and others. Some of the ridings can be traced back to the early sixteenth century and can boast an almost uninterrupted history since then. Other events are more recent inventions, generally less than a hundred years old. An equivalent event in England is known as Beating the Bounds.

This book traces the history and development of the Scottish ridings from the sixteenth century to the present day. Clearly, some definition of common land or 'commonty' is required at the outset. At its simplest, common land is land possessed in common by different proprietors. There are several different types of common in Scotland, but this book is primarily concerned with burgh commons. Burghs were established in Scotland from the twelfth century onwards by both the Crown and local barons. Most burghs received extensive territories for the use and support of the inhabitants and these property rights were burgh commons. The uses of the common land are explored more fully in chapter two, but these included the right of certain people to graze cattle or sheep, to cut peat for fuel, and to gather wood, heather and other raw materials. Burghs depended on these privileges for their survival and prosperity, and constant vigilance was needed to secure them. To protect the common from unlawful encroachment from other landowners, the burgh authorities made regular and formal inspections of the boundary lines and markers that defined the limits of their land. Because these boundaries were often very extensive, many participants made the inspection of the marches on horseback.

Burghs across Scotland once rode their marches as a matter of course. In the sixteenth century, ridings took place in Edinburgh, Glasgow, Aberdeen, Stirling and Dundee, and also in smaller towns such as Haddington, Rutherglen, Arbroath and Inverness. Generally, these ridings survived until the eighteenth century when they gradually petered out. Today, only a few towns outside of the Borders continue to hold ridings. Linlithgow Marches Day has taken place annually since at least 1541 although, like many other ridings, it was interrupted in the twentieth century for the two world wars and the General Strike in 1926. Musselburgh Riding of the Marches was first recorded in 1682, since when it has taken place approximately every twenty years (although from 1936 the town has also had an annual Honest Toun Festival). Similarly, Lanark Lanimer Day (or Landmark Day) was first recorded in 1570 and has an almost unbroken history to the present.

Riding of the Marches

every 21 years

OFFICIAL PROGRAMME

1956

PRICE **2/6**

MUSSELBURGH

12TH TO 18TH AUGUST

Opposite: Musselburgh Riding of the Marches is said to have taken place every twenty-one years since it was first recorded in the late seventeenth century. *(Author's collection)*

Right: The Callant and his supporters at Jedburgh in 1964. *(Robert D. Clapperton Photographic Trust)*

However, there is no doubt that the home of the ridings is the Scottish Borders, that region immediately to the north of the Anglo-Scottish frontier. All of the Border towns now stage a summer riding of some kind and these can be divided into two basic types. First, there are the 'genuine' or 'real' Common Ridings, which have a direct line of development from the original Riding of the Marches. It is uncertain which of the Borders ridings is actually the oldest, but Selkirk Common Riding, which now attracts the most riders, has the earliest records, beginning in the early sixteenth century. The first record of Hawick Common Riding is from 1640, although the event is probably older. Langholm Common Riding has been held annually since 1816, although it is known that a less-formal inspection of the marches occurred previously. Finally, Lauder Common Riding can be traced back to the seventeenth century, although the event fell in abeyance in the nineteenth century, only to be revived in 1911 for the coronation of George V.

The second group of Borders ridings has a slightly different emphasis from the original Common Ridings, although they also have an element of the town 'riding-out'. These ridings were instituted in the late nineteenth and twentieth centuries, generally in towns that did not possess common land and therefore had no tradition of riding the marches. These towns have developed ridings based on important events in their history. For instance, Galashiels Braw Lads' Gathering focuses on, amongst other things, the granting of the town's charter. Jedburgh (or 'Jethart') Callants' Festival involves a re-enactment of the Raid of Reidswire (1575), a cross-Border skirmish in which local men played a prominent role. Peebles Beltane Festival revives the tradition of a medieval summer fair and a Riding of the Marches. Invented ridings of this kind usually include visits to important places in the local vicinity. Melrose and Kelso have ceremonies at their local abbeys, now ruined, whilst Coldstream stages a ride to the battlefield of Flodden (1513). All of these ridings copied the older Common Ridings and are sometimes, rather unkindly, described as artificial or 'ersatz' festivals.

There is one general feature of the ridings to mention at the beginning that is so obvious that it could be easily overlooked: namely, that the ridings are a celebration of the ancient partnership between human beings and horses. In his book *The Role of the Horse in Man's Culture*, Harold B. Barclay has written:

> *With the possible exception of the dog, no animal has attracted man more than the horse, and with no other animal has man developed such an intimate relationship. The horse is alert, agile, sleek in form and movement, and possesses sufficient intelligence to respond to man, to trust him and to work with him.*[1]

Since earliest times, men and women have loved horses. They provide their riders with the thrill of speed and power, and they can also be highly affectionate to anyone with enough skill and patience to earn their trust. As E.H. Edwards wrote: 'There is no rapport so deep as that possible between horse and rider.'[2] Horses are not naturally aggressive animals, although human beings have adapted them to use in warfare and on the battlefield. Horses have long been a symbol of authority, wealth and social status, the basic reason being that a mounted person looks down on a pedestrian whilst the latter is forced to look up. It is only very recently that horses have lost most of their economic and social functions and become primarily linked with recreation and leisure. It is significant that the earliest references to the ridings almost always state that the marches were *ridden* (although some people also took part on foot).

This book is interpretative, not encyclopaedic. Its purpose is to trace the development of the ridings from the sixteenth century to the present, drawing out general themes and common features and placing them in their historical context. The ridings are a complex subject, having acquired many different meanings and functions over time, some of which have lapsed or been superseded. For example, in the modern ridings the inspection of the marches, which was the original purpose of the event, now takes place only in a symbolic way. The principal rider may cut a turf to mark the site of a boundary, but riders rarely go around the entire marches as they once did. This book will show how the ridings have evolved in the face of changing social environments and how their ability to adapt has been the key to the ridings' survival. The ridings reflect the society in which they have taken place, having been used to promote many different values and ideals over the centuries. They have survived, and continue to flourish, because they cater for the real needs of individuals and communities. Chapter one provides a detailed introduction and overview of the modern ridings, explaining their main features and the nature of these events. Subsequent chapters trace the history of the ridings from the sixteenth century to the present day.

Studying the Ridings

The literature of the ridings is, paradoxically, both plentiful and sparse. Local writers have written a great deal about individual events, but often this material is highly derivative. On the other hand, because the ridings are very private events and not well known to the outside world, they have attracted little serious attention or academic study.

The principal primary source for the study of the ridings is the records of various burgh councils, such as minute books, court books and treasurers' accounts. In some cases, these have survived from the sixteenth century, providing a fascinating insight into town life in early modern Scotland. The ridings are often mentioned in these records and occasionally there are

We are off to ride the common! Riders at Hawick sing the *Old Song* before the day's ride, pictured in 1965. *(Robert D. Clapperton Photographic Trust)*

details of physical locations of boundaries and the marches. Unfortunately, burgh records of this kind tended to be very repetitive, using the same wording year after year and rarely describing actual events. A slightly different angle on the ridings is provided by the records of various craft guilds, such as the Shoemakers Guild of Selkirk, which provided the backbone of the ridings.

Local newspapers are an important source of information about the ridings. In the Scottish Borders the local press took off in the mid-nineteenth century, with the beginnings of such papers as the *Southern Reporter* (1855), the *Hawick Express* (1870) and the *Hawick News* (1882). In contrast to official burgh records, newspapers often gave very detailed accounts of local ridings. Speeches at various functions were reported word for word and many of the ceremonies were fully described. The local press also gave extensive coverage to various controversies surrounding the ridings and protagonists used the columns of the local press to air their opinions and debate the issues. The later nineteenth century was also a rich period for local historical studies and many of the standard works of British local history were written around this time. Two books of particular relevance to the current study were Robert Craig's and Adam Laing's *The Hawick Tradition of 1514*, which was published in 1898, and Thomas Craig-Brown's *History of Selkirkshire*, which was published in 1886. These books, and many others like them, contain much useful material on the ridings. They are also, incidentally, beautifully manufactured books. Likewise, the annual *Transactions of the Hawick Archaeological Society*, which first appeared in 1856, contains a wealth of information about the history and folklore of the Borders, including material on the ridings.

The ridings have attracted little academic interest, although there is one notable exception in Gwen Kennedy Neville's *The Mother Town. Civic Ritual, Symbol and Experience in the Borders of Scotland*, which was published in New York in 1994. Neville's book, which contains little actual history of the ridings, focuses on Selkirk Common Riding, using it as a model to trace the development of the concept of the town in Western culture. I hope that this book will be seen as a complement to Neville's work. The ridings can be placed in a broader historical context thanks to several academic studies of British popular customs that have appeared since the 1970s. I have listed the most useful of these in the bibliography at the end of this book. Unlike earlier collections of folklore, which merely recorded events, these recent studies have examined the general themes and motives underpinning popular customs. The evidence for popular customs like the ridings is often limited or inadequate because they were regarded as trivial and insignificant. It is only very recently that historians have recognised that the study of popular customs, like that of sports and games, can provide a rare and valuable insight into the individual and collective mentality, thus giving voice to the mass of people who are otherwise historically silent.

1

The Modern Ridings

'This day, we hae done a guid thing!'
– Common Riding phrase

This chapter provides an overview of the modern ridings, but it should begin with a warning. Anyone who attempts to write a general description of the ridings is almost certain to offend local opinion. The modern ridings are complex events, full of variations and special features, and local people like to stress the unique nature of their own event. Someone reading the following description will probably shake his or her head and say: 'But that's not how it's really done!' Nevertheless, whilst recognising local sentiment, the modern ridings follow a broadly similar pattern to each other and it is possible to give a general account of them. Most of this chapter provides an outline of the ridings, drawing parallels between them and highlighting their common features. It explains some of the emotions which the ridings arouse and why they are important. The chapter concludes by examining gender issues and recent controversies over women's involvement in the ridings, which, if nothing else, show the strength of feelings involved in these events.

But before embarking on a description of the modern ridings, what characterises the towns where these events take place? In general, they are small and compact, most having a population of less than 10,000 people, although some are slightly larger at between 12-20,000 people. Many of these towns are rather isolated from the main Scottish centres of population in Edinburgh and Glasgow. The heartland of the ridings is in the Scottish Borders and even now travel in some parts of the region is frustratingly slow. There are no motorways, only a few stretches of dual carriageway and public transport is limited, especially since the late 1960s when the Borders was deprived of a railway link with the rest of the country (although there is endless talk of the line being restored). Partly as a result of their size and isolation, the towns are homogeneous communities, what locals would describe as being 'close-knit'. There are strong kinship connections and locals often stress their links with other families. The feeling is that 'everyone knows, or is related to, everyone else'. Incomers to the towns often have to bear a certain stigma, which they might find very hard to shake off. It is not unknown for people to have lived in a town for many years but still to be labelled as an outsider. In Peebles and other places, the local population divides itself between the 'gutterbluids', the established natives of the town, and the 'stooriefits', who are the resident incomers.

Light industry and tourism now dominate local economies, but towns retain a close link with the land and farming. Many locals have an instinctive feel for the countryside, even if their direct experience of it is only through recreation. Although the towns have greatly expanded in recent years, in part due to commuter pressures from Edinburgh, the countryside remains very accessible in these places, only a few minutes walk away from town centres. This is an important factor in the survival of the ridings because it encourages the ownership of horses, and people can keep horses relatively cheaply and easily. In many cases, the principals in the ridings own their own horses and are already experienced and talented riders. There are numerous stables in the immediate vicinity of the towns and there is plenty of space to ride and exercise in safety. It is not uncommon to see a horse and rider passing through the quieter streets of the Border towns. It is also inexpensive to take riding lessons. Unofficial horse racing or 'flapping' is very popular in the Borders and people sometimes club together to buy shares in a racehorse.

A highly localised patriotism flourishes in the Scottish Borders, which is often validated as a legacy from the days of Anglo-Scottish warfare. Local people are proud of their traditions and take a keen interest in their history. In the towns, there is a strong sense of civic pride, partly created by their isolation, which means that locals feel distinct and superior to others. This has created intense rivalry between the towns, best summarised in the popular saying, 'I'd rather be a lamppost in Hawick than provost of Gala'. The main outlet for these rivalries is on the rugby field and clubs are the focus of great civic pride. It says much for the intensity of local rivalries that a Border League was established over seventy years before the introduction of a national competition. Local derbies are fiercely competitive and teams can compensate for a disappointing season by beating their rivals.

Preparing for the Ridings

This section provides a general description of the modern ridings, starting with the build-up to events. Working behind the scenes are various committees of interested local people, who try to ensure the smooth running of the ridings, such as the Hawick Common Riding Committee or the Selkirk Common Riding Executive. Low-key preparations for the ridings take place throughout the year, but events really begin several weeks beforehand when the leading participants or 'principals' are chosen and made known to the town. Their identities are the cause of much speculation and are an open secret by the time of the official announcement. The most important appointment is the person who will be the symbolic leader of that year's riding and who will have the honour of carrying the town flag on the day itself. In almost all cases, a man will fill this position. The correct nomenclature for these riders is very important and is strictly observed:

Coldstream	The Coldstreamer
Duns	The Duns Reiver
Galashiels	The Braw Lad
Hawick	The Cornet
Jedburgh	The Jethart Callant
Kelso	The Kelso Laddie
Lanark	Lord Cornet
Langholm	The Cornet
Lauder	The Cornet
Melrose	The Melrosian
Musselburgh	The Honest Lad
Peebles	The Cornet
Selkirk	The Royal Burgh Standard Bearer

Each riding has its own principal to lead the event. *From top left clockwise:* Cornets at Peebles, Hawick, Langholm and Lauder. *(Scottish Borders Tourist Board/Scottish Borders Museum and Gallery Service (Selkirk Collection))*

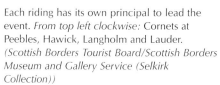

LAWRENCE EWART. — CORNET. — 1930.

The Selkirk Royal Burgh Standard Bearer (left) and the Galashiels Braw Lad and Lass (right). *(Scottish Borders Tourist Board)*

It can be seen that many towns appoint a 'Cornet'. The term was first recorded in the sixteenth century and seems to have been borrowed from the military, a Cornet being a commissioned officer in an army cavalry troop who carried the colours, similar to an ensign in the infantry. As early as 1705, the Hawick town council nominated James Scott 'to be corronett for the yeare'.

There are several different methods by which a Cornet or Standard Bearer is chosen. In some towns, the organising committee is responsible for finding a suitable candidate. Alternatively, previous post holders might make the choice, either by themselves or with a little prompting from behind the scenes. In Hawick, the choice of the Cornet lies solely with the Cornets of the previous two years. More democratically, some towns have a public election. In Langholm, the selection of the Cornet is made at a public meeting and a vote is held if there is more than one candidate. In Musselburgh, where everyone is entitled to a vote, the election of the Honest Lad is said to attract a higher return of votes than a General Election. In all cases, the Standard Bearers and Cornets are expected to have the same personal qualities. They should be young, of good character, a native of their town, preferably born and educated there, and actively involved in their community, perhaps being a member of a local sports club or a youth group. They should also, of course, be at least a competent rider. They must have taken part in several ridings before, ideally since a young age, and have shown an enthusiasm for their festival and the position of principal rider. For example, a profile of Lee Matthews, the Hawick Cornet of 1995, shows the background of a typical principal:

Cornet Lee James Matthews (22), 12c Myreslawgreen, Hawick, is the son of Mr and Mrs Jim Matthews. The Cornet's father, Jim, has been an avid mounted supporter of Hawick Cornets all through his life. The 1995 Cornet is employed as a frameworker with Pringle of Scotland. Lee first followed when he was 11 years old. Educated at Drumlanrig Primary School and Hawick High School, he is a keen sportsman, having played rugby for Hawick PSA, YM and Hawick Harlequins. Lee is a member of Hawick Conservative Club, also Mosstroopers and Burns Clubs and sees his appointment to Cornet as being a boyhood ambition achieved.[1]

In many of the ridings, the principal must also be a bachelor and is expected to remain so for his period 'in office' (possibly for two years or three ridings). Whilst the principal has a female partner to accompany him at some functions, he is, in this sense, married to the town and to the riding, like a priest is married to his church. The principal might receive an offical allowance to help him with his expenses over the coming months, but this is often pitifully inadequate and he might have to show some ability to cover his costs. For this reason, the principal often has connections with the small business community and is often related to local shopkeepers, tradesmen or farmers. There is no doubt that in the past some individuals were excluded from trying to become principal simply because they were unable to afford it. Writing in 1881 but recalling the early nineteenth century, 'Old Hawick Callant' commented that the Cornet: 'was chosen from among the small famers and tredemen's sons, generally of the wealthier classes. It was not everyone who could be Cornet. It was very expensive. It cost Andrew Dickson [the Cornet in 1817] £300 [Scots] to support the honour of his position.'[2]

However, in the modern ridings the office of principal is not very exclusive socially. Many young men (and their families) make great financial sacrifices to become principal, often lumbering themselves with considerable debts for years to come. In fact, money, status and education are far less important than the willingness to show commitment to the riding. What distinguishes many principals is their utter ordinariness. Whilst several of the newer ridings occasionally have difficulties in filling their posts, there is great competition and rivalry in the older Common Ridings to attain the position of principal and it takes several years of dedication and involvement before a young man becomes eligible. For example, Ian Rodgerson, the Selkirk Standard Bearer of 1986, had ridden the marches eighteen times before he was finally chosen.[3] In 2003, Gary Guthrie had waited eleven years before his turn finally came.[4] It is considered a great honour to be appointed principal and the position is much valued and cherished. An important social function of the ridings is that they provide local people with an opportunity to acquire prestige and recognition within the confines of their community.[5] For the principal, the riding is almost certain to be the most memorable day of his young life. He will briefly be the focus of everyone's attention, like a bride on her wedding day. In 1983, Hawick Common Riding took place the day after a General Election. Fulfilling a shrewd election promise, Archie Kirkwood, the new MP, took part in the riding but the day still belonged to the Cornet. The notion of being 'king for a day' is an ancient feature of popular customs like the ridings and is one to which we will return.

The formal selection of the principal takes place several weeks before the riding, either on 'picking night' or at an 'investiture' or a 'sashing' ceremony (where the principal is presented with his sash of office). In Selkirk, the new Standard Bearer is 'chaired out' in a ceremonial procession by the Common Riding Committee and ex-Standard Bearers. In Hawick, the Cornet-elect, having accepted the office, leads a walk around the town and visits the site of the old tollhouses nearest and furthest from his home. The evening ends in a congratulatory reception called a 'smoker'. To help him perform his duties over the coming weeks, the principal is accompanied by some kind of bodyguard or guide. In many cases, his immediate predecessors are appointed as his Right- and Left-Hand Men. In Selkirk, the Standard Bearer is supported by a small group of 'Attendants', and he must have been an Attendant himself for at least one year before he can become Standard Bearer.

The Hawick Cornet and his Right- and Left-Hand Men. *(Ian Landles)*

The Selkirk Standard Bearer and Attendants. *(Robert D. Clapperton Photographic Trust)*

An older, married man often guides the principals, such as the Hawick Acting Father (right), who in this case ought to speak to the Cornet about choosing a top hat. *(Ian Landles)*

The principals at Hawick with their lasses, pictured in 1965, enjoying the Scottish summer. *(Robert D. Clapperton Photographic Trust)*

Above: The Peebles Beltane Queen. *(Scottish Borders Tourist Board)*

Left: Women take great pride in their roles in the ridings. Hawick Cornet's Lass Rosemary Aubrey Wilson and the flag in 1927. *(Scottish Borders Museum and Gallery Service (Hawick Museum Collection))*

In some cases, an older married man accompanies the principal, such as the 'Acting Father' at Hawick, who is charged to keep a friendly paternal eye on the younger spirits.

All of these positions, the most important in the ridings, are occupied by men. There are some roles for women, but generally these are supportive of men. The principal is expected to have a female partner to accompany him at functions like the riding ball. She may be permitted to ride with him around the marches and she may also have some duties of her own, such as bussing the town flag. However, unlike the principal, she is not appointed by the town but by the principal to be 'his lass'. It is rare for a woman to be chosen in her own right, although there are exceptions. In Galashiels, the town selects the Braw Lass to accompany the Braw Lad, and in Musselburgh the Honest Lass is one of the principals in the annual Honest Toun Festival. Both of these events were instituted in the 1930s. Pre-pubescent girls are chosen as Festival Queens in Lanark and in Peebles. But even in these towns, the symbolic leader is always a man. It is very rare, but not entirely unknown, for a woman to carry the town flag. As we will see, one of the criticisms of the ridings is that they reinforce traditional gender roles, putting men in the spotlight and women in the background. It should be stressed here that the women who take any of these roles, whether independent of men or not, have great pride in the positions that they occupy. Like their male counterparts, they consider themselves very honoured to have been chosen.

The principal and his entourage take part in a variety of events in the period leading up to the riding. The principal takes his mounted followers on practice rides, which are known as 'ride-outs'. Most towns have one or two of these, although Hawick has an extended series of rides to neighbouring villages and farms. Ride-outs often incorporate visits to sites of local significance or commemorate historic events. In Duns Reiver's Week, the Reiver and his supporters ride to Duns Law, where a service is held to commemorate the signing of the National Covenant in 1639. Likewise, the Gala Braw Lad and Lass and their supporters ride to the site of the first parish church of Galashiels. Ride-outs can also include a meeting or 'tryst' with the principals of other towns. The Galashiels principals and the Selkirk Standard Bearer meet together at a special 'Spurs Night', which includes a dinner and dance, and the presentation of traditional gifts. Since 1931, the principals from Galashiels and Lauder have had a gathering at Threepwood crossroads, where medallions are exchanged. Similarly, the Jethart Callant meets the Kelso Laddie at the village of Morebattle, roughly halfway between the two towns. Ride-outs may also involve a formal visit to the seats of the local nobility, often to ask permission to ride on their land. The Kelso Laddie and his supporters ride to Floors Castle where the Duke of Roxburghe entertains them. Likewise, the Coldstreamer and his followers visit the Hirsel, the ancestral home of the Earls of Home.

The ride-outs are often impressive spectacles, attracting large numbers of mounted supporters. Some of the rides require a certain stamina and endurance on the part of riders to be completed successfully. The Mosspaul ride at Hawick measures twenty-four miles over rough moorland.[6] Similarly, the Redeswire ride at Jedburgh is a twenty-five-mile return journey from Jedburgh to the Redeswire on the Anglo-Scottish border. Riders who complete some of the rides for the first time are presented with commemorative badges. In Hawick, those who complete the Mosspaul ride are presented with a badge, which bears the image of a horse's head, and are enrolled in a club called the Ancient Order of Mosstroopers, which promotes the Common Riding (the Ancient Order was actually formed in 1920). Badges are also presented to riders who complete the Jedburgh Redeswire Ride for the first time. Ride-outs of this kind are something of an initiation test for those about to take part in the main riding. There are no rules that a rider must have completed a ride-out before he or she can take part in the main event, but there is some social pressure to 'earn your badge'.

The ride-outs set the scene for the main ridings, which are now timed as a matter of convenience. In the Borders, ridings are always held in the same order on alternate weekends to avoid rivalry between towns and to allow principals and others to attend neighbouring events. (There is however some overlap. Melrose and Peebles, and Duns and Jedburgh hold their events in the same week.) The dates of the modern ridings are calculated as follows:

Hawick	Thursday, Friday and Saturday after the first Monday in June
Selkirk	Friday after the second Monday in June
Melrose	Third full week in June
Peebles	Third full week in June
Galashiels	End of June, sometimes the first weekend in July
Jedburgh	Ends second Saturday in July
Duns	First full week in July
Kelso	Middle of July
Langholm	Last Friday in July
Lauder	Ends first Saturday in August
Coldstream	First full week in August

Outside of the Borders, Lanark Lanimer Day is held on the Thursday 'between 6 and 12 of June'. Linlithgow Marches is held on 'the first Tuesday after the second Thursday in June'. Ridings are held in the summer months when in theory it is warmer and drier, thus encouraging more people to take part. Unfortunately, as is well known, the Scottish summer regularly fails to deliver. Bad weather at the ridings is a very old complaint. In 1858, the horse racing at Hawick Common Riding was hit by a sudden thunderstorm, which had disastrous results for Hawick's 'bright-eyed daughters':

> *Gay dresses, which a few minutes ago swept along the turf in graceful folds, were huddled over shoulders … petticoats bedraggled and streaming as if fresh from the washing tub; their extremities, boots and stockings of one clayey hue. Bright ribbons and flowers parted with their tints, which mingled with rosey complexions made sweet faces appear as if tattooed.*[7]

The week of the riding usually begins with a special church service called the Kirking. Here, a blessing is given on the coming event and the principal and his lass are presented with Bibles. The service may be held in the principal's own church (if he has one), but it often takes place on the oldest religious site in the town, even when the buildings are ruined. Peebles Beltane Festival, for example, begins with a united service held amongst the medieval remains of the Old Cross Kirk. The Kirking is a rare religious interlude in the course of the ridings, although it is customary to say a prayer when the wreaths of remembrance are laid at the war memorial and also to say a grace before formal meals. The Kirking is not an old feature of the ridings but was introduced in the later nineteenth century as part of a wider effort to sanitise these unruly events. The Kirking of the Cornet at Hawick was introduced as recently as 1887. The secular nature of the ridings contrasts with the custom of Beating of the Bounds in England, where the bounds of the parish are perambulated and a priest often leads the procession. The Riding of the Marches is likely to have had some religious and perhaps superstitious input before the Scottish Reformation in the 1560s. It is possible that the Reformation altered some of the character of the ridings, removing much of their religious symbolism.

Following the Kirking, various events take place in the week of the riding. In some towns, the riding is part of a more general Civic Week, which might include concerts, sports events and competitions designed to enhance civic awareness. Practice rides may also take place during the week. The principal and his supporters are kept busy at this time. They are expected to undertake a round of visits and engagements to hospitals, old people's homes and schools, where the principal asks the head teacher to give pupils a holiday for the forthcoming riding. A significant feature of the week is a reception for the 'exiles', people born or raised locally who moved away but who have returned for the riding. These people may have been away for many years, but now they are coming back to their 'true home'. Exiles can include people who live in other parts of Scotland and the rest of the United Kingdom and Ireland, but the real exiles are those who come from foreign countries. Every year, individuals and families come from all over the world for the ridings, although most are from the United States of America, Canada, Australia and New Zealand. The presence of the exiles, and that of other people who are normally absent, lend the ridings much of their poignancy and significance. A typical family reunion occurred at the Gala Braw Lad's Gathering in 1994:

> Evidence of the Gathering being a time of reunion was certainly evident. The Chalmers family – brothers Eric and Roy, and sister Mabel – have not met up together since 1957. Younger brother Eric (47) of 3 Elm Grove said: 'Our celebrations have been going on for two weeks', while 58-year old Mabel, from Canada, recalled walking down the street at early Gatherings. However, the most poignant response came from 59-year-old Roy, who comes from New Zealand: 'This is still home to us … and always will be'.[8]

Exiles have a special status in the ridings. Their names are listed in the local press and special songs have been written in their honour. In Langholm, the local band used to meet the last train to arrive before the Common Riding, which was full of local exiles, and to escort them through the town. The band still goes to the site of the station, even though the trains stopped running long ago. In Selkirk, there is a special Colonial Society, made up of Selkirk exiles from across the globe and which has a special flag that is carried in the procession on the Common Riding morning.

For all those associated with the ridings, the period leading up to these events is a time of anticipation and increasing excitement, rather like the approach to Christmas. Towns get much busier than normal, the streets are brightly decorated with coloured flags and bunting, the travelling 'shows' arrive and there is a great deal of activity as people get ready for the big day. Towns have their own permanent colours, such as blue-and-yellow at Hawick or red-and-blue at Selkirk, which are worn proudly by local people during the ridings and which are displayed in shop windows and hung from buildings. Preparations for the ridings have to

An important part of the principals' duties is that they visit local schools and encourage young people to support the ridings, as shown here in Hawick in 1956 (above) and Galashiels in 1963 (below). *(Robert D. Clapperton Photographic Trust)*

Hawick
Common-Riding

Songs and
Ceremonies

* * *

List of Cornets from 1703 to present time

Several towns have their own songbook, full of local songs and poems in praise of the town.
(Author's collection)

be made well in advance and this requires careful foresight and planning. Here we find the traditional role for women in the ridings: to be, in Gwen Kennedy Neville's description, stage managers and organisers of events rather than the principal actors.[9] Women are responsible for making the domestic arrangements that allow the ridings to run smoothly. This traditional division of roles has been criticised as being appallingly old-fashioned. As one irate eighteen-year-old girl complained about Hawick Common Riding in 1985: 'It is totally male-orientated ... The women are expected to be tartan Cindy dolls. They've been pushed into the outskirts to be bystanders, makers of the packed lunches and to pick up the pieces when the men lie drunk in the gutters.'[10] However, there is more here than institutionalised sexism. Often, women are perfectly happy to play their part and stay in the background looking after everyone. Indeed, they can be downright patronising towards their male counterparts. 'Let them have their fun', say some of the women. They know that without their support, the men would not get very far. In response to these criticisms, it might be argued that the various Common Riding Committees and Executives, who actually run the events, are composed largely of groups of men, who are highly-committed and give freely of their time. The ridings would not take place without their hard work.

The approach to the ridings is also a time of music and song. Several towns have local songbooks, containing songs and poems known only to local people. Favourite local songs are sung and heard repeatedly in the course of the ridings, although rarely at other times of the year. For instance, Peebles has its *Beltane Festival Song*; Melrose, *Here's Tae Melrose*; Jedburgh has *Jethart's Here*; and Kelso, *Kelsae, Bonnie Kelsae*. At Selkirk, people are roused in the early morning with the playing of *Hail, Smiling Morn* whilst the town has the signature tune *The Souters o' Selkirk*. It is fair to say that most of the songs have few claims to musical artistry. They are sentimental and full of local patriotism, but inhabitants are as proud of them as they are of the ridings. In the Borders, a few of the songs may derive from the old ballad tradition, although most originated in the late nineteenth century. The riding songs have several general themes, such as the love of the town and the desire to return to it, the beauty of the local countryside, and the reasons why the town is superior. There are also songs that are just plain odd. The Hawick Common Riding favourite *Pawkie Paiterson's Auld Grey Yaud* is about, of all things, a talking horse on its way to the slaughterhouse. The songs are a powerful symbol of unity and of membership. As one former Cornet said: 'Lose the songs and you lose your community'.[11] Songbooks are sold locally and recordings can be bought, but every native claims to know the words of the songs 'by heart', having been taught them in schools or informally at home. Traditional Scottish songs also feature in the ridings, such as *Scot's Wha Hae*, *The Flowers of the Forest* and *Auld Lang Syne*.

Shortly before the riding, a formal proclamation or crying is made that the marches are about to be ridden and that townspeople (or male burgesses) are expected to attend. An honorary official makes the announcement, sometimes by walking through the streets to alert the inhabitants. In Linlithgow Crying of the Marches, the town crier, resplendent in a plumed hat, black velvet jacket and knee breeches, marches along the High Street accompanied by a drummer and an army of schoolchildren. Similarly in Selkirk, the Burgh Officer 'Cries the Burley' by walking around the streets the night before the Common Riding. In some towns, the proclamation is made from a balcony of the town hall. Proclamations of this kind are a relic of the days when news was conveyed mainly by word of mouth. Now wholly symbolic, they state that all burgesses and inhabitants are to attend the riding and anyone who is wilfully absent will be fined. Participants are to take part in their best clothing or apparel and nobody is to molest or hinder the authorities as they go about their business.

Another important moment is the formal presentation of the town flag to the principal, who is instructed to carry it safely around the marches and then return it to the burgh authorities. The principal may also be presented with a special sash as a symbol of office. In Hawick, the Cornet is given the flag at a Colour Bussing ceremony in the town hall, which takes place 'the nicht afore the morn'. Here, the Cornet's Lass ties ribbons on the head of the staff of the flag before it is presented to the Cornet. The tradition of 'bussing' a flag happens in all the ridings and is said to imitate the ancient practice of women decorating their men as a sign of affection and good fortune before they went away to war. In all towns, the flag is central to the local riding. It is the symbol of the town, representing its honour and traditions. The flag is treated at all times with reverence and respect, as if it were a holy relic. In 1994, the Hawick Cornet said: 'After receiving the Banner Blue from the Master of Ceremonies, it was like being given a holy grail – it will not bring me eternal life but it will give me eternal happiness'.[12] Few people are permitted to handle the flag and those who do are made fully aware of their privileged position. Occasionally, outside bodies, such as central and local government (who really should know better) or tourist boards, are guilty of great insensitivity about the ridings. In 1995, the Black Tower in Hawick, an old coaching hotel that incorporated a medieval tower house, was opened as a tourist centre. A logo device was introduced to promote the new attraction, which used the image of the Common Riding flag. The new device was very unpopular with many locals, who argued that their sacred emblem had been cheapened for commercial purposes. Unsuccessful requests were made to the tourist board to have the image redesigned or removed. The incident revealed the gulf that can exist between market-driven organisations and purely local institutions, a division that has become apparent many times in the history of the ridings.

Above: Crying the Burley at Selkirk announces the forthcoming riding. This photograph of the Burgh Officer and the flute band is from 1934. *(Scottish Borders Museum and Gallery Service (Selkirk Collection))*

Below: Nicht afore the morn. The Cornet's walk around Hawick in 1957, where he is accompanied by supporters and eager schoolboys. *(Robert D. Clapperton Photographic Trust)*

Bussing the Flag at Lauder, above, and Kelso, below.

(Above: Robert D. Clapperton Photographic Trust)
(Below: Scottish Borders Tourist Board)

The Colour Bussing at Hawick is one of the great events. The Cornet's Lass ties the ribbons on the flag in 2002, above, and the Gallery looks on in 1965, below.

(Above: Derek Lunn Photography)
(Below: Robert D. Clapperton Photographic Trust)

Common Riding Day

Common Riding Day or Marches Day begins in the very early morning, testifying to the pre-industrial origins of the ridings. A band plays through the older streets to waken the inhabitants, such as the special 'Rouse Parade' by the Selkirk Flute Band, which begins at 4.00 a.m. Langholm Common Riding begins with a race for foxhounds, which is considered to be one of the most important events in the sport. By contrast, Hawick Common Riding begins with the mysterious Snuffing ceremony, where small packets of snuff are fought over by a boisterous crowd. The exchange of snuff was a traditional expression of companionship, like sharing a bottle of whisky. Several Scottish towns retain a municipal snuffbox for use on ceremonial occasions. A Snuffing ceremony also takes place at Annan Common Riding, where the snuffbox is passed around the riders.

Some ridings begin with an official breakfast for the principals and their guests, which may be hosted by the honorary provost. This is an enjoyable occasion when everyone anticipates the day ahead. Speeches are made and songs are sung, the first of many renditions of the day. The breakfast is an official send-off for riders and originated in the days when riders went around the whole boundary and needed to build up their strength for the journey. Throughout the town, there is an almost tangible sense of excitement. It is often remarked that 'everything is different on Common Riding day'. The town is an island out of time, as if the rest of the world has ceased to exist. People busy themselves with last minute preparations and have little concern for anything else. As one report about Lanark Lanimer Day said: 'If people switched on the news, it was not to hear about the international situation. What worried Lanark was the weather forecast.'[13]

At Hawick, the Common Riding begins with the mysterious Snuffing ceremony. Wullie Kennedy prepares the snuff mull in 1907. (*Scottish Borders Museum and Gallery Service (Hawick Museum Collection)*)

Following the breakfast, the stage is set for the day's ride. This usually begins with a formal procession or parade, which may start from the site of the market cross. A musical band playing local tunes heads the procession. Towns have several different types of band and each of these is likely to be involved in the riding at some point. In Selkirk, there is the Silver band, the Pipe band and the Flute band. Likewise, Hawick has a brass Saxhorn band and the Drums and Fifes. Flute bands of this kind are a unique feature of the ridings, although they are often associated with religious extremism. The Common Riding flute bands might have originated as symbols of Protestantism and the British military, but today they do not have any sectarian links. For locals, the flute band is like the clatter of horses' hooves: one of the essential sounds of the ridings. As the dramatist O.H. Mavor ('James Bridie') commented in 1950: 'I used to think fifes sounded like piddling in biscuit tins, but, when they played *Teribus*, they are really spirit-stirring all right.'[14] In the ridings, each band is expected to follow a strict code of performance. In Hawick, the Drums and Fifes play specific tunes in certain streets. In some cases, the procession includes civic dignitaries and their guests, who are chauffeur-driven and who do not take part in the actual ride. In Selkirk, members of the ancient craft guilds such as the Hammermen, Weavers, Fleshers and Merchants, head the procession, marching in pre-determined order with their colourful banners. But in all cases, pride of place is given to the principal and his equestrian guard. The principal is the man of the moment, the local hero representing the honour of the town. His importance is emphasised by his special costume, which includes an embroidered sash of office, coloured rosettes and ribbons and perhaps an old-fashioned top hat, a bowler or a Scottish tam-o'-shanter. In Langholm, the Cornet wears special brown gaiters whilst in Jedburgh the principals wear scarlet riding jackets. The most distinctive uniform of all belongs to the Hawick Cornet, who wears an eighteenth-century-style top hat, a dark green tailcoat, white breeches and a crimson sash.

A cavalcade of mounted supporters follows behind the principals. In 2003, there were estimated to be over 260 horses at Hawick, over 350 horses at Selkirk and 335 horses at Lauder. The age range of the riders is anything from under five to over seventy and for many of them this is the only time of the year when they would consider riding a horse. The enthusiasm for taking part encourages many novice or unskilled riders, 'wha clap their spurs to toe in place of heel'.[15] The atmosphere is cheerful and good-humoured but also dignified. Riders are smartly dressed and are expected to wear specially designed ties, riding-jackets, stout boots and headgear. Brightly coloured or flippant clothes, such as tee-shirts or shorts, are not permitted. Riders are also not allowed to smoke cigarettes during the formal ride. In Hawick, the riders wear sprigs of oak leaves attached to their lapels, perhaps as a symbol of strength and courage.[16] Processions include visiting principals from other towns, who can be recognised by their different coloured rosettes. At Langholm, uniquely, the annual choice of colours is the same as those worn by the winning jockey at the Epsom Derby. In Selkirk, the Standard Bearer gets to choose his own colours as well as those of the town. There is great rivalry between the towns in the Borders, but they dutifully support other ridings. It is an important part of a principal's responsibilities to represent his or her town at other ridings. An eager crowd of townspeople and visitors watch the procession, cheering the riders on and wishing them a safe return. With its flags, horses and stirring music, the procession has a strong military feel about it. Watching the riders as they pass through the town, it is difficult not to think of them going away to war.

The procession is the prelude to the main business of the day: the Riding of the Marches. Leaving the confines of the town for the first time, the riders engage in a fierce gallop called 'the charge' or 'the chase'. This has no real purpose except to release excess energy and excitement. It is a thrilling spectacle. In 1981, one native of Langholm said: 'I've heard television commentators say that the Derby is the greatest horse race in the world, but I say they're folk of very limited experience – they've obviously never seen the Langholm Charge!'[17] Things gradually settle down when riders head into the countryside. The modern ridings are, of course, largely symbolic events. Riders rarely go around the entire boundary as they once did, although the original purpose of the event has not been entirely forgotten.

The principals and riders at Hawick in 1956 (above) and Selkirk in 1968 (below) off to ride the marches. *(Robert D. Clapperton Photographic Trust)*

Above: The Silver Band at Selkirk *(Scottish Borders Tourist Board)*

Below: The standards of the ancient craft guilds are carried at Selkirk, shown here in 1978. *(Robert D. Clapperton Photographic Trust)*

Opposite: Leaving the confines of the town, the Cornet's Chase at Hawick is a spectacular mounted charge into open country. *(Scottish Borders Tourist Board)*

Riders at Hawick Common Riding, young and old.

(Above and left: Scottish Borders Tourist Board. Below: Ian Landles)

Riders at Lauder head into the countryside (above) and Coming in at the Toll in Selkirk. *(Scottish Borders Tourist Board)*

Riders at the Galashiels Braw Lads' Gathering make a spectacular fording of the River Tweed. *(Scottish Borders Tourist Board)*

Above left: Cutting a sod of earth to mark the boundary lines is one of the oldest rituals. The Hawick Cornet carries out this ancient duty in 2003. *(Derek Lunn Photography)*

Above right: In Musselburgh, the Turf Cutter cuts sods of earth at specially designated stations. This photograph shows Robert Fairnie, the finely dressed Turf Cutter in 1956. *(Author's collection)*

Centre: In Hawick, the Cornet dips the staff of the flag in the river to mark a boundary line. *(Scottish Borders Museum and Gallery Service (Hawick Museum Collection))*

Right: The lasses at Hawick pretend to enjoy their curds and cream in 1962. *(Robert D. Clapperton Photographic Trust)*

Riders often visit the furthest extremity of the common, the point furthest from the town, where the principal cuts a sod of earth to mark the limits of the burgh territory. In Musselburgh, turfs are cut at various points on the old boundary line by an official Turf Cutter, who casts the divots with a hearty cry of 'It's a' oor ain'. In Hawick, the Cornet fords to the middle of the river where he dips the staff of the flag in the water to mark the site of a boundary.

During all of the ridings, regular halts are made for refreshments, often an important part of the day's traditions. In Selkirk, riders gather at the Three Brethren cairns and drink various toasts. In Hawick, riders are entertained at St Leonard's farm where they are served dishes of 'curds and cream' or curds and whey, which is known locally as 'soor dook'.[18] They are also given a special cocktail of rum and fresh milk. Likewise, participants at Linlithgow drink 'Blackness milk', fresh milk liberally laced with whisky. These traditions have strong agrarian roots. In many communities, the opening of the commons for spring grazing was marked with the preparation of a 'syllabub', which consisted of the milk of separate cows mixed in a bucket with some form of alcohol. Unusual and distinctive features of this kind help to emphasise the special nature of the day. However, despite the widespread use of alcohol, it would be mistaken to see the ridings as just drunken processions on horseback. Total inebriation is frowned upon and a rider who has lost control through drink will be castigated and left behind in disgrace. Indeed, many of the rides have potentially dangerous moments and cannot be undertaken too lightly. One of the worst accidents occurred in 1958 when the Selkirk Standard Bearer was drowned at the Braw Lads' Gathering when attempting to cross a flood-swollen river. Galloping on hard roads has obvious dangers, particularly for inexperienced riders. Likewise, rain can make the earth slippery and the ride uncomfortable. Riders are regularly thrown off their mounts and occasionally there are broken bones and other injuries.[19] It is also not unknown for horses to be injured and to have to be destroyed.

Once the riding is complete, the riders come back to the towns. In Selkirk, the riders return with a thrilling, high-speed gallop called 'Coming in at the Toll', where they are cheered home by a large crowd. This is followed by the unique ceremony of 'Casting the Colours' in the Market Square, where the Selkirk Standard Bearer and members of the craft guilds take it in turn to cast flags. The last flag to be cast in this way is that of the Selkirk Ex-Servicemen and once it has been lowered there is a two-minute silence, broken only by the playing of *The Liltin'*, a lament for the dead of the battle of Flodden (1513) and of all wars. Even for a non-native, there is no moment quite like this and few events in the ridings can match it for intensity and heightened emotion. As one report had it in 1994:

> *It was the Colonial Society Standard Bearer, Ernie Hume, who gained one of the most rousing receptions. Symbolising just how passionate the casting ceremony can be, the 55-year-old designer – who left Selkirk 30 years ago to set up home in Maryland, USA – was clearly moved by the occasion. Wiping a tear from his eye, he said: 'When I heard them play* The Liltin' *I thought back to when I used to sit on my father's shoulders right here. I can remember him taking his cap off and I saw he was crying. I couldn't understand why then … but I can now.'*[20]

Warfare has had a huge impact on Scottish communities and one of the universal features of the ridings is a visit to the local war memorial, where the principal or Festival Queen lays a wreath of remembrance on behalf of the town. It is often remarked that the principal is about the same age as those listed on the memorial. In Selkirk, the Act of Remembrance takes place before the actual riding but in Hawick the Wreath Laying by the Cornet takes place the day after the main events. Sombre and serious, these ceremonies commemorate all local men and women who have died in wars, but especially those who fell in the two world wars. They reflect the strong feelings of loss experienced through war and the need for constant vigilance against outside threats. However, there is nothing xenophobic about these ceremonies. They honour men and women who gave their lives for the nation as well as the towns.

Selkirk Common Riding concludes with the unique ceremony of Casting the Colours in the Market Square, pictured here in 1898. *(Scottish Borders Museum and Gallery Service (Selkirk Collection))*

All of the ridings incorporate an act of remembrance at the local war memorial. Pictured in 1964, the Lauder Cornet lowers the flag in silent tribute. *(Robert D. Clapperton Photographic Trust)*

Throughout the course of the ridings, local and national loyalties regularly overlap and bolster each other. Local allegiances are in the foreground but the nation is never diminished. The Union flag and the Scottish Saltire are flown from the town hall and public buildings, toasts are drunk to the reigning monarch, and in many cases the playing of the British National Anthem concludes the formal events. Likewise, although many of the ridings commemorate incidents from the Anglo-Scottish wars, including the calamitous Scottish defeat at Flodden, there is little hostility towards England. The ridings are uniquely Scottish but they are not anti-English. The local attitude was summed up recently when a Border farmer was asked if he was Scottish or British. 'First of all, I'm Jethart,' he replied. 'Then I'm a Borderer. Then I'm Scottish. Then I'm British. But it depends where I am and what I'm doing at the time.'[21]

In most ridings, there is an accompanying programme of horse racing, athletics and games. In Selkirk, horse racing is held 'at the Rigg' whilst in Hawick people go 'up the Moor'. There are special ceremonial races for horses that have ridden the marches and others for genuine racehorses only. The Scottish Borders is the heartland of British 'flapping', which means horse racing on unlicensed tracks and not recognised by the Jockey Club, the custodians of the rules of racing. The Common Riding meetings are the highlights of the annual flapping circuit. Townspeople and visitors flock to the courses, whether they have an interest in racing or not. Car boots are opened, picnic hampers produced and the good work of the previous few days is shared. There are also tents and marquees that sell food and drinks. Old friends and families gather together and there is much fun and amusement as normal inhibitions are lowered. This is the real purpose of the day.

Meanwhile, the principal has to complete his official duties and report back to the authorities on the state of the marches. Originally, he would have informed them of any encroachments or other problems, but today he simply reports that all is in good order. In some towns, he has to sign the burgh map. The honorary provost congratulates the principal on his conduct during the riding and presents him with some kind of memento, such as a gold medal. It is also the principal's duty to return the flag to the safe keeping of the burgh authorities. This is a poignant moment, signifying that the principal's riding is now over. Alex McVittie, the Langholm Cornet of 1919, spoke for many: 'To be Cornet gives you an inexplicable feeling, it is very emotional: the handing in of the flag brings tears to your eyes'.[22] In some towns, the flag is then publicly displayed for a short period as a symbol that the riding has been successfully completed. In Hawick, the Cornet handles the flag for the last time when he displays it from the balcony of the town hall. In a short and moving ceremony, the band plays a hymn-like invocation whilst the Cornet lowers the flag and the mounted supporters stand in their stirrups as if to attention. Festivals like the ridings are often said to encapsulate the human lifecycle and at this moment it is difficult not to think of death and loss.

In all towns, the ridings conclude with a 'greeting dinner' in honour of the town, the riding and the principals, and also with the official ball, where dancing continues well into the wee small hours. The ball is an annual social highlight in the town: tickets are hard to come by and are highly prized. The ball is an important opportunity for display: women wear long gowns and men wear dinner suits or kilts. For most people, the ball is a rare opportunity for glamour and to dress up, just as the riding is one of their few chances to ride a horse. Those involved might be thought of as belonging to a temporary aristocracy, arousing feelings of respect, admiration and envy. In Hawick, members of the public pay to watch the Common Riding Ball from a balcony. The ball blends together modern and traditional dancing, including Scottish country dances. There are special dances like the Cornet's Reel, which are reserved for the principals and their partners only. In Hawick, the final dance takes place at sunrise on top of the Moat Hill (a Norman motte and bailey castle), where the principals greet the sunrise and the new day. Some fanciful suggestions have been made to explain this peculiar tradition, such as it being a remnant of the ancient Druids, but as one level-headed Victorian wrote, 'probably the visit is only the outcome of a little hilarity on the part of the Cornet and his lads'.[23]

In Selkirk and Hawick, an important part of the day is a visit to the racecourse. 'Up the Moor' in Hawick, 2003 (above) and 'At the Rig' in Selkirk, c. 1910 (below).

(Above: Author's collection)
(Below: Scottish Borders Museum and Gallery Service (Selkirk Collection))

Horse racing at Hawick Common Riding. These meetings are the showpiece of the annual 'flapping' circuit. *(Scottish Borders Tourist Board)*

The principals dance a reel at the Hawick Common Riding games in 1962. *(Robert D. Clapperton Photographic Trust)*

With its fancy dress and children's parade, Peebles Beltane Festival is the most colourful of the modern ridings. *Top left clockwise:* the straw man, Braveheart Junior, the Beltane Queen and corporate Fat Cat. *(Scottish Borders Tourist Board)*

The Peebles Cornet greets the crowd. *(Scottish Borders Tourist Board)*

The Children's Court at Peebles. *(Scottish Borders Tourist Board)*

The return of the flag to the town authorities is always an emotional occasion, as shown here at Hawick in 2002. *(Alastair Watson)*

The Hawick Common Riding Ball begins with the Grand March led by the principals (above) and dancing the night away (below). *(Derek Lunn Photography)*

In Hawick, Common Riding Friday ends with a visit to the ancient Moat Hill to watch the sunrise. *(Scottish Borders Museum and Gallery Service (Hawick Museum Collection))*

For people not fortunate enough to attend the ball, the evening is spent with friends and family or by visiting the fairground ('the shows'). The fair arrives in town at the beginning of the week and stays for the duration. It has an unusual relationship with the riding: it is an important part of it, but it is also aloof and separate. The fair does not originate locally and it has no local roots. None of the people who work in it are local and they have little knowledge of the riding. Similarly, nobody in the town knows where the fair comes from or where it goes once the riding is finished. Both sides keep their distance and only come together when business transacts. Local people know that a visit to the fair is a sure way to lose their money, but in true festival spirit no one really cares.

The riding may extend over two days, usually Friday and Saturday, but like Christmas Day and Boxing Day, the second day has an air of anticlimax and weariness. By the end of the second day, even the most avid supporter is beginning to wilt. The Sunday at the end of the riding is recovery day. The town is subdued and quiet, nursing a collective hangover. The atmosphere is captured in Robert Murray's witty poem *The Reckoning (The Sunday after the Common Riding)*:

> *Can they be the kirk bells ringin?*
> *Weel, aw canneh gaun the day*   aw – I, gaun – go
> *Aw'm no in the tid for sermons,*   tid – mood
> *So aw'd better bide away.*   bide – stay
> *Eh, but my een ir drumlie,*   drumlie – muddy, discoloured
> *An ma heid is unco sair;*   sair – sore, painful
> *Oo must have been gaun a dinger*   dinger – high spirits
> *Baith at the Haugh and at the Muir.*[24]   baith – both

Friends and visitors gradually disperse and after a few days the town gets back to normal. However, the riding sticks in the memory and is a major topic of conversation for weeks to come. It is extensively reported in local newspapers, which give spreads of photographs of the riding, virtually the same every year. The inevitable comment is made in the newspapers and in the town that it is only fifty-two weeks until the next riding.

This kind of general description of the ridings is inevitably flawed because it captures little of their complexity or the passions that they arouse. It might appear to some observers that the ridings are little more than horses and a picnic: at best, they are a pleasing anachronism, at worst, an excuse for excessive drinking and boorish behaviour. But for those who have grown up with a particular riding and who take part in it every year, they are far more important than this. Locals often say that the ridings are 'of the spirit', that they are not just about spectacle but are to be experienced and that they are 'better felt than telt'. As one Hawick Common Riding poem puts it:

> *It's no' in steeds, it's no' in speeds,*
> *It's something in the heart abiding;*
> *The kindly customs, words and deeds,*
> *It's these that make the Common Riding.*[25]

The ridings are private events, organised by and for local people. In the 1970s, Borders Regional Council published a booklet to promote the ridings to tourists, but warned that, 'these are not events staged for visitors but rather community celebrations for the townspeople and their friends'.[26] Towns make little effort to promote the ridings, apart from some advertising in local newspapers and shop windows. The tourist industry often expresses frustration and regret at this apparent failure. In 1996, a member of the Scottish Borders Tourist Board complained: 'So much more could be done to promote the Common Ridings. It is an opportunity missed as far as tourism is concerned. Borderers are extremely proud of their heritage, but are not willing to get involved in the promotion of it.'[27] The truth, of course, is that the ridings have very little for the tourist industry to exploit. Indeed, casual visitors might wonder what all the fuss was about. The ridings have impressive processions and traditional displays, but generally are short of pageantry and colour. Nothing much has changed since the 1920s when *The Border Magazine* observed: 'Those looking for spectacle and merry-making will be disappointed.'[28] In fact, visitors and non-natives are destined to feel out of place at the ridings. 'The living loyalty of the native is to be seen then moving on every face, and one feels almost an intruder upon the mysteries performed in a sacred place.'[29] This is not to say that visitors are unwelcome but, as Alan Massie has pointed out, they will soon realise that they are joining a family.

Like all families, the ridings have their own patterns of behaviour, their own way of doing things, which can seem strange, perhaps incomprehensible, to others. The Common Riding songs, for instance, are familiar to local people and are powerful expressions of identity and belonging, but are largely unknown outside of the towns. Similarly, locals say that their riding is 'in the blood', resembling the passionate allegiance others may feel towards a football team or a religion. It is an accepted part of life. It is part of them. As *The Border Magazine* correctly observed:

> *You must be bred into it, or caught young and inoculated. The 'cult' of the Common Riding*
> *is of the spirit. Every son or daughter is supremely happy at the Common Riding but a whole*
> *lot of them would be hard pressed to explain why. It's the Common Riding and that is held*
> *to be sufficient.*[30]

What is important here is the local response to the ridings: the way people speak about them and the part that they play in their lives. The riding is a significant reference point for local people, often being one of the most memorable events of the year.

By golly, it's the
Peebles Gollies, source
of much controversy at
the Beltane Festival.
*(Scottish Borders
Museum and Gallery
Service (Tweedale
Museum Collection))*

Local people are very protective of their riding and are suspicious when someone tries to meddle in it. Recently, the underlying traditionalism of the ridings has caused them some problems. They have been accused of insularity and of being out of step with the rest of the world, often lacking in political correctness. But opponents rarely appreciate the strength of local attachment to the ridings and that outside criticism is likely to be counter-productive. This was clearly illustrated in the run-up to Peebles Beltane Festival in 1991, when one woman (a Peebles exile) objected to the use of golliwog costumes in the parade. These, she argued, were unacceptably racist, offering to replace them at her own expense. Predictably, locals ensured that there was a bigger golliwog presence than ever. On the morning of the event, *The Scotsman* reported: 'The 1991 Beltane has seen a "save-the-golly" campaign, specially printed golliwog tee-shirts and a golly song which is already selling like hot-cakes. The Green Tree Hotel has changed its name to the Golliwogs Rest for the Festival.'[31] This could easily have been seen as popular racism when in fact there was no intention of causing offence to anyone, except perhaps the woman who made the original complaint. Instead, this was a reaction against outside interference in a private event, showing the strength of local attachment to small parts of tradition. And besides, when it comes to the ridings, the outside world can think what it wants.

Gender Issues in the Ridings

Nowhere has the depth of feeling towards a riding been so clearly demonstrated than over the issue of women's involvement in Hawick Common Riding. Earlier in this chapter it was shown that women have an ambiguous role in the ridings. They are entitled to participate in most events, but they tend to be on the margins and often play secondary roles. Generally, they occupy a traditional position, to be the supporters of men, dismissed by the critics as 'the makers of the sandwiches'. This is not to say that women are downtrodden and miserable, or that the riding towns are more backward and sexist when compared with other places. Most women look forward to and enjoy the ridings as much as men, for example often spending a lot of money to obtain new dresses to take part in the ball and other functions. Nevertheless, women rarely become principals in their own right and in some cases they are excluded from dinners and other gatherings. In short, the ridings are men's events, and women who take part in them are often treated as honorary men. But in Hawick Common Riding, until very recently, women were not allowed to take part in any of the ceremonies on horseback.

In 1996, Hawick Common Riding was thrust into the national spotlight for its prohibition on women riders, although the issue had been simmering for several years before this. The explanation for the ban on women riders was that it had 'aye been', that they had never taken part on horseback before and that the Common Riding would be damaged, and perhaps destroyed, if this was changed. In fact, a little digging in the archives showed that the ban on women riders was a bogus tradition and that women had taken part on previous occasions. In 1914, a woman called Miss Monteath was recorded as having ridden on the Common Riding Friday, 'astride in a graceful and gallant manner'. Curiously, nobody seems to have objected to her presence and the Cornet even thanked her publicly for her support.[32] Women continued to ride in the 1920s and were only stopped after 1931 when one woman fell off her horse and broke her leg. Subsequently, a few isolated protests were made. In 1955, Jean Mckenzie, a nineteen-year-old dairymaid from Melrose, disguised herself as a boy and rode with the men at one of the ride-outs. Her disguise was eventually uncovered and in some quarters the incident was not treated as a joke. Writing to the *Hawick News*, 'Supporter' described it as a 'mean trick', but on the other hand the Glasgow-based *Daily Record* was highly amused. Under the heading 'Bravo Jaunty Jean!', it was claimed that, 'she has struck a blow for her sex and brought colour to the prosaic modern day'.[33] Women's involvement in the Common Riding attracted occasional interest and some derision, although, like the golliwogs issue in Peebles, this was usually counter-productive. Maverick actions aside, it seems that women had little choice but to passively accept their lot.

The participation of women in the Common Riding really became an issue in 1988 when Mrs Myra Turnbull, a Conservative member of Borders District Council, became Hawick's first female provost. Whilst nobody was against her appointment (at least not publicly), her official role in some Common Riding events created problems, as these events were traditionally for men only. In particular, the provost was expected to chair a gathering in the St Leonard's Hut, a barn outside of Hawick where riders gather at the Common Riding to sing songs and drink together. Those involved say it is the highlight of the day, although like a rugby club dinner, 'it is no place for a lady'. As one man put it in 1990: 'Everybody likes Myra, but the Hut is not the place for her. There has never been a woman in there. No way is there ever going to be. It has aye been like that.'[34] Thus, despite her position, Mrs Turnbull was forced to wait outside the building until the men had finished. The case became something of an annual *cause célèbre* for the national media. Newspaper photographs showed the poor woman clad in her ermine robes of office stuck outside in the rain whilst men pushed past her or barred her way. Unintentionally, Mrs Turnbull had become a martyr for women's rights and a symbol of the need for change. When interviewed, she tended to be rather evasive, preferring to maintain a diplomatic silence and perhaps not willing to rock the boat.

Lady Jane Grosvenor (second from left) and Mrs Myra Turnbull (second from right), Principal Guest and Honorary Provost at Hawick Common Riding in 1994, but not welcome in the Common Riding Hut. *(Ian Landles)*

Inside the Hut, traditional male bonding but no place for a lady. *(Alastair Watson)*

However, her decision in 1994 to invite Lady Jane Grosvenor, Duchess of Roxburghe, to be principal guest at the Common Riding might have been a deliberate act of provocation. (Despite her impeccable aristocratic credentials, Lady Jane was not permitted to ride a horse.) The shabby treatment of Mrs Turnbull highlighted the issue of women's involvement in the Common Riding and led to wider calls for women to be allowed to take part on horseback. Local opinion was divided on the issue. Some women defended the status quo whilst others supported change. In 1994, *The Scotsman* quoted one woman who said: 'You wonder why, when Nelson Mandela is achieving racial equality in South Africa, it's so hard to get sexual equality in Hawick.'[35] Unfortunately, any appeal for change fell on deaf ears. The Common Riding Committee, who were charged to look after the event, stubbornly ignored the issue, perhaps in the hope that it would go away.

Matters finally came to a head in 1996 when two women, Ashley Simpson, a twenty-three-year-old factory packer, and Mandy Graham, a twenty-one-year-old mill-worker, announced that, whatever the consequences, they would take part in the Common Riding as mounted supporters. Both were skilled horsewomen, having worked in livery stables and with hunters and polo ponies. 'We have wanted to support the Cornet all our lives,' they said.[36] Their announcement split the community and a heated debate about women's involvement took place between the 'traditionalists' and the 'reformers'. In a heartfelt speech, one former Cornet dismissed the women as 'suffragists full of vision of their own glory', adding:

> It is not the public or the Press that dictate tradition. Tradition is dictated by what happened in the past. Centuries ago the men of Hawick fought and died to protect their women and children. It was the women who suffered and wept when the warriors didn't return. The answers are all there in tradition, if these co-called reformers care to look. You cannot re-invent history, so you cannot change tradition.[37]

It is important to stress here that the controversy was not a simple division of the sexes. Some women were vehemently opposed to change, arguing that despite the ban on female riders, women already had an important role in the Common Riding. One Cornet's Lass said: 'The leaders of other Common Ridings are envious of how much involvement the Hawick women principals have in the ceremonies. The greatest honour of all is when the Cornet's Lass ties colours to the burgh flag. It's the only festival where women are allowed to touch the flag.'[38] As the 1996 Common Riding approached, tempers became increasingly frayed. The two women were openly vilified and abused, whilst one local councillor who supported their case claimed to have received death threats. Likewise, the 1996 Cornet, speaking on behalf of the Common Riding Committee, claimed: 'We have been verbally attacked and spat at, described as Nazis and chauvinists. None of it is justified.'[39]

In the week preceding the Common Riding, events took a bizarre and rather sinister twist. Following an announcement that the two women would take part in a preliminary ride-out, a local solicitor and member of the Common Riding Committee sought an interim interdict to forbid the women from carrying out their threat. The application asked the sheriff to forbid the two women from 'molesting, annoying and embarrassing' the Cornet, and 'encouraging any others of the female sex to join the cavalcade or any other in the month of June'.[40] The plea fell on unsympathetic ears and the sheriff dismissed claims that the women's presence could lead to public disorder, arguing that the application was wholly lacking in substance and ordering the men should pay costs. Legally, nothing could prevent the women from taking part in the ride-out.

On 1 June 1996, amidst unprecedented rumours that the ride-out would be cancelled, Ashley Simpson and Mandy Graham, plus two other women, showed the courage of their convictions and appeared at the muster-point on horseback, accompanied by their rather unlikely guardian, Norman Pender, a former Scottish rugby prop. Taking up position at the rear of the cavalcade, the women were cheered by some spectators and verbally abused by others.

As the procession made its way out of the town, headed by a distraught Cornet, a group of traditional women formed a human barricade across the street, successfully isolating the four women riders from the main body. Thankfully, despite the depth of feeling and tension of the occasion, there were no arrests or injuries, although police later charged one councillor for threatening behaviour towards the women.

The national and international media had a field day. Events were prominently featured on television news bulletins and the newspapers, giving Hawick more media exposure than it had ever had away from the rugby field. Neighbouring towns happily weighed in at the town's expense. In Peebles Beltane Festival, the fancy dress parade had several locals dressed as the women riders, one of whom bore the message 'Hawick women can't ride, but – it's aye been – they make a good cup of tea!' The two women at the centre of the dispute were invited to be guests of honour at Annan Common Riding. In August, the Common Riding even featured at the Edinburgh Festival Fringe where Innerleithen poet Howard Purdie performed as the Reverend Jeremiah Ayebeen delivering hellfire sermons on the theme 'Rampant Bampotism in Hawick'. There was much truth in the comment that the whole affair would have made a great Ealing Comedy. Both parties retired from the ride-out badly shaken, although the women riders had undoubtedly won the moral victory. Fortunately, as the actual Common Riding came round, common sense prevailed and both sides called a truce. The women agreed not to take part in exchange for a pledge of immediate talks with the Common Riding Committee about women's involvement (a pledge which was later reneged upon). The 1996 Common Riding went ahead as normal, much to everyone's relief, and demonstrating that the event was more important than the issue. As one man said: 'Those girls behaved with great dignity, but they are right not to ride today. Our Common Riding is very special to us and the day belongs to everyone and should not be spoiled. If some things have to change, it should be done with common sense and good will.'[41]

Following the Common Riding, an Association of Lady Riders was formed to fight for women's involvement in the Common Riding. A rival organisation was also set up called The Supporters of Hawick's Customs and Traditions, which pledged to resist change. It included six women on the steering group. In late 1996, a public referendum was held to settle the issue, but the result was inconclusive because of a boycott by the reformers and a low turn-out. Interminable arguments continued to rage until eventually, with both sides on the point of exhaustion, a compromise solution was reached. Women would be allowed to take part in most of the preliminary ride-outs and also to follow the Cornet on the Saturday of the Common Riding. The biggest concession was that they could take part in the most important of the ride-outs to Mosspaul. However, women would not be allowed to follow the Cornet on the Common Riding Friday, the main day of the event, and the singing of the songs and speeches in St Leonard's Hut would remain a male preserve. The Association of Lady Riders subsequently disbanded and it seems unlikely that the agreement, which arguably still left women on the margins, will be challenged in the foreseeable future.

Liberal observers have been baffled by the Hawick case. It is, they say, typical of provincial backwardness and parochialism, a pathetic last stand against progress. How on earth could people be so wrong? It was like those strange women before the First World War who argued against women being given the right to vote. It is worth noting that the Hawick case was not entirely unique. Similar arguments have taken place about the exclusion of women from other popular festivals, such as the Kate Kennedy procession in St Andrews and from the Viking fire festival of Up-Helly-Aa in Shetland. The dispute shows that traditional customs like the ridings, which originated in the days when sex roles were more strictly defined than today, do not always fit comfortably with the standards of modern liberal society. Perhaps the closest parallel was with recent controversies in the Church of England over the ordination of women priests. As Jonathan Petre has observed:

Above: Amidst angry scenes in May 1996, traditionalist women form a human barricade across Hawick High Street to prevent women riders taking part in a ride-out. *(Alastair Watson)*

Right: Lurid headlines followed the ride-out dispute in 1996. *(Hawick News)*

A town divided after shocking ride-out scenes

Cornet Alan Wear—reduced to tears.

PIONEERING LADIES.—Denise Pairman (left) and Mandy Graham prepare for their historic ride to Denholm on Saturday.

Message from Provost Hogg

The following statement was issued yesterday afternoon (Wednesday):—

I am delighted to confirm that agreement has been reached between the Common-Riding Committee and the two ladies, Mandy Graham and Ashley Simpson, who originally raised the issue of female mounted supporters.

They have agreed that for the remainder of the 1996 celebrations they will not take part.

In return the Common-Riding Committee have agreed and I, as chairman, have given an undertaking that a meeting will be convened immediately after the Common-Riding to counter the whole issue in a calm, positive and responsible manner, to see if an acceptable solution for future years can be reached. This agreement is in the best interests of our town.

(Signed) Provost Tom Hogg.
(Countersigned)
Mandy Graham and Ashley Simpson.

Film makers

Media students at the Borders College in Hawick have produced a new 20-minute film, "The Jouk" which they hope to enter in national film competitions.

Common-Riding cash

Hawick Common Good Fund working group has recommended a £5410 grant for this year's Common-Riding.

BENHOLM DAME.—Ashley Simpson ready to end the female ride-out ban.

Continued on back page

The issue of women priests aroused deep emotions in people who had not darkened the door of a church since childhood except at weddings and funerals, perhaps because the debate exhumed unresolved tensions and prejudices about the role of women in society that were supposed to have been long buried. For some, the notion of women priests aroused deep antagonism, even a sense of indecency. Others were so consumed with outrage at the perceived injustice to women that they stopped their ears to any argument against female ordination. Most people were, however, bemused by the ferocity with which normally mild-mannered churchmen and women engaged in battle.[42]

Defenders of the status quo in Hawick argued that they were protecting the Common Riding and that they only had the best interests of the event at heart. If the ritual was tampered with, it may lose its potency. Change sometimes has to happen, but it should occur gradually and with the agreement of the whole community. The big weakness of the reformers' case was the fear factor: there were no guarantees that the Common Riding would not be damaged if women were allowed to take part. Significantly, both sides agreed that the decision to change rested solely with local people. Traditionalists were anxious to shift the blame for the controversy onto outside influences, in particular the media, who were accused of sensationalist reporting. It says much that the controversy was suspended during the actual Common Riding and not allowed to interfere with the event. When the media appeared on the day of the Common Riding, there was no story to report, except the riding itself. The Lady Riders' dispute showed the depth of feeling that the ridings create and their importance to local people.

2

'Fable Shaded Eras': Riding the Marches, c.1500-c.1690

Like many other aspects of Scottish history, our knowledge of the Riding of the Marches essentially begins in the sixteenth century. Some of the earliest references to the ridings include Selkirk (1509), Aberdeen (1525), Linlithgow (1541), Peebles (1556), Lanark (1570), Glasgow (1574) and Edinburgh (1583). There are also later references to ridings at Hawick (1640), Rutherglen (1664) and Musselburgh (1682). These dates, of course, refer only to when the ridings were first recorded in town books or official records, and it is likely that most of them had taken place long before they were first mentioned. It is impossible to know when individual ridings actually began, but a few of them might date back to the earliest foundation of burghs in the twelfth century. Perhaps the ridings evolved from much older ceremonies about land ownership and demarcating boundaries. The Romans, for instance, worshipped a god of boundaries and frontiers called Terminus. The festival, Terminalia, was held on 23 February and involved sacrifices at boundary stones consecrated to Jupiter. In England, the use of a procession to settle a boundary dispute has been traced back as early as 896. The English custom of 'beating the bounds' of a parish might have originated in Auvergne around 470.[1] The custom was linked with Rogationtide, the three days before Ascension Day, the fortieth day after Easter when Christ ascended to Heaven. Processions went around the parish boundaries to call for God's blessing on the land and also to check the site of the boundaries. In lowland Scotland, the Riding of the Marches had become widespread by the early sixteenth century. This chapter will examine the early Scottish ridings, covering the period roughly between 1500 to 1690. The chapter begins by looking at the main social functions of the ridings, why these events took place and what they were intended to do. The second part of the chapter provides a detailed account of the form and style of the early ridings.

Social Functions of the Ridings

Before examining the social functions of the early ridings, it is worth briefly considering factors that encouraged a sense of community in Scottish burghs. One of the most important of these was the general insecurity of life. People faced many uncertainties and dangers, such as war, plague, harvest failure and fire, all of which could bring disaster. In the Scottish

Borders, the closeness of the frontier with England and a general tendency towards lawlessness only made matters worse. In 1451, the lands and privileges of Peebles were confirmed by James II because the town's charters and other documents had been destroyed by war. The renewal of Selkirk's charter in 1536 took into account that all previous charters had been lost because of war, pestilence and fire.[2] Threats of this kind meant that there was a need for constant vigilance and a deep mistrust of strangers. People were forced together for mutual defence, which in turn created a sense of shared responsibility. In the burghs, this also led to feelings of distinctiveness and of living in a separate community.

Individuality naturally flourished in the burghs but there were many instances of co-operation and interdependence amongst townspeople. The idea of a community as a coherent body of people bound together by common rules and often sharing a common purpose was well established in Europe before the end of the twelfth century. For example, the Berwick guild statutes of 1249 prescribed the framework of government for the 'commune' of the town, declaring that the entire community, the whole body of the burgesses, would elect the mayor and aldermen.[3] Community was very important if a burgh was to survive and prosper. Municipal affairs and trading exchanges both required a degree of harmony and consensus to be effective. In everyday life, people had to be looked after and cared for, especially when they were babies, very old or sick, which encouraged the development of neighbourliness.

This is not to argue that life in the burghs was always peaceful, tolerant and harmonious. Relationships were often very strained and there was a constant threat of casual violence. Nevertheless, there were many factors at work that encouraged a sense of community. Local trade and craft guilds played an essential role in the development of civic life. Even more than the town council, they gave expression to the communal feelings of most townspeople. Medieval guilds were rather similar to modern trades unions. They were organisations, clubs or fellowships of people who shared common interests, such as merchants or artisans. Guilds were formed for the mutual protection and charity of members, to maintain craft standards and often for communal worship. Much of guild life was concerned with convivial friendship and there was great stress on coming together for regular feasts and celebrations. Guilds organised solemn and less formal processions in burghs, often on holy days in honour of their patron saint.

There were also many tangible signs of community within burghs. The focus of burgh life was the market place, which was the centre of local trade and a meeting place for local people and for visitors. Proclamations and official announcements were made from the market cross. Facing onto the market place was the townhouse or the tollbooth, which was a mark of civic pride. The building of a new townhouse in Aberdeen at the beginning of the fifteenth century was the responsibility of the whole community and every inhabitant was required to contribute one day's work to the construction or to pay 4d.[4] The townhouse combined the activities of burgh administration, legislation and justice. Some burghs were too poor to afford a townhouse and instead held meetings in the open air, sometimes in the churchyard. The burgh church was another focus of municipal pride. Corporate identity was given further expression by the possession of a burgh seal. By 1400, at least thirty-two burghs in Scotland had their own seals.[5] Burghs held other items of common property, including musical instruments and flags. All of these implied common interests and responsibilities on the part of the community. For safe keeping, burgh charters and other precious documents were kept in common chests and the keys held by reliable burgesses ('thre fathfull menes').[6]

Another important item of common property was the common land. Scottish burghs depended on a mixture of trade and agriculture for their survival. The average burgess was both townsman and farmer, and there were strong links between urban and rural life, giving communities a great interest in the ownership of common land. The common had many important uses. It provided grazing for sheep and cattle, and might provide hay or winter fodder if the land was good enough. In some places, the common was only rough or hill grazing, but still useful because sheep or cattle could be moved to it during growing time on

A dispute at the Selkirk riding in 1541 led to the murder of the local provost, John Muthag, still commemorated in Muthag Street in Selkirk. *(Author's collection)*

the better lands. Some burghs employed a common herd who was expected to restrict grazing at various seasons of the year. The common was also a valuable source of natural resources. It provided wood and peat for fuel and sometimes coal. It also provided a range of raw materials for many different aspects of burgh life. In poorer burghs, almost all of the buildings were thatched with heather taken from the common. In Selkirk, a house with a slate roof ('the sclaithouse') was sufficiently rare to be given a special mention in the burgh records.[7] The common provided timber, which was an essential building material, and wood for making equipment and utensils. Only burgesses were allowed to collect fuel or heather from the common, and then only in a carefully controlled way.

The principle function of the Riding of the Marches was to protect the boundaries of the common and to check any encroachments upon it by neighbouring landowners or others, some of whom might also claim rights to use the same land. The inspection of the boundaries was made routinely or when an encroachment was reported. In some burghs, special 'liners' or 'landemires' were appointed to show the true sites of the boundaries. In May 1536, participants at the Selkirk riding found that a neighbouring landowner had built a stone wall that encroached on the common. The liners were consulted and following their advice a cairn of stones was built on the boundary.[8] Likewise, after a riding in 1574 the 'outlandemeris' informed the burgh council of Glasgow about various faults on the common, including turfs cast upon the Summerhill, 'be quham we misknaw'.[9]

Communities dealt with these kinds of encroachments very severely. Unauthorised buildings and walls were pulled down and destroyed. In July 1524, the community of Selkirk chose thirteen aged and well-advised men to ride the north common on their behalf. They found a yard built unlawfully at Philiphaugh and walls erected at two other places. The yard and the walls were destroyed and the perpetrators had to promise that they would never try to use the land again.[10] Similarly, in June 1539 the community of Selkirk demolished a house that had been built without permission on the common.[11] Communities issued 'letters of cursing' against those who destroyed boundary dikes and cairns. In October 1529, the burgh council of Selkirk decreed that the 'brekaris' of barrows, if known, were to repair them, and if not known they were to be cursed by the local vicar and the barrows repaired at common expense.[12] When communities found that crops were being unlawfully grown on their land, they took action and trampled them down. On 3 June 1539, the community of Selkirk was ordered to destroy corn planted on the common by one Simon Fairlie. Nine days later, the 'haile communite' went to the north common and rode all over the growing crops and destroyed them. Fairlie promised publicly that he would never occupy the common again.[13] Occasionally, neighbouring landowners and others deemed guilty of encroachment did not accept judgement so passively. In Selkirk, the most serious incident of encroachment led to the murder of the provost, John Mithag, and one of his bailies, James Keyne. They were murdered on 25 July 1541 by three kinsmen of a local laird and claimant to the common called Ker of Greenhead. One of them, James Ker, was said to have unlawfully ploughed on the common, and Selkirk won a decreet of the Lord of Council against him. Mithaig and Keyne were murdered when they were riding to Edinburgh for the third production of proofs.[14]

Riding the marches not only gave communities the opportunity to check encroachments, but it also provided them with a mental map of their lands. At this time, there were few plans or surveys and knowledge of the extent and nature of land ownership could be gained only by making regular physical inspections. It was important for communities to maintain a collective knowledge of their lands and to hand this information down to future generations. Therefore, when the commons were ridden, communities made a point of taking some of their oldest members. Old people were believed to have acquired honesty and wisdom during the course of their lives. Their presence leant authority to the ridings and their greater experience made their decisions harder to challenge. In 1536, the riding of Selkirk south common included thirteen 'aged, knowledgeable and worthy men'. Likewise, the riding of the north common included 'the vothiest and best agit men of our burgh'.[15]

It was important to involve older members of the community in the ridings but their usefulness partly depended on young people taking part (which, of course, meant only young males). The ridings were an opportunity to impress on younger members of the community some knowledge of the boundaries and also the need to protect them.[16] However, there might have been another reason for trying to involve young men in the ridings, namely that this kind of event provided a convenient outlet for their natural vitality and exuberance.

It was shown in the previous chapter that young unmarried men, aged between fifteen and twenty-five, retain a special status in some of the modern ridings. The Standard Bearer or Cornet is almost always a bachelor and must remain so during his period in office. Married men are allowed to take part in the ridings, but the main supporters are seen as being the unmarried 'lads' or 'callants'. It is accepted that during the riding the lads have some licence for minor misbehaviour. As a Hawick Common Riding song puts it: 'What though her lads are wild a' wee/And ill tae keep in order.'[17] The division between married and unmarried men in the ridings has a long history. In Hawick, it was once the tradition to hold separate dinners for married men and the Cornet and his lads. It is also likely that the unmarried men rode in a separate group from the married men. Records of Hawick Common Riding from the early eighteenth century regularly stress 'the young unmarried men and lads of the said toun'.[18]

The divisions made between married and unmarried men can also be found in many other British and European customs and folk festivals. For example, at Shrovetide, the three days before the beginning of Lent, there were numerous ancient football games (actually more like modern rugby) and other sporting contests that were played between bachelors and married men. Marriage was seen as a significant dividing line in life. It meant giving up youthful independence for joint responsibility, which implied certain changes in attitudes and behaviour. In other words, marriage meant becoming an adult. In sixteenth-century Edinburgh, only married men were considered responsible enough to become burgesses. A surprising feature of life from the fifteenth century onwards was that the middle and lower classes of both sexes married remarkably late. It has been suggested that between 1500 and 1800 the average marriage age for males in England was between twenty-six and thirty years old.[19] The delay was caused by the need to save money for household goods and for young men to complete their apprenticeships. There were also more parental and community sanctions on relationships than generally exist today.

This extended period between puberty and marriage meant great sexual denial on the part of young men and women. The suppression of natural impulses often led to frustration and stress, which in turn might create problems of social control if they were denied some form of release. Contrary to accepted belief, it is not a recent phenomenon that young people are awkward and often indulge in anti-social behaviour. Popular customs like the ridings had many different functions, but in part they might have acted as a kind of safety valve for a rigidly hierarchical society to let off pressures and potentially destructive tensions. Today's teenagers and adolescents are often directed into sport in the belief that it will develop their personal qualities and that it will keep them out of trouble. For much the same reasons, young people were encouraged to channel their energies into popular customs and civic ceremonies.[20] Commonly during these events, normal rules of behaviour, including deference to authority, were temporarily relaxed or suspended. Often, unmarried men would use these occasions as an opportunity to assert their right of 'misrule' both against older, married groups and perhaps against the wider social and spiritual hierarchy.

It is difficult to know if unmarried men and youths had a special role in the early ridings. One indication that they were involved is the importance attached to the position of Standard Bearer or Cornet. The tradition of appointing a young unmarried man to lead the ridings is of an uncertain date, but it may be very old. The earliest reference comes from 1703 when a man called James Scott was chosen as Cornet of Hawick. The appointment of 'mock kings' of this kind was a feature of many ancient folk festivals. It was associated with summer and winter customs, especially the May games. The crucial point was role inversion, where a young and otherwise insignificant person became the symbolic leader of a community for a limited period. The process has been described as 'liminality', which in Victor Turner's words:

> is frequently found in cyclical and calendrical ritual, usually of a collective kind, in which, at certain culturally defined points in the seasonal cycle, groups or categories of persons who habitually occupy low-status positions in the social structure are positively enjoined to exercise ritual authority over their superiors.[21]

In the sixteenth century, many Scottish burghs appointed mock kings for civic events. They were known by different names in different places: for instance, Edinburgh had an 'Abbot of Narent' and a 'Lord of Inobedience'; Peebles, 'the Abbot of Unrest'; and Aberdeen, 'the Abbot and Prior of Bonaccord'. Intriguingly, from the late fifteenth century, the tradition of the mock king was often blended with the popular cult of 'Robin Hood', which was widespread in Scotland until the Reformation. In 1508, Aberdeen appointed 'Robert Huyid and Litile Johne' who had been previously known as the Abbot and Prior of Bonaccord.[22] No one really knows how the name of the famous outlaw became associated with the tradition of the mock king. It has been suggested that 'Robin' may originally have been based on a character in French rustic plays called *pastourelles*.[23] Gradually, he was adopted into the summer revels, and the close link between these and forests led to the connection between the Lord of May and Robin Hood the outlaw. In Scotland, Robin Hood received royal approval. In 1503, James IV made a special payment to the Robin Hood of Perth.[24]

Whatever their names, these traditional figures have many striking parallels with the principals of the modern ridings. In Aberdeen, the appointment took place annually in April or May and the duration of office was either for the summer or the whole year. Appointees were often the sons of prominent burgesses and they were expected to be young men of good character. It was considered a great honour for a young man to be chosen for office. In 1531, the position in Aberdeen was described as 'ane office of honor'.[25] Towns extended their patronage to appointees, who, in some cases, were paid for their efforts. In 1555, new burgesses in Peebles had to pay their burgess silver 'to my lord Robene Hude'.[26] The fact that the authorities gave their blessing to these appointments suggests that they remained largely in control of events and they were not as subversive as first appears.

Mock kings were expected to perform their duties to the satisfaction of the burgh authorities. These duties are generally unspecified, although in 1552 the Lords of Bonaccord in Aberdeen were responsible for keeping the town in 'glaidnes and blythtnes' by organising dances, fairs, plays and games.[27] In Aberdeen, they also had a role in organising civic processions on holy days, royal visits and other 'neidfull times', which is likely to have included the Riding of the Marches. All adult males in Aberdeen were expected to give their support to the abbots. In May 1507, it was decreed that all 'youthis, burgeis and burges sonnys' were to follow the abbots at holy day processions. Anyone who did not take part was to pay a fine.[28] Mock kings were closely associated with festivities and revels, which sometimes incurred the displeasure of burgh authorities. As early as April 1445, the burgh council of Aberdeen town complained about 'diuerse enormyteis' that had taken place by the abbots in the past and tried to make them behave themselves by not paying their fees.[29] In 1552, the Lords of Bonaccord were condemned for holding many 'grit, sumpteous, and superfleous' banquets during their reign and especially in May, which was thought neither 'profitabill nor godlie'.[30] It is also significant that in 1555 the Scottish Parliament prohibited the Robin Hood processions, although six years later they were still being organised in Edinburgh by apprentices and merchants' servants. Despite the Reformation, some of the functions of mock kings seem to have continued under a different guise. In the mid-seventeenth century, Aberdeen appointed a young man as bearer of the town's standard at the Riding of the Marches. For instance, on 15 August 1662, Robert Gray, son of Thomas Gray, 'sometyme provost of Aberdein', was chosen to carry the flag.[31] It does not seem too improbable that the modern Standard Bearers and Cornets are the descendants of the old abbots and lords of misrule.

Another function of the pre-Reformation ridings, which admittedly is largely speculation, is that they might have attempted to gain some form of supernatural protection for the burgh and its lands. It is very difficult for us to appreciate that popular customs often tried to influence natural forces. Primitive football games, for instance, were not only recreations but rituals designed to work some good for the community, in particular to ensure future prosperity and fertility. In some Border villages, newly married couples donated a ball or the bride started the game with a token kick.[32] Similarly, in many summer customs, children and young people were decked with flowers and vegetation to bring about the rebirth of nature after winter. At Rutherglen Riding of the Marches, it was customary 'time out of memory' for participants to deck their hats with broom. It was once a feature of Lanark Lanimer Day for the young men or 'birks' and members of the trade guilds to march in procession bearing branches of trees.[33]

In the Middle Ages, it was believed that a formal procession around an area of land would purify and protect it. In part, this was a very human response to an insecure and hazardous world. The food supply was precarious, harvests often failed, and there was a constant threat of war, plague and other natural disasters. In these circumstances, it is unsurprising that people, who were otherwise impotent and helpless, turned to ritual in an attempt to control an unpredictable environment. Before the Reformation, participants in the ridings might have carried holy objects as they went around the burgh lands, perhaps candles or bells, which were supposed to frighten away evil spirits. Wealthier burghs might have had their own holy relics, which were brought out and displayed in important processions. However, the most likely object to have been carried was a banner painted or embroidered with the image of a saint.[34] The worship of the saints was an essential feature of pre-Reformation society. It was believed that the saints had powers to relieve the adversity of their followers on earth. They were seen as intercessors who could obtain benefits from God for those who venerated them, either privately or in a group. By taking a saint's image around the marches, participants hoped that the saint would encourage God to show favour upon them and provide their lands with divine protection.

An Outline of the Early Ridings

The previous section examined the functions of the ridings until around 1700. The main purpose was, of course, to check the boundaries of the common land and to prevent any encroachment upon them. The ridings might have been used as an outlet for the natural energies of young people and to prevent social disorder. In addition, they might have been an attempt to obtain some control over an unpredictable earthly environment. The next section will try to give an overview of the early ridings and to answer the question, what were they actually like? It is possible to give a general picture of the early ridings, although it should be remembered that burghs were always keen to stress their individuality and what happened in one riding might not necessarily have happened in another.

The timing of the early ridings was rather unusual. Unlike today's ridings, which take place according to a schedule planned well in advance, burghs seem to have been fairly flexible about the dates of their ridings. In the early sixteenth century, Selkirk Common Riding did not take place on a fixed day of the year but instead ridings were held on random dates. In 1522, Selkirk north common was ridden on 8 August but in 1535 it was ridden on 19 May and in 1536 on 1 May. The purpose of the ridings was to protect the burgh lands and they took place when an encroachment was reported or when trouble threatened. On 6 July 1536, the burgh council of Selkirk ordered that a riding would be held on the following Sunday because a neighbouring landowner had built a wall on some of the town's land and the community had to go and knock it down.[35]

Other burghs were also flexible about the timing of their ridings. In 1576, the council of Aberdeen decreed that the town's 'landimaris' would be ridden annually in mid-April, but in 1599 the date of the riding was switched to May. By 1623, the timing had changed again and the riding took place in August.[36] The modern ridings are generally summer festivals but originally ridings were held at other times of the year. In 1579, the Edinburgh riding took place on 31 October, the eve of All Saints' Day or Hallowe'en, when all merchants, craftsmen and others in the town were to accompany the authorities on an inspection of 'thair meithis and boundis'.[37] In Stirling, the annual riding took place in early March and was linked with the election of a new burgh council. On 18 March 1611, it was decreed that the town's marches would be visited the following Monday following the election and admission of the new provost, bailies and council. In 1653, the Stirling riding took place on the first Tuesday of March.[38]

Participants had to have some warning that a riding was about to take place and that they were expected to take part in it. In December 1583, the Edinburgh town council decreed that the burgh marches would be inspected on the day of the Trinity Fair and that 'intimatioun to be made the day before'. On 10 June 1584, the 'nichtbouris' of Edinburgh were instructed to meet together the following Saturday at 5.00 a.m. at the provost's house and to be ready to inspect the marches.[39] In some towns, the town drummer alerted people by playing through the streets and crying the riding. In 1599, the town drummer gave the inhabitants of Aberdeen twenty-four hours' notice that a riding was about to take place.[40] In June 1572, the inhabitants of Peebles were expected to convene 'at the stryking of the swische' (at the sounding of the drum, or possibly the trumpet).[41]

However, although certain members of the community were obliged to take part in the ridings, it appears that some people were less than enthusiastic and failed to appear. Burgh authorities faced a constant problem trying to ensure that everyone who was supposed to take part in the ridings actually did so. In June 1578, the burgh council of Glasgow complained that only a very small number of 'honest men' had fulfilled their civic duties and accompanied the provost and the bailies at the last inspection of the marches. Non-appearance of this kind was considered a serious offence by the burgh authorities and fines were levied on absentees. The response of the Glasgow council was to threaten a fine of 8 shillings on anyone who did not show for the next riding.[42] In 1584, the burgh council of Edinburgh decreed that individuals would be fined 8 shillings if they did not appear at the riding on the Trinity fair.[43] In 1640, the burgh council of Hawick ordered that anyone missing from the Common Riding without good reason would be fined 40 shillings.[44] Attendance might be checked from specially compiled lists or rolls, which were reviewed at certain points during the riding. In 1641, the burgh council of Dumfries paid 12 shillings to two men to buy paper and write the town-roll at the next riding.[45]

Most ridings probably began at the market cross, which was the centre of the local community. Certain items of burgh property would have been used to establish the drama of the occasion and to enhance the power of corporate institutions and their officers. Banners and flags were an important symbol of authority and it is likely that these were prominently displayed at the ridings. Before the Reformation in the 1560s, these might have included banners that bore the image of a saint, which were believed to radiate special protective powers and to lend some supernatural authority to the marches. Craft and trade guilds had their own banners that were carried whenever the guild went in procession, a custom that still survives in Selkirk Common Riding. Burghs also had their own flags. In the early seventeenth century, Aberdeen purchased a new flag made of red and white taffeta, which had the town's coat of arms and the motto *Bon Accord* embroidered in the middle. The new flag was a replacement for one made in 1561 that had become 'all lacerat and revin, and nocht seiming to be borne.'[46] In May 1626, the burgh council of Glasgow chose two men to carry the 'tounes cullouris' at the next muster day.[47]

Another symbol of authority that might have been taken was a halberd axe. Halberds were long-shafted weapons consisting of an axe blade and a pick and topped by a spearhead. In 1660, the burgh council of Peebles paid to have an iron halberd specially cast and rust-proofed with fine oil.[48] In some of the modern ridings, halberdiers dressed in official uniforms still lead the procession. Until the late eighteenth century, some of the riders would have carried weapons of their own, such as swords, daggers and pistols. In 1599, participants at Aberdeen were ordered 'to be in reddines in armes' for their next riding.[49] Riders might also have worn some pieces of armour, if they had been rich enough to own any.

Some of the participants in the early ridings have already been mentioned: the provost, the bailies and other members of the town council, the liners who inspected the boundary lines, and representatives of the craft guilds. Some records state that the ridings involved the burgh community or the 'haill communite'. This might have referred only to the burgesses or members of the burgh, which usually meant about a third of adult males in any one burgh. But occasionally the records are more specific and suggest that other people were also involved. In June 1532, the burgh council of Selkirk decreed that all 'burges and induellaris' aged between sixteen and sixty were to take part in the next riding. Anyone who did not take part would be fined and there were different penalties for burgesses and others.[50] In this instance, it seems that the riding was not restricted only to the burgesses but encompassed all adult males of the right age group.

The ridings were intended to represent the unity or oneness of the community, although in practice they underlined social divisions and inequalities. Many people were deliberately excluded and could only watch from the sidelines, a reminder of their lowly status. The largest group who did not take part was, of course, women. Occasionally, a woman held the position of burgess or had an important role in the local economy, but they had no place in the urban hierarchy.[51] There is little doubt that until the late nineteenth century the ridings were exclusively male. Other people who were probably excluded were non-burgesses, old people, casual visitors, and the sick or infirm. At best, their purpose was to provide an audience for the main event. Most children would not have taken part although, like today, some participants might have made a point of taking their sons with them in an attempt to provide continuity and show them the boundary lines. Whilst many people were excluded from the ridings, there is some evidence that others from outside a burgh could be involved. In 1586, the burgh council of Lanark hired a horse for a messenger to go to Linlithgow to see if the provost would come and ride the Lanark marches. The council clearly thought that the Lanark riding was impressive enough to invite an important visitor to take part in it, which suggests that the town was staging an event that it wanted to promote.[52]

It is significant that many of the early records state that the marches were *ridden*. For instance, in July 1524 the whole community of Selkirk 'raid' both the north and south commons.[53] In October 1576, the burgh council of Aberdeen ordained that the town's marches were to be 'ridden anes auerie yeir'.[54] In October 1579, the inhabitants of Edinburgh were ordered to accompany the provost, bailies and council 'on horsbak'.[55] The use of horses in the ridings was partly a practical measure because the marches were often a long way. In Selkirk, the perimeter of north common extended for fourteen miles and the south common was twenty miles. People were more accustomed to walking long distances than today, for example by going to and from church each week, but walking around the marches could be awkward and very tiring. It was much easier, quicker and more dignified to make the journey by horse. Until the invention of mechanised transport, horses had an essential part in many aspects of human activity. They were used in many different ways and there were a variety of horses for different tasks, from sleek war-horses to work- and plough-horses. The French chronicler Jean Froissart recorded ponies and bay horses in the fourteenth-century Borders. A good horse was a symbol of power and authority. Like motorcars, they were status symbols, reflecting the social standing of their owner. The sixteenth-century historian John Leslie wrote that the Border Reivers believed that anyone 'that gangis upon his fute' was abject and utterly contemptible. Like other animals, horses were often treated badly but they were also highly prized. Leslie wrote that the Reivers valued horses above all other material things and that they didn't care much about other 'househaldde geir' as long as they had access to fast horses.[56]

However, it is unlikely that all participants in the early 'ridings' were mounted. Some people would have been unable to meet the running costs of a horse and have had to take part on foot. In June 1584, the burgh council of Edinburgh decreed that the town's marches should be visited 'on fute', although in this case the marches were not very extensive.[57] In June 1574, the burgh council of Glasgow made a 'perambulatioun' of the town's marches. In May 1588, the council and community of Lanark inspected their marches on 'hors and fuit'.[58] One individual who might have made the journey on foot was the turf-cutter, a man who carried a spade and who cut turfs at certain points to mark the boundaries. Likewise, the burgh musicians might also have walked. There has always been a close association between popular customs and music. Music was accessible, public and could transform a harsh reality into a sense of resilience, determination and hope. It is likely that musicians took part in the early ridings, in part to draw attention to the mounted procession and make it seem more impressive and important. In the modern ridings, a brass or pipe band generally supplies music, but bands of this kind were introduced in the nineteenth century. Hawick and Selkirk Common Ridings also feature flute and drum bands, a musical combination that was known in the sixteenth-century Borders.[59]

A fascinating insight into the musical world of early modern Scotland is provided by Robert Sempill's poem *The Life and Death of Habbie Simson, the Piper of Kilbarchan*, which was written in the mid-seventeenth century. Sempill's poem captures the rough folk-energy of popular customs and the central role of music in these events. Habbie played his pipes at fairs, feasts, weddings, football matches and horse races. He was something of a local hero and was greatly loved by children ('gaitlings'), old men ('carl') and young women ('whan he play'd, the lasses leuch'):

> *So kindly to his neighbours neast*
> *At Beltan and St Barchan's feast*
> *He blew, and then held up his breast,*
>   *As he were weid:*   weid – mad
> *But now we need not him arrest,*
>   *For Habbie's dead.*

> *At fairs he play'd before the spear-men,*
> *All gaily graithed in their gear men,*   graithed – attired
> *Steel bonnets, jacks, and swords so clear then*
>   *Like any bead:*
> *Now wha shall play before such weir-men*   weir-men – men of war
>   *Sen Habbie's dead?*[60]

Many Scottish burghs employed their own musicians like Habbie Simson. In 1487, there were 'commoun pyperis' in Edinburgh.[61] In 1522, inhabitants of Aberdeen were obliged to pay the minstrels 'thair meit and wagis', and anyone who failed to do so would be fined.[62] Musicians had the duty to play a morning alarm call and to announce the night curfew. In 1540, the burgh council of Aberdeen appointed two brothers as the common minstrels and they were expected to play in the morning and evening, 'and vder tymmis neydfull, concerning the toune.'[63]

Musicians were also supposed to play at fairs and other events, which included the Riding of the Marches. In 1575, the burgh council of Lanark paid two minstrels called George Simson and John Watson 'for ganing throw the common'. This seems to have been successful because six years later John Watson was appointed the town minstrel to play the drum through the town in the morning and evening. The drum was rated as a valuable piece of common property because on rainy days Watson was to play a pipe instead, protecting the drum from water damage.[64] In the seventeenth century, the burgh council of Peebles paid two men called 'Hew Blak and Gairden' to play the drum and pipe about the commons.[65] At the Dundee riding of 1727, the burgh council paid £3 Scots to 'ane hautboy and violine'.[66] Musicians were burgh officials and they were supplied with special uniforms. In 1607, Stirling supplied 'George Crafude, drummare, and John Forbes, pyper, each with a pair of woollen trousers. In 1622, the town provided the drummer and piper with complete uniforms of red coats, trousers and stockings, 'wrocht in gude fassoun.'[67] In May 1706, Linlithgow bought coats for the drummer and piper in preparation for the riding.[68]

How were the marches actually defined? There were few maps and plans and many people were illiterate anyway, therefore much depended on physical markers on the ground. One method of defining boundaries was by using prominent natural features, such as rivers and streams. Part of the boundary of Selkirk north common was defined by a steam called Philipburn that led to a waterfall on Lamelaw hill.[69] Other features that marked the boundaries were the crests of hills and other natural ridges, woods, hedges and solitary trees. In 1556, a prominent willow bush marked part of the boundary of Peebles common.[70] The sites of wells or springs were also used. These sites had a significant role in folklore. They were believed to have magical powers, bringing health and vitality from the earth itself and being a gateway between this and other worlds. It is significant that in 1579 the practice of making pilgrimages to holy wells was prohibited by an Act of Parliament, principally because 'pagan' survivals of this kind were seen as rallying points for Catholicism. At the Riding of the Marches however, the primary function of wells was to provide refreshment for thirsty riders and their mounts.

Artificial features were also used to define the boundaries. Special boundary ditches were cut, walls and 'march dikes' were erected, and rows of trees were planted, especially elder trees or bourtrees. Large stone cairns were built to mark the site of a boundary, such as the Three Brethren cairns on Selkirk north common, which are mentioned in sixteenth-century records

Marking the northern extremity of Selkirk common, the Three Brethren cairns are mentioned in sixteenth-century records and are still visited at the Common Riding. *(Author's collection)*

and are still visited at the Common Riding.[71] Every time riders visited the cairn a few more stones were added to the pile. Features of the agricultural landscape might have a dual role. A cattle enclosure and the wall of a cornfield marked boundaries of Lanark common.[72] Likewise, stone and wooden crosses were used although they were principally objects of devotion. In 1556, a boundary of Peebles common was defined by 'Hammildone croce'.[73] Features that long pre-dated the existence of the common were also employed. At Hawick, the burgess role was read on the 'Ca Knowe' or Call Knowe, a small mound near the furthest point of the common. The site, which was also known as the Heroes' Grave, was excavated in the early nineteenth century and found to contain an ancient stone cist and human bones.[74] Until recently, most people had little idea about the origins of prehistoric sites such as burial mounds and standing stones. They only knew that they had been there longer than anyone could remember and that they were very old indeed. By using ancient places in this way, communities invested their marches with an air of timeless authority that was very difficult to refute.

Another method of defining the boundaries was by the erection of special march stones or 'witter stanes'. These stones were set up at regular intervals from each other, usually in places where there were no other features to distinguish a boundary line. Stones were inspected during the ridings and special ridings were held for the purpose of erecting new stones or to replace those that had been damaged. On 25 May 1535, the inhabitants of Selkirk went to the north common and, on the advice of the oldest and wisest burgess, set up stones to mark the division between lands belonging to Selkirk and Carterhaugh.[75] In the seventeenth century, the burgh council of Stirling ordered that every new burgess or guild member was to pay the town treasurer 24 shillings Scots for the erection of new march stones. Each stone was to be three foot long and a foot square, 'with the year of God hewin in figures on the upmost end'. This was a successful scheme because a few years later the council decreed that 'thair is noe more neid of stains' and instead new burgesses were to give a donation to buy arms for the burgh arsenal.[76] However, the authorities always had to be vigilant because march

67

Aberdeen has the best surviving examples of march stones in Scotland, which were erected in the eighteenth century, but on the site of much earlier stones, some of which still survive. CR stands for City Royalty. *(Author's collection)*

stones were often removed or damaged. Following an inspection of the marches in June 1574, the burgh council of Glasgow was told about a stone that had been removed leaving 'ae greit space' in the common.[77]

March stones had to be distinctive and obvious. When the council and community of Peebles inspected their marches in June 1556, they passed, amongst others, from two grey stones to a white stone, and then past 'ane red hedit stane' down a stream to another grey stone.[78] Sometimes, march stones were painted or made from brightly coloured stone, such as white quartz. The stones that bound the common of Dundee in the seventeenth century had the town's badge of a lily sculpted on them and also the date of their erection ('1619').[79] Similarly, the stones on the Rutherglen common were shaped, 'somewhat resembling a man's head, but the lower part is square.'[80] One of the stones in Aberdeen was marked with a letter 'P' for the property of Aberdeen. Other stones had the mark of St Peter's keys. Also in Aberdeen, there were special stones with saucer-like depressions. These were filled either with molten lead and embossed with the burgh seal, or with wine that riders drank direct from the stone.[81] Similarly, in eighteenth-century Hawick a depression in the keystone of the Auld Brig was used as a mill for distributing snuff. Sharing food and drink in this way was an important expression of group solidarity. By using a march stone as a communal drinking cup or a snuffbox, membership of a community was cleverly emphasised.

As we have seen, by regularly walking or riding around the boundaries, communities gave themselves a mental map of the layout of their lands, which could be drawn upon when there were disputes about the position of a boundary. To further impress this knowledge on individuals and on the collective memory, the ridings often involved some element of physical induction. New burgesses were picked up and swung against special dumping or 'doupin' stones, a practice that survived in some ridings until well into the twentieth century. In Lanark, first-time participants were forcibly immersed in the Ducking Hole in the River Mouss so that they would remember the point where a boundary met the water. In some ridings, boys and young men were physically beaten at certain important places on the journey, as happened in the Aberdeen riding of 1755:

> The young men were taken to each of the march stones, and there subjected to that peculiar mode of flagellation which, at the present day, is employed in order to embue the mind with a knowledge of Greek, Latin, and English Grammar.[82]

Thomas Wilkie, a collector of popular customs in southern Scotland in the early nineteenth century, recorded that similar methods were used when new march stones were erected:

> It is a common custom when March-stones are set up, for sons of the proprietors of land in the vicinity, to be asked to stand as witnesses. After the stone, or stones are fixed, these young men are laid hold of, and their ears are cruelly punched, by the lairds of the lands newly marched. This is to make them remember the transaction of the stones placed.[83]

In 1764, a group of old men were consulted to settle a dispute over the boundary of Wilton common, near Hawick. One of them, James Scott, remembered that when he was young he saw the boundary being established. What had stuck in his mind was that one of the participants slapped a boy standing near him, 'and said to him he would mind the marching forty years after.' The young Scott ran away in terror, but true enough he never forgot the site of the assault or the boundary.[84] Behaviour of this kind, which now seems appallingly cruel, was intended to transmit knowledge by physical experience, in this case by linking a particular place with a traumatic event. There are also hints of an initiation rite, which are often violent and designed to test courage and endurance. Another method of impressing people with knowledge of the boundaries, which was no doubt a lot more popular, was by giving them money, sweets or other treats at important places.

Once the serious business of inspecting the marches had been completed there might have been time for some fun and relaxation. Many of the ridings would have concluded with some kind of corporate dinner or a feast, a practice that survives in modern events. Participants would have been encouraged to feel a strong sense of community and belonging with each other. Burgh occasions of this kind often involved huge amounts of food and drink. Alcohol, in particular, was part of every public and private ceremony. It broke down social distinctions and provided a temporary escape from the strains of everyday life.

For obvious reasons, the principal leisure activity associated with the ridings was horse racing. Racing is an ancient sport and one that developed naturally in a world where horses had great economic and social value. Horses were status symbols and there was rivalry between different owners to establish who had the fastest horse. This in turn led to the development of organised race meetings. In Scotland, there was great national enthusiasm for racing, encouraged by the Stewart kings who took the sport to their hearts. James IV had his own stable and, as the accounts of the Lord Treasurer make clear, he regularly bet large stakes on the outcome of races.

In the seventeenth century, burghs were keen to lend their support to local meetings. In 1653, the council of Peebles provided a saddle 'worth ten merkes mony' as a prize for races at the Beltane fair. Later, the town paid for an engraved silver cup and a silver quaich inscribed with the town's coat of arms.[85] Councils made great efforts to promote their local meeting and paid messengers to go to other towns and announce the races. In 1661, Peebles burgh council paid two boys to carry a letter to Selkirk to proclaim the races.[86] Similarly, in 1656 Selkirk burgh council paid for a messenger to hire a horse and ride to Kelso with news of the Common Riding races. Race meetings were popular because they were social as well as sporting occasions. Little is actually known about the side-attractions but there might have been a heady mixture of music, dancing, travellers and other visitors, and a good deal of eating and drinking.

Other athletic competitions may also have taken place at the end of the ridings, such as footraces, wrestling, weightlifting and tug-of-war. In 1663, some sheets of paper were awarded as a prize in the boys' race at one of the Peebles ridings.[87] Sports of this kind were not just contests of strength and skill but also acted as a shop window for young men to display their prowess and bodily vigour. In part, this was to appeal to the limited number of available girls but also to local chieftains and leaders, who were always trying to find imposing bodyguards and warriors.

Like their modern equivalents, the early ridings were a complex historical mix. It is not known when or how the ridings originated but these events were a feature of civic life in the burghs by the early sixteenth century. The principal purpose of the ridings was, of course, to check the boundaries of common lands and to prevent any encroachment upon them. Burgh authorities took the ridings seriously, using them to promote a sense of community and common responsibilities. The ridings were also used as a crude educational tool to transmit knowledge of the boundaries between generations. As in many other popular customs, it is possible that young unmarried males had a special role in the ridings, perhaps as symbolic leaders. The ridings provided an outlet for their natural energies and in turn acted as a means of preventing social disorder. It is also likely that the early ridings had an element of fun about them, which would go a long way to explain their survival and enduring popularity. They were an opportunity to put on a show, to dress up and impress, to enhance social status and gain prestige, to take part in events like corporate feasts, races and games and, most importantly, to share in a common experience.

3

'O Flodden Field!':
The Common Riding and the
Battle of Flodden

Tradition, legend, tune, and song,
Shall many an age that wail prolong
— Sir Walter Scott, *Marmion*

No work on the Scottish Common Ridings would be complete without some consideration of the battle of Flodden Field and the various Common Riding traditions that stem from it. Flodden was fought on 9 September 1513 between an English army led by Thomas Howard, Earl of Surrey, and a Scottish army under King James IV. The day was a military disaster for Scotland. It was reported that 10,000 Scots were killed in the battle, including the king and a large number of the Scottish nobility. The memory of that dreadful defeat is still perpetuated in the ancient Common Ridings of Selkirk and Hawick, and also in the modern Coldstream Civic Week.[1] Selkirk and Hawick have a tradition that many local men went to fight in the battle and that very few survived. Hawick Common Riding also recalls the months after Flodden when the young men or 'callants' defended the town and captured the flag of an English raiding party.

These traditions about Flodden have become central to the local Common Ridings and to some extent they have come to obscure the original purpose of the ridings. Indeed, the Common Ridings are sometimes said to be 'about Flodden', forgetting the rather more mundane tradition of inspecting the burgh marches. But are these traditions historically accurate or just local invention? And how have they come to be so closely associated with the Common Ridings? This chapter will assess the Flodden traditions of Selkirk and Hawick by examining them in the light of surviving evidence about the battle. The chapter begins by looking at the tradition of local involvement and loss at Flodden, especially that of Selkirk, and then considers the state of the Scottish borders after Flodden and the Hawick Common Riding tradition of 1514.

Left: Instituted in 1952, Coldstream Civic Week features a ride-out and service at the Flodden battlefield. *(Ian Landles)*

Opposite: Pictured here in 1899, the Casting of the Colours in Selkirk is said to represent a lone survivor of Flodden. *(Scottish Borders Museum and Gallery Service (Selkirk Collection))*

The Borders at Flodden

In Selkirk Common Riding, the highlight of the day is a simple ceremony called 'Casting the Colours', which takes place immediately after the Riding of the Marches. On a covered dais erected in the Market Square, the Standard Bearer 'casts' the burgh flag in figure-eight motions about his body to the old tune *The Souters o' Selkirk*. Although it has striking similarities to some Italian customs, the Casting is said to imitate a solitary survivor of Flodden who, on his return to Selkirk, swung a captured banner around himself to indicate the nature of the defeat. Other bearers cast their flags, including those of the Selkirk craft guilds and merchants. When the flag of the Selkirk Ex-Servicemen has been lowered, there is a profound and emotional silence broken only with the playing of the lament *The Flowers of the Forest*, which is known locally as *The Liltin'*. As the local saying goes, 'there is not a dry eye in the Market Square'.

The earliest reference to a Selkirk tradition about Flodden was made around 1722 by a writer called John Hodge:

> *King James IV, on the way to Flodden, where he engaged the English army, had from the burgh of Selkirk eighty well-armed men commanded by the town-clerk, who were all, except for the clerk, cut to pieces. The clerk only returned, and brought with him one of the English banners and a halbert axe, which are yearly carried before the magistrates at the riding of their common.*

This tradition was firmly established by the end of the eighteenth century and therefore pre-dates the popular interest in the battle created by the success of Sir Walter Scott's *Marmion*,

which was first published in 1808. Reverend Thomas Robertson, minister of Selkirk, recorded the tradition in the *Old Statistical Account*, although in this version '100 citizens' were said to have followed 'the fortune of James IV on the plains of Flowden'.[3] Sir Walter Scott briefly considered the tradition in *The Minstrelsy of the Scottish Border*, which seems to have been the only thing he ever wrote about the Border Common Ridings. Scott used the tradition given in the *Statistical Account*, adding that it contained nothing that was 'inconsistent with probability'.[4] The modern version of the tradition is little changed to the one recorded in Hodge's manuscript.

An important part of the Flodden traditions of Selkirk and Hawick is that each town sent a large number of men to join the campaign. The military arrangements of sixteenth-century Scotland certainly required this. The army of the day was a 'citizen army', with military service demanded of all able-bodied men between the ages of sixteen and sixty.[5] This was for a maximum of forty days in a single year. Each man was expected to supply his own provisions and weapons, the latter fixed according to his status. Periodic *wappenschawings* or weapon displays were ordered by local sheriffs and barons to ensure that those living within their area possessed the appropriate arms. Such arrangements made for an inexpensive army but also one with severe limitations. There was little effective machinery to enforce the regulations and much depended on the willingness of subjects to co-operate. This would have created many problems in a notoriously lawless area like the Border marches, where, in Thomas Rae's words, 'national feeling was almost meaningless, [and] many men refused to recognise the suzerainty of the monarch on either side of the frontier'.[6] The infamous Border Reivers flourished at the time of Flodden and they would have been wary or unwilling to put their lives at risk for a cause they did not recognise.

But not everyone in the Borders defied the law so blatantly. For the inhabitants of the Border burghs in particular, there would have been considerable social pressure to take up arms. Indeed, a royal burgh like Selkirk might have considered it a matter of local pride and honour to supply men for the king's army. An entry in the *Selkirk Burgh Court Book* dated 2 August 1513 does give detailed instructions for a forthcoming *wappenschawing*, which suggests that the town was preparing to fulfil its obligations and send some men to join the campaign.[7]

However, even if the Border burghs satisfied the military requirements, this does not validate the Common Riding traditions about heavy losses at the battle. We should remember that Flodden was the unfortunate conclusion of an otherwise successful campaign. Prior to the battle, the Scottish army had spent nearly three weeks in England, capturing Norham Castle and occupying the valley of the River Till. The length of this campaign caused severe problems in the Scottish army, notably of supply and motivation. Norman MacDougall, the biographer of James IV, has written that 'it was difficult, if not impossible, to keep the host in the field for much longer than a week to ten days, a fortnight at the very most, in spite of the theoretical forty days' service'.[8] Officially, each man was supposed to bring provisions for forty days but it is more likely that individuals carried enough food for only ten or twelve days, after which time the army began to melt away through desertion. The problem was compounded in the Flodden campaign by poor weather and disease, the great scourge of armies of this time and which had dogged the Scottish army since assembly. Moreover, by capturing Norham Castle, the Scots had fulfilled an old ambition and won a major victory. For many soldiers, it would have seemed that the job was done and that they could go home. Thomas Ruthal, the Bishop of Durham, gave the exaggerated figure that 20,000 men left the Scottish army at the siege of Norham.[9] Several days before Flodden, the burgh council of Edinburgh complained that 'all maner of personis' were returning from the king's army.[10] Norman MacDougall has suggested that it might have been easier to keep the service of the contingents from the royal burghs for the full forty days. On 2 August 1513, the Aberdeen burgh council authorised the raising of a tax of £400 Scots to provide a small force to support the king.[11] But there is no evidence that Selkirk, a much poorer royal burgh, made similar arrangements and, as the Edinburgh desertions suggest, payment of this kind may not have been very effective.

Any attempt to determine the fate of the Border contingents at Flodden involves much speculation and conjecture. The records of the battle are often contradictory and there are few references to the Border levies. At the beginning of the battle, the Scottish army arranged itself into great square and diamond-shaped formations called 'battles', each being 'an arrowe shotte' (about 200 yards) from its neighbour.[12] These were not random concentrations of men, but complex constructions of smaller units recruited through a family, lineage or feudal relationship, and grouped around a flag or a leader or united by a common war cry.[13] At Flodden, some or all of the Scottish Borderers fought together on the extreme left of the army under the command of Alexander Lord Home and Alexander Earl of Huntly, two men who had many family connections with each other. The chronicler Robert Lindsay of Pitscottie wrote that Home and Huntly fought 'witht the borderaris and countriemen to the number of ten thowsand'.[14] Another near-contemporary writer, George Buchanan, said that Home was in charge of 'the March men'.[15]

Alexander Home was the leading Border noble at this time and he would have been able to exert great influence, particularly after his appointment to the wardenship of the Scottish east and middle march in 1511.[16] An important part of Home's remit was to muster the Border marches in times of war and for this purpose he had at his disposal all the men of his marches who were liable for military service. Home had his own military court with the right to prosecute cases of non-attendance, thereby increasing the pressure on people to join the campaign. However, it cannot be said that the Selkirk contingent definitely fought under Home. As tenants of a royal burgh, they might have fought under the direct command of the king rather than the warden.[17] The animosity between Selkirk and the earldom of Home expressed in the traditional Selkirk Common Riding song *The Souters o' Selkirk* has been taken as evidence that the Selkirk men did not fight under Home (a Souter is an old Scots word for a shoemaker and a native of Selkirk):

> It's up wi' the Souters o' Selkirk
> And down wi' the Earl o' Home,
> And here is to a' the braw laddies,
> That wear the single soal'd shoon:
> It's up wi' the Souters o' Selkirk
> For they are baith trusty and leal;
> And up wi' the lads o' the Forest,
> An' down wi' the Merse to the deil.[18]

Significantly, the Shoemakers Guild in Selkirk had no corporate identity until 1601 and the earldom of Home was not created until 1604.[19] As Thomas Crawford concluded: 'Not too much should be made of the tradition that the song refers to the brave service of 80 burgesses of Selkirk at the battle of Flodden ... But the appeal to intensely local loyalties is obvious.'[20]

The first hand-to-hand fighting at Flodden took place on the left of the Scottish army, where Home's force met Sir Edmund Howard who was leading the men from Cheshire, Lancashire and Yorkshire.[21] Home and his force swept all before them in this initial assault. At the sight of the approaching line of Scots, most of the English seem to have turned and ran, leaving Howard with only a small force to fight his way to safety.

Home and Huntly were unable, or unwilling, to capitalise on their victory to help the rest of the Scottish army. Before they could wheel round and make a flank attack on the English centre, their advance was checked by the arrival of Thomas Lord Dacre, the warden of the English marches, and his force of Border horsemen. What happened next has always been something of a mystery. Andrew Lang, historian and native of Selkirk, confessed: 'I have never been able to understand the conduct of Home's Borderers at Flodden.'[22] Some sources suggest that Dacre 'like a good and an hardy knight' charged his men into Home's division and put the Scots to flight, thus saving Sir Edmund Howard and preventing the collapse of the English right wing.[23]

However, other writers suggested that Dacre's role at Flodden was rather less honourable. Rumours spread after the battle that Dacre had been reluctant to get involved in the fighting. The chronicler Edmund Hall wrote: 'The lord Dacre with his company stood styll al daye unfoughten with all'.[24] In October 1513, the Bishop of Durham agreed that 'many reports had been circulated to his dishonour' and suggested that the king send a letter in Dacre's defence.[25] It may be significant that similar stories were spread against Alexander Home. He was said to have refused Huntly's plea to go to the aid of James IV and that he had held his ground as the rest of the Scottish army was cut down. In 1516, these accusations were used against Home when he was convicted of treason and beheaded:

> This deed gave rise to more general admiration than grief, for Alexander was already most notorious among the people as stained by treachery because in the English war he had not gone to the aid of his countrymen when they were distressed and falling in front of the camp of which he was in command.[26]

Both Home and Dacre led formations that were composed largely of men from the Border marches. In pitched battles like Flodden, Border soldiers were known to be wary about attacking their neighbours because they did not want to upset the complicated system of cross-Border relationships and feuds. As a result, unofficial 'arrangements' were sometimes made between Border soldiers to ensure that they did not harm each other. At the battle of Pinkie on 10 September 1547, the English Borderers wore special armbands and letters embroidered on their caps:

They said themselves the use thereof was that each of them might know his fellow ... howbeit, there were of the army among us (some suspicious men perchance) that thought they used them for collusion, and rather because they might be known to the enemy, as the enemies are known to them (for they have their marks too), and so in conflict either each to spare each other, or gently each to take other.[27]

It is not known if a similar understanding was made at Flodden, but it would explain the reports of mutual inaction between the two sides.

In addition, some of Home's men seem to have quickly lost interest in the battle after their victory over Sir Edmund Howard. Armies at this time were notoriously difficult to control and after an initial victory soldiers often drifted off in the hunt for loot and plunder. It is known that Home's division took some English prisoners, who were later ransomed.[28] There were also complaints after the battle that the thieves and robbers of Tynedale and Teviotdale had stripped the English baggage train. It may be relevant that the earliest versions of the Selkirk tradition always refer to items having been brought back from the battlefield: for example, an English flag, a sword, a halbert or a horse. The *Old Statistical Account* says that the Selkirk men returned 'loaded with spoils taken from the enemy', which perhaps records a folk memory about the battle.[29] The only reference to Flodden in *The Burgh Court Book of Selkirk* is an entry for 29 October 1521 which records an argument between two men about an English horse brought back from Flodden.[30] This entry is also, of course, evidence of one Selkirk man who was present at Flodden and who returned after the battle.

However, the attacks on Home and Dacre were made sometime after Flodden and might have had more to do with political rivalries rather than what happened at the battle. Many of the English nobility were known to be jealous of Dacre's close relationship with the Earl of Surrey. Lord Home was one of the few Scottish nobles to survive Flodden and was a convenient scapegoat for the defeat. Pitscottie's assertion that Home and Huntly lost 'few of thair men either hurt or slain' does not agree with casualty lists. These show considerable losses amongst the Scottish Border nobility, including members of the Home family; John Murray of Fala Hill, the Sheriff of Selkirkshire; and John Scott of the Haining, the local laird of Selkirk.[31]

Unfortunately, the best source for the period, *The Burgh Court Book of Selkirk*, contains almost nothing about Flodden. This has appeared to some historians, 'as if a silent oath had been taken that the dreadful day should be forever blotted out of record'.[32] An entry for 2 August 1513 gives instructions for a *wappenschawing*, but there is nothing recording those from Selkirk who took part in the campaign or those who failed to return. Common Riding tradition says that eighty burgesses went from the town and that a man called Fletcher was the only 'Souter' to come home. However, a number of names that figure in the pre-Flodden pages of the *Burgh Court Book* can also be seen afterwards. As Thomas Craig-Brown wrote: 'the clerk's handwriting remains the same, old names are repeated in lists of members, orders about the watch are given in much the same terms as formerly'.[33] More importantly, the *Burgh Court Book* shows that there is no dramatic increase in the creation of new burgesses for the period after Flodden, which is what would have occurred if a large number had been killed. In an average year the town appointed only one or two new members: 1536 was exceptional as forty-six new burgesses were created to raise money to pay for the confirmation of Selkirk's charter as a royal burgh. But one new burgess was created in 1513 and only one in 1515. There is nothing to indicate a sudden surge of replacements.[34]

The Flodden statue of Fletcher casts a long shadow at Selkirk Common Riding. *(Scottish Borders Tourist Board)*

The Borders After Flodden

The battle of Flodden also features prominently in Hawick Common Riding. In 1898, two lawyers, Robert S. Craig and Adam Laing, published *The Hawick Tradition of 1514: The Town's Common, Flag and Seal*, which set out to examine and verify 'the facts bearing on the time-hallowed tradition of 1514'. Craig and Laing summarised the Hawick tradition as follows:

> [After Flodden] *in Hawick few men were left to defend the town. It was at the mercy of the English, who in the year of Flodden and in the subsequent year, over-ran the country pillaging and killing. One such party did in 1514 approach the town of Hawick and threaten it. In default of their elders, mostly slain at Flodden with Drumlanrig, their local leader, the younger men of the town rose to the occasion. They went out as far as Hornshole, some two miles farther down the river, encountered the enemy there, routed them and took from them the flag they carried. This flag, or at least a replica of it, has been carried annually at the ceremony of the Riding of the Common ever since.*[35]

Craig and Laing claimed that the tradition was well known locally at the end of the eighteenth century. The earliest reference to the tradition is in *The Common Riding Song*, the words of which were written by Arthur Balbirnie in the 1790s:

At Flodden field our fathers fought it,
And honour gain'd though dear they bought it;
By Teviotside they took this Colour,
A dear memorial of their valour.[36]

Balbirnie's song is still sung at the Common Riding, where it is now known as *The Old Song* (the new song being James Hogg's *The Colour*). Another early reference to the tradition is contained in Robert Wilson's *History of Hawick*, which was published in 1825. Wilson had been Cornet in 1799 and was a political radical, and he used his book mainly to discuss the issues of the day rather than historical events. Wilson, like some later writers, embellished the tradition with some 'details', such as 'two hundred stout men ... who shouted unanimously to be led into battle [against] the enemy, about forty in number.'[37] In 1826, John Mason also recorded the tradition in *The Border Tour*, one of the earliest travel guides to the Scottish Borders, an area that had become a popular holiday destination thanks to the work of Sir Walter Scott:

> *The marches of the land belonging to Hawick are annually perambulated by the magistrates,*
> *followed by every inhabitant who can meet with a horse to bestride. In the centre of the*
> *cavalcade is a burgess, or the son of a burgess, called the Cornet, bearing the town standard,*
> *on which is inscribed '1514', a similar flag having been taken in that year from a marauding*
> *party of the English by the inhabitants.*[38]

Poets and songwriters are largely responsible for the impressions we have of Flodden. This is particularly apparent with the Hawick Common Riding song *The Colour*, or as it is more commonly known *Teribus*, the words of which were written in the early nineteenth century by James Hogg, a Hawick stocking-maker and self-educated working man. Hogg's twenty-four-verse epic (thirty-nine verses if we include his less well-known work *Flodden Field*) has become *the* standard account of the Hawick tradition. Selected verses from it are sung repeatedly in the course of the modern Common Riding.

Hogg's song was written 300 years after Flodden and it cannot be used as reliable historical evidence. As one local writer put it: 'The author has assumed considerable poetic licence, and drawn pretty much on his imagination.'[39] At best, the song is 'fictional reportage' written in a style like the old Border ballads. However, it has been noted that Hogg's *The Colour* and Balbirnie's *Common Riding Song* do have strong similarities.[40] Both have the same tune and contain lines and phrases that seem to correspond. The two songs were written around the same time so one writer might simply have copied from the other, but it is also possible that both writers were drawing on an old ballad or song that they both knew but which is now lost. There is no doubt that they used an old tune. When he was asked about his song, Hogg retorted: 'Its air's eternal.'[41] Francis H. Groome, the compiler of the *Ordnance Gazetteer of Scotland*, wrote about *The Colour*: 'The music dates from the most ancient times, and describes more than any other air, the wild and defiant strain of the war tramp and the battle shout.'[42]

Unfortunately, there is no sign of the 'missing' ballad in George Caw's *The Poetical Collection*, which was published in 1784 and was one of the first books to be printed in the Borders. Neither is there anything in Sir Walter Scott's famous collection of Border ballads *Minstrelsy of the Scottish Border*, although Scott was deeply suspicious of Hawick because of its radical political sympathies. Nevertheless, *The Colour* and *The Common Riding Song* do seem to follow in the tradition of the old Border riding ballads. One of the functions of the ballads was to pass traditional stories and tales between the generations, and often ballads were based on real events. Writing in the sixteenth century, John Leslie described that the Border Reivers took great pleasure in their own songs and music, and used ballads to learn about 'the actes of thair fowrbearis.'[43] Ballads were sung, and cherished, because they gave a heroic tinge to their environment and society. The defeat of an enemy raiding party and the capture of their flag was just the kind of thing to be immortalised in a ballad. Whilst the songs written by Hogg and Balbirnie are both of relatively recent origin, they retain many of the characteristics of the older ballad tradition. They are folksongs that tell a story, focussing on a single event with a minimum of comment and descriptive setting. Moreover, they are learned from others rather than by reading. Even today, local people know these songs because they hear them from relations, friends or teachers or by taking part in the Common Riding each year.

It is possible therefore that there was an old ballad about Flodden and that Hogg and Balbirnie were drawing on an ancient folk memory about the battle. Battles were significant and often traumatic events and were not easily forgotten. This was certainly the case with another of the great Border fights, the battle of Ancrum Moor, which was fought in 1545. At the beginning of the nineteenth century, Thomas Wilkie, a collector of Border folklore, visited the battlefield and discovered that even after 250 years stories were still being told about the battle:

> The people there, being in the immediate neighbourhood of the scene of action, give a more circumstantial, and consequently a more interesting account of the battle than any of our historians ... William Fiddis, an old man, said he had heard his grandfather say, that the farm-house of Morridge-hall was the place where the wounded men were carried into; and that the most bloody part of the engagement was on a ridge running northward from that house.[44]

Folk memories of this kind are clearly very durable but there is also a tendency for them to blur facts and invention together, making them unreliable as historical evidence but at the same time more difficult to refute. For example, the Hawick tradition says that at Flodden 'the barony of Hawick lost its Lord of the Manor [Sir William Douglas] and 200 men'.[45] This specific statement regarding losses at Flodden is worth a closer look. In George Ridpath's *Border History*, which was published in 1816, it is reported that on the eve of Flodden, the Earl of Angus departed from the Scottish camp leaving behind him his two sons, who 'fell in the battle with 200 gentlemen of the name Douglas'.[46] In the *Annals of Hawick* by James Wilson, which was published in 1850, it is related that 'Sir William Douglas of Drumlanrig ... with 200 gentlemen of that name were killed in the engagement'.[47] However, in *Upper Teviotdale and the Scotts of Buccleuch* by Jane Rutherford Oliver, which was published in 1897, there is this assertion:

> The muster from Hawick is stated ... to have been about two hundred, who marched under the banner of Douglas of Drumlanrig ... Sir William Douglas was killed in the battle, and it is asserted that his followers were nearly exterminated.[48]

Thus, from the original statement that 200 men of the name Douglas were killed at Flodden, a tradition has been manufactured that the same number of Hawick men fought and fell there!

All that can be said for definite is that there is a tradition in Hawick about Flodden that is closely associated with the Common Riding. The tradition was well known at the end of the eighteenth century and is likely to be much older. Some writers have embellished it with fanciful details, but the basic story is that after Flodden an English raiding party was defeated and their flag was taken. But is the tradition accurate? Did it really happen? Whilst there are no records of the event, it is possible to use other evidence to provide at least some of the historical background to the tradition.

An important part of the story is that in the aftermath of Flodden, the Scottish marches were defenceless and were laid waste by English raiding parties. James Hogg's *The Colour* states:

After Flodden was decided,
Surrey had his troops divided,
Turned them loose to lawless plunder—
Heaven just! Why slept thy thunder.

At the word each fiend advances,
Flodden's blood yet dimmed their lances;
Entering hamlet, town and village,
Marked their way with blood and pillage.[49]

The image that the Border marches were devastated after Flodden is crucial to the Hawick tradition because it emphasises a great local victory at a time of national calamity. As the song puts it: 'Scotia's boast was Hawick's callants.' However, the picture of widespread destruction in the Borders is largely inaccurate. There was no invasion of Scotland after Flodden and there is no indication of increased English activity in the Scottish marches immediately after the battle. Flodden had been a decisive battle and a major English victory, but, in the words of Geoffrey Elton, 'surprisingly little was done to follow it up'.[50]

The absence of an English invasion is partly explained by the great cost of military campaigning. It has been estimated that in the first six years of Henry VIII's reign, the English Treasury of the Chamber, the major financial office, had paid out over a million pounds, 'of which some two-thirds went on war and nearly half in a single week of 5–12 June 1513'.[51] The English army at Flodden took the king's pay and Thomas Howard, Earl of Surrey, was acutely aware of the need to save money. Thus, on 14 September 1513, Surrey dismissed the greater part of his army, boasting that he saved the Exchequer the wages of 18,689 men for a fortnight.[52] Henry VIII was still waging war in France at this time and to launch a second campaign in Scotland would have been financially and militarily disastrous. Henry was currently enjoying some success, having won the infamous 'battle of the Spurs', when the French cavalry fled so rapidly. He had no intention of throwing it all away with a pointless war in Scotland. A notoriously vain man, Henry would have been envious that he had been eclipsed by the stunning victory of his subordinates.

In addition, Flodden had been fought in mid-September and it was around this time of year that armies began to think of suspending their activities for the coming winter. This was mainly a problem of supply. Armies could not be expected to live off the land during the winter months, especially in the barren frontier marches. There had already been severe problems during the Flodden campaign when the English army had ran out of beer and been reduced to drinking puddle water.[53] Surrey's victory at Flodden had been a brilliant defensive action and achieved against the odds but he was too wise and wily to push his luck any further by launching a hasty invasion of Scotland. He probably could not have mustered the force for an invasion anyway. The English army was weary from a long, hard campaign and now, with the battle won, most of the force would only have wanted to go home.

In the absence of a major invasion of Scotland, Thomas Lord Dacre of Gilsland, the English warden of the marches who had fought at Flodden, was left to guard the frontier and keep the Scots in good order. Henry VIII's orders to Dacre have not survived so it is difficult to determine the official policy regarding Scotland and the marches. Dacre was probably expected to put the Scots on the defensive by subjecting them to a series of destructive raids. Fortunately, most of Dacre's correspondence from this period has survived. It provides a fascinating insight into the life of a Border warden and is the ideal source for assessing the extent of frontier activity in the months after the battle.

The first reference to English actions in the Scottish marches comes in Lord Dacre's letter of 22 October 1513, six weeks after the battle.[54] These raids were small in scale, although the writer claimed no less annoying to the enemy. On the following day, Dacre recorded three raids into Annandale and four raids into Teviotdale.[55] Detailing the latter raids, Dacre reported the burning of Howpaslot Tower on the Borthwick water near Hawick and winning a good haul of sheep, goods and 'insight' (furniture); an attack upon Carlanrig taking about eighty cattle; and a great raid made by the men of Tynedale and Redesdale, who burnt the village of Ancrum and took sixty prisoners. Dacre did not mention the fate of the fourth raid although, like the other three, it was probably in the vicinity of Hawick.[56] On 29 October, Dacre reported two further expeditions. On the night of Tuesday 24 October, he sent sixty of his own tenants from Gilsland to Eskdalemuir, where they burnt seven houses and took some cattle. On the morning of Thursday 26 October, Sir Christopher Dacre, the brother of the warden, and a band of his followers burnt Stakehughe Tower and the surrounding area, 'continewally birnying from the breke of day to one of the clok after noon'.[57] Finally, on 13 November, Dacre wrote to Henry about a 'Great Raid' into Liddesdale and the Scottish middle march.[58]

These are all the raids recorded by Lord Dacre for the period between the battle of Flodden in September 1513 and the signing of the peace treaty between Henry VIII and Louis XII of France in August 1514. There is no reference to any attack made upon Hawick, although it is clear that English raiding parties were in the vicinity of the town. No doubt, Dacre hoped that his reports would greatly impress his superiors. The Bishop of Durham, for one, favourably commended him on the many injuries he had done to the Scots.[59] Some historians have subscribed to this view. George MacDonald Fraser claims in his popular Border history *The Steel Bonnets* that the Scottish marches, 'could hardly have fared worse if Henry had brought all-out war north of the Border'.[60]

In fact, rather than a crushing blow, these raids seem to have followed the old pattern of cross-Border reiving. They were generally targeted against isolated farmhouses and towers, clearly with one eye on a speedy exit before the Scots could organise and respond. Many of these places were just over the frontier from the English west march, where the Dacre family had its main properties. The closeness of England suggests that these locations had little economic or strategic importance. Writing to the distant council of England, Dacre reported that he had burnt the town of Canonbie as if he had won a major military victory.[61] Several years earlier however, James IV had visited Canonbie during his 'raid upon Eskdale' to root out local outlaws and found it so poor and wasted that it could not supply the royal party with any supplies.[62] Likewise, Dacre recorded that he had burnt several towers and farms in Teviotdale. These however were very isolated places and vulnerable to attack. The near-contemporary ballad *Jamie Telfer of the Fair Dodhead* describes a similar raid upon a lonely settlement only a few miles from Howpaslot Tower, which Dacre had burnt in 1513. According to the ballad, the luckless Jamie Telfer could do nothing to prevent the intruders taking his cattle and belongings, since his only defence was 'ae auld sword without a sheath/That hardly now would fell a mouse.'[63]

Lord Dacre's willingness to attack only soft targets is underlined by his mood of caution when Henry ordered him to make larger, more destructive raids upon the Scottish marches. On 20 October 1513, Dacre acknowledged 'the King's desire' for him to make raids upon the three Scottish marches.[64] It is clear that Dacre had great reservations about these raids. He wrote back reminding Henry that Richard III, Duke of Gloucester and former warden of the west march, had always thought that making an expedition into Teviotdale was a great enterprise, even with all his allies and supporters. Dacre's hesitancy about making an invasion of the Scottish marches came from his long years of experience in Border warfare. He knew that big invasions of this kind required careful organisation and planning, and that there were many dangers about hanging around in their enemy's territory. In 1523, the younger Earl of Surrey, the son of the Flodden hero, wrote a vivid description of a raid upon Jedburgh. Surrey's letter clearly described the kind of situation that Dacre was afraid of. Surrey wrote that Jedburgh was the most dangerous place that he had ever known. During the night, the fiendish Scots continually ambushed and harried the English camp, causing the horses to stampede and great distress and alarm amongst his force:

I dare not write of the wonders that my Lord Dacre and all his company saw that night, six times, of sprights and fearful sights. They all say that the devil was among them six times. I assure your grace, I found the Scots at this time the boldest and hottest men that ever I saw in any nation.[65]

Surrey might have been writing an official dispatch but he could not hide the terror that his army had gone through during the raid. In 1513, Thomas Dacre was fully aware that an invasion had the potential to go horribly wrong. But it does not seem to have occurred to him that the Scots would be any weaker after their defeat at Flodden.

Another reason for Dacre's unwillingness to make raids into Scotland at this time was his own weakness as warden, particularly of the English east march. His appointment to the wardenship of all three marches in 1511 had represented, in S.M. Harrison's words, 'rather a lack of any more suitable candidate than a reflection of Dacre's particular talents'.[66] The main problem was finance. There is no record that Dacre ever received an official salary and as a result he constantly struggled to fulfil his remit. In a letter of May 1514, he countered criticisms of his wardenship, writing: 'Right harde and impossible it is for suche a poure Baron as I am, to make resistance and kepe the King's subgeitts ... without great help and assistance.'[67] Dacre's problems were made worse by his failure to get on with the Northumbrian gentry. In the east march, the Dacre family was thought to be little more than a gang of Border brigands. Loyalties lay firmly with more established heads, especially the powerful Percy family. Dacre complained that he had, 'no strienth ne help of men, freynds, ne tennants, within the same est Marchies ... non of them doo seruice for me'.[68] Likewise, when reporting the 'Great Raid' of November 1513, Dacre complained that many prominent men of the east march had promised to support the raid but had failed to turn up at the appointed meeting place.

It appears therefore that English raiding after Flodden was very limited. Lord Dacre faced many difficulties that prevented him from getting deeply involved in Scotland. Henry VIII was away on campaign in France and had other things on his mind. Thirty years after Flodden, English raiding destroyed much of southern Scotland during the infamous Hertford Raids of 1544 and 1545, but there is little to suggest that raiding on a similar scale took place after Flodden. Indeed, it is possible that the memory of the Flodden period and the Hertford Raids became confused over the course of time. Oral traditions often tend to telescope events, pushing them together and missing out the 'uneventful' times in-between. The notion that the Borders were devastated after Flodden may in fact be a folk memory of much later events.

But where does this leave the Common Riding tradition about the defeat of a raiding party and the capture of their flag? A careful reading of Lord Dacre's letters suggests that the tradition may have some truth. On 13 November 1513, Dacre wrote to Henry VIII informing him that he had recently made a 'Great Raid' in Scotland with a force of 4,000 horsemen and 400 'fute men with bowes'.[69] Contemporary figures of this kind are notoriously unreliable and can only be taken to mean 'a very great number'. Nevertheless, the English force was important enough to occasion a lengthy report from the warden. Unusually for a Border raid it also included a slow-moving company of infantry. Curiously however, despite its strength, the Great Raid doesn't seem to have achieved very much, apart from burning some isolated towers and hamlets and taking plunder, as Dacre put it, 'of no gret substance'. Perhaps to their surprise, the English came up against a defensive force that was sizeable, vigilant and only too ready to attack the would-be spoiler. As Dacre later recalled, 'the Scots persewed us right sore ... bekered with us, and gave us hand stroks.' Resistance came from several different sources. As the English crossed the valley of the Rule Water to the south of Jedburgh, they were harried by a force that included members of the unruly Turnbull family or clan. Three Scottish 'standards' then appeared, making a pincer-like assault upon the English:

That is to say, David Karr of Fernehirst, and the lard of Bongedworth upon the oon side, and the sheriff of Tevidale on the othre side, with the nombre of Dcc men or mo.[70]

As the English fled for home, the Scots were further strengthened by the appearance of their own warden, Alexander Lord Home, with 2,000 men and four other standards (unfortunately unnamed). 'And so the countre drew fast to theym,' as Dacre gloomily concluded.

We can only speculate on the extent of co-operation and organisation amongst the various groups of defending Scots. They had had some time to prepare for the raid thanks to a system of warning beacons placed on local hilltops. The appearance of Lord Home is significant and must have given Dacre an unpleasant surprise. It was Home's sworn military duty as warden to continuously harry and drive any invaders back over the Border. His presence suggests that the normal Border defensive systems were working effectively in November 1513. But the success of the operation against the English might have had more to do with traditional Scottish impetuosity rather than organisational genius. The usual reaction to raids of this kind involved excitement, vigour and haste. Writing sometime around 1521, the Scottish historian and theologian John Major captured the spirit of this brave, but often reckless, defence:

> The nearest chief gathers the neighbouring folk together, and at the first word of the presence of the foe, each man before mid-day is in arms, for he keeps his weapons about him, mounts his horse, makes for the enemy's position, and, whether in order of battle or not in order of battle, rushes on the foe, not seldom bringing destruction on himself as well as the invader.[71]

But whatever the extent of co-operation amongst the Scots, there is no doubt that they put up an effective resistance to a major English raid. The invader had been sent home with a good bloody nose, apparently having achieved very little. There is no sign of weakness or submission amongst the Scots, even though the Great Raid had taken place just two months after their dreadful defeat at Flodden. With the failure of the Great Raid, English activity in Scotland seems to have largely petered out. There is no record of Lord Dacre ever having fulfilled his intention of making a great raid upon the Scottish east or west marches, despite his assurances to the king. In a letter of 17 May 1514, Dacre gave a list of 'towyns and howsys' in Scotland that had been destroyed by raids.[72] Most of these had already been mentioned in previous letters, suggesting that Dacre was going over old ground, perhaps in the hope that his superiors would not notice.

The earliest accounts of the Hawick Common Riding tradition refer to the period 'sometime after Flodden' and not to the year '1514'. This is similar to the ancient Border ballads, which sometimes specify a certain day or a month but rarely mention the year of an event. Likewise, the oldest surviving replica of the captured flag has the contemporary date '1707' and not the date of a historical event. However, there is no need to contest the main point of the tradition, namely that a raiding party was defeated. It might be relevant that Lord Dacre's letter of 23 October 1513 refers to four raids into Teviotdale close to Hawick but records the success of only three parties. Alternatively, the tradition might have originated in the Great Raid of November 1513. Hawick's local superior, Sir James Douglas of Cavers, the Sheriff of Teviotdale, was part of the Scottish defence. After the raid, some of the English force went home to Hexham in Northumberland. The arms of the Priory Church of St Andrew at Hexham bear a gold cross on a blue background that is very similar to the 'Banner Blue' of the Common Riding.

It was shown in chapter one that flags and banners have a central role in the modern ridings, where they are treated with great reverence. For centuries, flags and banners were functional objects in a world that was largely non-literate and where messages had to be conveyed by symbols. They were part of the international sign language of heraldry and they had important military functions, such as acting as a rallying point for soldiers or symbolising authority. The Scots prepared new banners for the Flodden campaign, including a special banner for the king and banners that bore the images of Saint Andrew and Saint Margaret, complete with special protective covers to keep the rain off.[73] Flags of this kind were often credited with magical properties and were treated as lucky charms. On the way to Flodden, the Earl of Surrey said

Left: A replica of the Hawick Banner Blue now hangs in Hexham Abbey, Northumberland, from where it might have originated.

Below: The image of Flodden was used to commemorate much later wars. The Hawick Acting Father lowers the 1514 flag at the war memorial. *(Ian Landles)*

Mass in Durham Cathedral and borrowed the holy banner of Saint Cuthbert to bring his side good fortune. The banner had been used in other campaigns against the Scots and the victory at Flodden was attributed to Cuthbert's intervention.[74] Flags and banners also had an important role in the chivalric code, which was still common currency at the time of Flodden. In August 1513, Lord Home suffered a severe mauling during the 'Ill-Raid' in Northumberland. The English chronicler Edmund Hall reported that Home lost many of his men and also his banner, implying that this had been an embarrassing blow to Home's prestige.[75]

Capturing the banner of an enemy was clearly a notable event and would have been celebrated and remembered. In the Borders, there were many legends about captured flags and banners. In Jedburgh, the Shoemakers Guild had a flag reputedly taken from the English at the battle of Newburn (1640). The rival guild of weavers had two flags, one from the English at the battle of Bannockburn (1314) and the other from the Highlanders at the battle of Killiecrankie (1689).[76] In Selkirk, 'Fletcher' returned from Flodden bearing a captured English banner. Closer to Hawick, old Cavers house, the home of an important branch of the Douglas family, held an ancient flag captured at, or before, the battle of Otterburn (1388).[77] Of course, some of these stories are very dubious and there is little doubt that flags and banners were often the subject of embellishment. Trade guilds, such as the Jedburgh shoemakers and weavers, made up stories about their banner to make it seem more important than those of their rivals, thus adding status to their guild.

In Hawick, the earliest references to a town flag date from the early eighteenth century. In 1706, the existing flag had become 'altogidder torne and useless' so the town council decided to buy a new one in readiness for the next Common Riding. A member of the council called Bailie Martin made a trip to Edinburgh to buy coloured silks and ribbons, and the council paid to have the new flag specially made. In May 1707 a merchant called George Deans became the first cornet to carry the 'new colour' at the Common Riding. The flag was treated as one of the town's most precious possessions as it was stored in the charter chest along with other precious documents.[78]

The importance of the Flodden traditions in several modern Common Ridings cannot be underestimated, although the historical evidence for these traditions is very ambiguous. It is likely that some men from the Border burghs fought at Flodden, either under the command of Lord Home or James IV. Some were probably killed at the battle but others would have returned home, perhaps bringing captured flags or other items back with them. There is nothing to support the stories about 'exact' numbers of men being lost at Flodden or for the traditional assertion that all the Border men were killed. Similarly, it seems that the Borders were not laid waste after the battle and that the Scots were still able to defend themselves and resist a major English raid. The Flodden traditions have been consistent since the eighteenth century, although over the years many fanciful details have been attached to them. It remains uncertain why these traditions should have become so closely linked with the Common Ridings, although like the ridings themselves they are a source of local identity and civic pride, stories that people like to tell about themselves and their town.

4

Form and Function in the Eighteenth-Century Ridings, *c.1690-c.1800*

In the eighteenth century, accounts of the ridings become more extensive and detailed, thus providing a clearer picture of the development of these events. Whilst many of the older features of the ridings continued, new themes and purposes started to emerge. This chapter will show that in the eighteenth century the ridings were a complex mix of civic and popular functions. The chapter begins by considering the civic functions of the ridings, showing how they were used to check encroachments on burgh lands, to consolidate authority and status in towns, and to cement social relations and group unity. Like other areas of national culture, the political dimension of the ridings was heightened in the eighteenth century. Local and national patriotism was closely associated, often to be reflected in the ridings, whilst in some cases the ridings developed links with radical politics. The chapter also considers the popular and recreational functions of the ridings. These events attracted widespread popular support, which sometimes led to conflict with civic authorities. The chapter explores the 'language' of the ridings, indicating the use of 'stage-props' and other artefacts to underline the importance of events. Finally, there is an examination of the decline of the ridings in the later eighteenth century, why these events survived in some towns but disappeared in others.

Functions of the Eighteenth-Century Ridings

In the eighteenth century, the primary function of the ridings remained the protection of the marches. Communities had several ways of dealing with encroachments on their lands. Immediate action might take place during the course of a riding. In June 1775, riders at Peebles found that some sheep belonging to a neighbouring farmer were being grazed on the common. Officials drove the sheep away and ordered the herd not to let them on the land in future.[1] Incidents of encroachment could also be attended to after a riding. It was customary for riders to provide the authorities with a report on the state of their lands. Following Hawick Common Riding in 1816, the Burleymen reported to the town council that several 'depredations' had been made on the town's land. The council took action and ordered that 'prominent measures should be taken to destroy these spoilers of the public property'.[2]

As well as annual ridings, communities also made less formal inspections of their lands. In 1737, the burgh authorities in Hawick, including some of the 'old burgesses' of the town, visited a disputed part of the common where they set up some march stones to establish the boundary.[3] Similarly, in 1776, the town council of Peebles appointed the magistrates and Dean of Guild to inspect a disputed boundary and to set up march stones to fix it 'in all time coming'.[4] Neighbouring landowners sometimes requested burgh authorities to clarify the boundary lines. In 1713, Walter Patersone, a farmer near Hawick, asked the town council to establish 'distinct meiths and marches' between his land and that of the town, which was agreed by the erection of march stones.[5] In 1779, following a request from a neighbouring landowner, the town council of Peebles made a formal perambulation to establish the line between the two properties.[6] During the ridings, the authorities had to be extremely careful that participants kept to the right line and did not encroach upon neighbouring properties, which might have led to a dispute. To prevent this from happening, burgh officials were sent out to mark the boundaries a few days before the riding. In 1755, the town council of Hawick ordered that the common 'shall be merched some days before the common rideing', employing four men with spades to cut turfs on the correct line.[7]

In the eighteenth century, public rituals and ceremonies played a major part in the way politics and society operated, both at local and national levels. Civic ritual could mobilise deep feelings of authority and consensus, and establish the power of corporate institutions. Burgh officials would often try to associate themselves with the Church in an attempt to underline their supernatural authority. Similarly, it was widely asserted that certain items of civic regalia, such as chains or robes of office, were magically imbued with corporate authority. The ridings gave burgh authorities and others the chance to enhance their position in the community. It was important to the image of their office that they should be involved. In Hawick, members of the town council were obliged to ride at the Common Riding or they would forfeit their position on the council.[8]

Contemporaries were fully aware that the ridings could be used for promoting both themselves and the institutions that they represented. In many towns, there were recurring arguments between various groups over their position in the ridings, often leading to bitterness and occasional violence. Craft guilds competed against each other for the prime position in the procession, which was at the front near the flag and the burgh authorities. Bringing up the rear was unpopular because it implied inferior status. At the Musselburgh riding of 1732, 'an unlucky difference' occurred between the incorporations of Weavers and Tailors over their positions in the procession, as the *Caledonian Mercury* reported:

> *The Taylors argued, That as the Precedency faln to them by Lot, no Opposition could now be offered in that Respect. 'Twas alledged on the other hand, That they (the Weavers) were Men, and as such, preferable at in all Events to Taylors. This signal Affront could not possibly be digested … while the Weaver Squadron were filing off to take the Post of Honour, with Capt. Scot at their Head, Adjutant Fairley (who acted in that Capacity on the Taylor Squadron) directed a blow at our Captain's Snout, which brought him to the Ground. Thus were the two Corps fiercely engaged; and nought was to be seen but heavy Blows, Hats off, broken Heads, bloody Noses and empty Saddles; till at last the Plea of Manhood seemed to go in favour of the Needlemen.[9]*

Captain Scot of the Weavers was taken prisoner and it was with great difficulty that the Weavers managed to escape without losing their flag. The Weavers tried to explain this humiliation by saying that the Tailors had been supported by the Butchers, 'and that they did not incline to embark with these Men of Blood'. There were similar disputes in other towns about the order of processions. In April 1767, the town council of Linlithgow recorded that recently there had been 'smal contests' between the Craft Incorporations, 'as to the parts of the street upon which they arrange themselves at the Cross upon their going and returning from the Marches'. After many arguments, the council finally devised a plan where the Crafts were to form themselves into 'two ranks' and the magistrates with the burgh flags would ride 'betwixt the Cordiners and the Weavers'.[10]

Another function of the eighteenth-century ridings, which might seem at odds with disputes of this kind, was the promotion of social ties and group unity. All communities have a compelling need to promote social harmony, to cement internal relations and reinforce a sense of group solidarity. The ridings re-affirmed these, in part through the shared experience of those who took part. Similarly, feasting together stressed fellowship and reinforced group awareness and expectations. During the ridings, many stops were made for refreshments and drinks. Describing Hawick Common Riding in the late eighteenth century, Arthur Balbirnie's *Common Riding Song* includes the verse:

> *At the Ca-knowe we halt a little;*
> *Slack our girths, and ease the cripple;*
> *Take a glass o' cheerin' whisky,*
> *Then down o'er Hawick Mossbrow fu' frisky.*[11]

In all cases, the ridings concluded with some form of corporate dinner and other entertainment. Balbirnie's poem says that after the Hawick riding the participants went to the town hall and spent the evening drinking, singing and dancing:

> *In the Town Hall all things are ready,*
> *Knives and forks we'll ply them steady;*
> *Push about the flowing glasses –*
> *Sing and dance and kiss the lasses.*

In Linlithgow, the annual Marches Day dinner was the social highlight of the civic year and involved considerable expenditure on the part of the council. In 1800, the council spent £9 18s 6d on hospitality at the Marches Day, as the treasurer's accounts illustrate:

To the Diken of the Fleshers for 2 lambs and 22 lb of Beef	£2 16s	
To the Diken of the Bakers for Tearts, Pyes and Loavs	£2 6s	
To 2 Gallons of Double Rum	£1 10s	
To 1 pint of Double Gin	8s	
To 4lbs of Sugar	4s	8d
To Beer	3s	8d
To Mr Alex. Mitchell	£1 5s	
To the Standart Bearers at the Brig	2s	8d
To the Millers at the Burgh Mill	2s	
To the Standart Bearers at Blackness	6s	
To the Castle (Castal Sogers)	10s	
To Clenin the hous at Blackness	4s	6d
To John Drummond for furning the hous with tabals	5s	
To Chirety	2s	
To 4 Broakin glesses	1s	6d[12]

The ridings also featured dinners and social gatherings for the trade and craft guilds. The conviviality of members had always been one of the most important functions of the guilds and the ridings were an opportunity for members to come together and celebrate their institution. In the 1790s, around a quarter of the annual expenditure of the Shoemakers Guild of Selkirk went on entertaining at the Common Riding. In 1796, for example, the guild had an annual expenditure of £7 13s 5d, of which £1 19s 2d was spent on a dinner, drink and music at the Common Riding, including 2s on the 'Lads' Ale' and 6s 6d on a fiddler, fifer

The flags of the ancient Selkirk craft guilds are still carried at the Common Riding. These photographs were taken in 1906 and show the Standard Bearers of the Shoemakers and the Tailors. (*Scottish Borders Museum and Gallery Service (Selkirk Collection)*)

and drummer.[13] In the early 1800s, the Shoemakers Guild of Linlithgow spent £2 on the annual dinner on the Marches Day, plus extra on music.[14] Back in Selkirk, the guild member who carried the banner at the Common Riding was expected to provide hospitality for his fellows. In 1721, Archbauld Watt of the Merchant Guild carried the flag and was to 'give ane entertainment upon the Common-riding day to the value of 20s. Sterling'. Failure to do so would mean losing his seat in the loft, 'his freedome of ye mortecloathe, and be extruded fra ye Companie'. In 1736, any member of the Merchants Guild who did not attend the Common Riding and the dinner of the guild would be fined 14s Scots. The guild treasurer would go to the shops and homes of absentees, 'and poind for same in cases of refusal'.[15]

Of course, this kind of excessive drinking and eating did not necessarily lead to social harmony. Getting drunk in a group might bring individuals closer together but their behaviour might alienate them from the wider community. In 1725, Hawick town council complained about, 'enormities, debates, and revellings committed at the Riding of the Marches ... both by old and young men, who were overtaken by excess in drunkenness'.[16] Sometimes, burgh authorities were sensitive to accusations of waste and often felt obliged to limit their spending at the ridings. In 1737, the town council of Stirling agreed not to spend any of the town's revenue at the Riding of the Marches because it was 'ane unnecessary burden on the toun'.[17] Similarly, in 1816 the town council of Hawick warned the Cornet 'not to incur any unnecessary expense in entertaining his company at the Common Riding', because the burgh authorities had to pick up the bill.[18]

Another function of the eighteenth-century ridings was the mutual association between local and national patriotism. Whilst the ridings were primarily concerned with local attachments, they were influenced by national developments. The accession of George III in 1760 led to the growth of national pride and patriotic sentiment in Britain. Unlike his father or grandfather, George was a thoroughly British monarch, a skilled royal showman who asserted a powerful nationalistic image. George aroused some hostility but he was also the focus of much patriotic adulation, especially after 1789 when royal celebrations throughout Britain increased dramatically in scale. In part, this was a response to the British defeat in America and also to the French Revolution and the threat of invasion by Napoleon and his armies.

Patriotic sentiment was not just engineered from on high. Civic authorities and the common people themselves were enthusiastic supporters of the British cause. For example, volunteer militia regiments attracted widespread popular support. By 1804, almost half a million British males were under arms. According to figures compiled by respective Lord Lieutenants, in May 1804, three out of five men between the ages of seventeen and fifty-five were under arms in Roxburghshire and Selkirkshire, amongst the highest response rate in Scotland.[19] Some traditions in the ridings date from the Volunteer period, such as the flute bands, which were (and are) a symbol of staunch Protestantism. In 1803, the Drums and Fifes of the Hawick Volunteers were given the prominent role of leading the Cornet's procession, a tradition that still survives. In the modern event, the band plays a tune called *Dumbarton's Drums*, which was originally the tune of the Royal Scots, the oldest regiment in the British army.[20]

Patriotism had both national and local uses. Urban authorities were keen to participate in national events because, in Linda Colley's words, they were a convenient vehicle, 'to advertise their town's particular affluence, identity and culture, as an outlet for civic pride as well as British patriotism'.[21] Arguably, the most important of these was the birthday of King George III on 4 June, which was widely celebrated with church services, corporate dinners, bonfires and fireworks. In Hawick, people living on either side of the River Slitrig tried to outdo each other with the size of their bonfires. In some towns, the king's birthday and the Riding of the Marches coincided and the two events were closely linked. In Linlithgow, the town council habitually issued joint instructions to the treasurer to make preparations for the king's birthday and Marches Day. In Lauder, the Common Riding took place on the same day as the king's birthday. Typically, the day begun with a church service, where the town council 'paid allegiance to their Sovereign Lord', which was followed by the riding and then a grand dinner to celebrate the health of the king and the prosperity of the burgh.[22]

Events of this kind were popular, but they were only one part of the story. The British monarchy stood at the head of a rigid social hierarchy, which some free-thinkers, inspired by new political ideas, had started to question. In Hawick, the burgh authorities were attacked for their extravagant waste of public money when celebrating the king's birthday. In the early 1800s, James Hogg, a stocking-maker, poet and political radical, used his *Common Riding Song* to satirise the event:

> *Sacred was the widow's portion,*
> *Sacred long from all extortion.*
> *Frugal temperance urged no cesses*
> *Birthday rants, nor Bailies' messes.*

Hogg's attack on the authorities caused the song to be printed in Kelso rather than Hawick because the only printer in Hawick, Robert Armstrong, had been a member of the town council and refused to handle the song.

In the late eighteenth century, the spotlight of political activity was turning increasingly towards the towns, either as Parliamentary seats or as the focus of county elections. Behind this development lay the struggle for control of the House of Commons and the emergence of party politics. In Scotland, the imagery of the ridings was used to express political allegiances, especially in the struggles for the reform of Parliament, which culminated in the Great Reform Act of 1832. The growing demand for the reform of Parliament was partly explained by the rise of an urban middle class, who had strong political aspirations. In 1832, the Whig government was ready to enfranchise the middle classes because, in William Ferguson's words, 'the middle-class was well-to-do, responsible, and educated, and only by granting its members representation as allies of the old governing class could the constitution be saved from democratic threats'.[23]

A good example of the new style of political activist was Robert Wilson, who had been Cornet of Hawick in 1799. In his writing, Wilson recognised the need for the security of property and for the 'middle orders of society' to have the right to vote, as this would be a safeguard against revolution and 'the hasty inflammability of the lower orders'.[24] Wilson and his fellow reformers drew inspiration from the Common Riding with its tradition of freedom from an over-bearing aristocracy. In the election campaign of May 1831, reformers from Hawick marched to Jedburgh to lend their support to the local Whig, Sir William Elliot of Stobs. The Drum and Fife band led the reformers, playing Common Riding airs as they strode along. Although their man was defeated in the ballot, the reformers claimed that they had won the moral victory. Elliot was carried shoulder-high through the streets of Jedburgh by the reformers, who sang Common Riding songs.[25] In many Border towns, the eventual passage of the Reform Act was widely celebrated, including local holidays, processions and open-air dinners. In Hawick, the Common Riding flag was flown prominently from the roof of the town hall.[26]

It is appropriate here to consider 'the most famous Borderer of all', Sir Walter Scott, and his attitude towards the ridings. It might be thought that Scott would have taken great pride in these ancient events. After all, here was a man deeply imbued with a sense of Scottish history and tradition, having made regular 'raids' into the darkest Borders to capture popular customs and ballads. Living in the Borders, Scott certainly knew about the ridings; Selkirk Common Riding took place almost on his doorstep. However, apart from a brief reference in *The Minstrelsy of the Scottish Border*, he seems to have written almost nothing about them.

This silence is remarkable and very revealing. Scott, it seems, turned up his nose at the ridings, partly because he felt threatened by their uninhibited nature but also because at this time the ridings were used as a vehicle for radical politics. Scott had little sympathy for the urban working classes, denying their right to be politically active and arguing that they should only obey their social superiors. He identified closely with his 'clan' and its chieftain, idealising the past and wanting to see a safe, ordered and deferential society. After his death in 1832, Scott achieved universal adulation but it is often forgotten that he was not entirely popular during his lifetime. Robert Wilson, the former Cornet of Hawick, had little time for Scott's romantic notions about the past and 'the previous motley annals of mankind', arguing that intelligent men should concentrate on the present. Wilson wrote that Scott, 'has attempted to revive the lifeless remains of feudal chivalry and nonsense ... What a pity it is that the original and cultivated mind of the baronet had not been directed to more noble pursuits!'[27] During the election meeting at Jedburgh in May 1831, Scott was abused and stones were thrown at his carriage by the 'blackguards' from Hawick and Jedburgh. John Lockhart, Scott's biographer and son-in-law, was horrified at the scene: 'The town was in a most contempestuous state: it was almost wholly in the hands of a disciplined rabble, chiefly weavers from Hawick, who marched up and down with drums and banners.'[28] It is also curious that Scott's great friend James Hogg, the Ettrick Shepherd, also wrote nothing about the ridings. A down-to-earth Border shepherd, Hogg was never averse to having a good drink or getting his hands dirty. In 1820, he turned down an invitation to attend the coronation of George IV because he would have missed St Boswells fair. Politically, Hogg was a moderate and a traditionalist, suspicious of both Tories and Whigs.[29] Perhaps the ridings were so familiar to Hogg that they were not worthy of comment.

The popularity of the ridings in the eighteenth century was not only restricted to burgh authorities. For many locals, including women and children, the ridings were occasions to anticipate with particular relish. Popular customs like the ridings provided a temporary escape from the harshness of the everyday world, giving people a sense of excitement and a chance to free themselves from boredom and weariness. Weeks and months of hard labour and deprivation were compensated for by the expectation of the ridings. For a brief period, food and drink were abundant, friendship and courtship flourished and the hardship of life was forgotten. Strong drink was an essential part of this temporary culture. Drunkenness was a regular feature of the ridings and many people indulged who were normally only moderate drinkers. Moreover, because normal inhibitions were temporarily lowered, popular customs like the ridings had a degree of sexual licence, offering young men and women the opportunity for encounters and liaisons. As R.W. Malcolmson has observed: 'Many fairs provided for the common people what masquerades afforded to the gentry and the nobility.'[30] Freed from normal restraints, young people could use these occasions to make new contacts or pursue existing ones.

Horseracing was another important recreational feature of the ridings and during the eighteenth century it underwent a significant transformation. The Jockey Club was formed in 1752 to regulate the sport. Courses were properly laid out and some of the classic British races were established, such as the St Ledger in 1776 and the Derby in 1780. Horse racing had a long association with the ridings, although local meetings of this kind were of limited quality. Few people could afford to maintain a thoroughbred but instead raced on the same horses that they used in the ridings, such as workhorses, ponies and even donkeys. Racing at this level was as much about social prestige as prize money. As Wray Vamplew observed: 'What greater ambition could there be than to ride one's own horse to victory at one's local meeting?'[31] Races were often run in heats to make the best of a small entry. In 1736, the town council of Peebles provided a purse of five guineas, 'and one given in compliments by the provost', for a race to be run in heats, the best of three, twice round.[32] Burgh authorities usually gave their support to local meetings, supplying some of the prizes from common funds. In 1725, Hawick town council gave £2 for the year's plate at the Common Riding.[33] In Peebles, the principal races were connected with the Beltane Fair at the beginning of May, although some races may also have taken place at the Riding of the Marches. In 1728, the town council provided a china bowl and fifteen guineas prize money.[34] Members of the local business communities also clubbed together to supply prizes.

Race meetings were important attractions, which drew people into towns. In the early eighteenth century, the town council of Selkirk willingly leant its support to the Common Riding races, 'considering the advantage a race would be to the burgh by the great confluence of gentlemen that would resort thereto'.[35] In 1802, James Hogg, the Ettrick Shepherd, visited the famous races at Leith, noting that the crowd was 'prodigious'. As he later wrote: 'I never expected to see so many people together in this world ... there being thousands on the sands betwixt the carriages and the scaffolds that could not see the heads of the riders.'[36] Writing about Hawick Common Riding in the early 1800s, Robert Wilson observed: 'The assemblage of people upon this occasion has been very numerous; principally, no doubt, on account of the excellent races which for these several years past have taken place upon the common.'[37] Burgh authorities went to great efforts to promote their local meetings. In 1736, the town council of Peebles ordered the council clerk to prepare advertisements for the local races and to send them to Edinburgh for insertion in 'publick news'.[38] In 1707, the races at Stirling were to be advertised in the '*Gazett*' six weeks in advance.[39]

Race meetings were important social gatherings, involving a certain festive licence as well as offering the opportunity of instant enrichment. In 1802, James Hogg visited a race meeting near Penicuik. He noted that the meeting had attracted a 'multitude' of people, some of whom were strangely dressed, and that it had been organised by 'a club of boys':

This was a holiday with them, that they would spend the evening in foot races and dancing; that these were the members so fantastically dressed with ribbons, which they had got from neighbouring girls, whom they, in return, would treat at their ball in the evening.[40]

Race meetings also included athletic events, such as sprinting, leaping, wrestling and other tests of strength and endurance, all accessible to people unable to afford a horse. In 1707, the races at Stirling included 'a man's foot race' for pairs of stockings, shoes and gloves.[41]

Popular support for the ridings amounted to more than a love of feasting and horse racing. The ridings were the products of a conservative culture, which appealed to the past to reinforce traditional rights and privileges, such as access to land or the right to gather resources. These were often zealously protected and any attempt at interference was likely to provoke a reaction. This sense of readiness to defend custom might extend to the ridings themselves. For example, in 1706 and in 1809, serious disputes took place at Hawick when the burgh authorities tried to change normal procedures at the Common Riding.

In chapter two, it was suggested that the appointment of young men as symbolic leaders of the ridings had many striking parallels with older customs of abbots or lords of misrule. By the eighteenth century, towns had different methods of choosing Standard Bearers for the ridings. In Lanark, the town council nominated the Lord Cornet in all years ending in odd numbers whilst the deacons of the crafts made the nomination when it was evens.[42] In Linlithgow, the privilege of carrying the town flag at the Marches Day went in an eight-year rotation cycle amongst the deacons of the various craft guilds, who would all have been married men.[43]

In Hawick, it was customary for the town council to make the final choice of Cornet, but for the young unmarried men to select the candidates from amongst themselves and submit a shortlist to the council. In June 1706, the town council did its usual duty and selected a man called Thomas Hardie to be Cornet. Unfortunately, for some reason, Hardie failed to turn up on the day of the Common Riding, leaving the town without a Cornet. Faced with an awkward decision, the town council agreed that the flag would be carried in turn by the oldest and youngest bailies that were present and that the 'young unmaried men' would not be allowed to carry the flag in future. The council's decision provoked immediate uproar amongst the young men and lads, who believed that their traditional privilege was being taken from them. Scuffles broke out as some of them tried unsuccessfully to wrestle the flag from the authorities. The lads then hastily made up 'ane mocke Colour' of their own, pursuing and harrying the council officials as they rode the marches:

deriding, mockeing, scoffing, and laughing at the old pencill, and bearers and cariers thereof, menaceing, threatning, and with many intollerable, injurious, and opproprious words, speeches, and carages publickly abuseing the present towne Counsell.[44]

It seems that the rebels had some popular support because the following day many inhabitants did 'holow out at windows, and to hoot the bailies' as they went about their business. The following year, the council decided to obtain a new copy of the flag and ordered that no other 'colour, pencell or standard' was to be carried at the Common Riding. However, the council, perhaps shaken by events of the previous year, backed down over the proposal not to appoint a Cornet and the tradition went ahead as usual.

Popular resentment towards the authorities in Hawick re-emerged in 1809, which became known as the year of the 'Disputed Common Riding'. The controversy was the result of the town council's attempts to restrict the Common Riding, especially the extent of corporate hospitality that took place during it, which was proving a drain on the council's funds. In May 1809, the town council put an end to pre-Common Riding meetings, including the official 'clothes making' where the Cornet's green jacket was made ready. The Cornet could retain the privilege of holding a dinner at the Common Riding, but invitations would be restricted

LIST OF CORNETS

1703 James Scott, called The Laird
1705 James Scott, West Port
1706 Bailie Hardie, because Thos. Hardie refused
1707 George Deans, merchant
1709 George Wight
1710 Wm. Gardener
1711 John Robson
1712 George Renwick
1713 James Purcell, wright
1714 Wm. Gladstanes
1715 John Stevensonne, weaver
1717 George Olifer, shoemaker
1718 Thomas Trumble, merchant
1719 Andrew Turnbull, merchant
1720 George Scott, wright
1721 Robert Howieson, merchant
1722 Robert Scott, merchant
1723 Name unknown
1724 Andrew Scott—Black Andrew
1725 Wm. Renwick, flesher
1726 James Dickson, merchant
1727 James Oliver, shoemaker
1728 Thomas Elliot, skinner
1729 Robert Boyd
1730 Gideon Ruecastle
1731 Wm. Richardson, cooper
1732 Name unknown
1733 Thomas Scott, shoemaker
1734 Robert Deans, flesher
1735 Wm. Turnbull, wright
1736 John Currie, skinner
1737 John Kedie, baker
1738 And. Turnbull, jun., mason
1739 James Wintrup, wright
1740 Geo. Gardener, shoemaker
1741 Chas. Tudhope, shoemaker
1742 Walter Purdom
1743 John Aitchison
1744 Francis Gladstones
1745 Robert Oliver, shoemaker
1746 A. Richardson, shoemaker

1747 John Wilkie, tailor
1748 Wm. Nichol, tobacconist
1749 W Tait, gardener
1750 Charles Stitt, merchant
1751 Wm. Kerr, merchant
1752 Wm. Oliver, shoemaker
1753 T. Turnbull, Esq., Fenwick
1754 Francis Aitken
1755 John Elliot, tanner
1756 Wm. Scott, baker
1757 John Robson, tailor
1758 William Oliver, merchant
1759 John Simpson, weaver
1760 G. Halliburton, wheelwright
1761 Walter Purdom, bailie
1762 J. Turnbull—Garlick Jock
1763 William Scott, tobacconist
1764 James Oliver, bailie
1765 Walter Scott—Black Wat
1766 Thomas Kedie, baker
1767 John Wilson, Deanfoot
1768 Wm. Oliver, Kirkwynd
1769 Wm. Scott, meal dealer
1770 G. Turnbull, West Port
1771 Archd. Paterson, cadger
1772 James Dryden, smith
1773 Walter Irvine, merchant
1774 Wm. Rodger, wright
1775 Robert Oliver, shoemaker
1776 Jas. Turnbull, clockmaker
1777 J. Richardson, wool merchant
1778 W. Robertson, carpet manuft.
1779 James Ekron—The Blast
1780 W. Burnet, shoemaker
1781 James Wilson, watchmaker
1782 Douglas Rodger, wright
1783 W. Turnbull, Esq., Fenwick
1784 James Oliver, baker
1785 John Wilson, tobacconist
1786 William Wilson, hosier
1787 James Oliver, tanner
1788 Wm. Scott, merchant
1789 Francis Scott, tobacconist

In Hawick, the list of Cornets goes back to the early eighteenth century. *(Author's collection)* and guests have to pay five shillings. These changes were very unpopular, not only because some people were being deprived of a free meal but also because the council was seen to be interfering with ancient rights and privileges. A petition was taken to the town council asking that the changes should be withdrawn, but it contained 'language highly disrespectable and improper' and was rejected, which only made the situation worse.[45] In a parody of a Common Riding song, James Hogg, a local poet, urged people to stand-up for their traditional rights:

> *Shades of heroes slain at Flodden!*
> *Shall your rights 'mong feet be trodden?*
> *Never! while a Border bowman*
> *Has a horse to ride the common.*

Rather foolishly, the town council turned cloak-and-dagger and held a secret meeting on the outskirts of the town, where they elected a Cornet, John Tully, a stonemason. Speaking for many others, Hogg was furious, commenting in his poem:

> *There our customs are arranged,*
> *Ancient modes for modern changed;*
> *If 'tis true as we've been told it,*
> *Their new Cornet here was moulded.*

> *If you love your ancient freedom,*
> *Their new Cornet never heed him;*
> *From among you chose a Cornet,*
> *Hand it down to sons unborn yet.*[46]

With Hogg's song as an anthem, an opposition Cornet – John Kyle, a merchant – was elected. Both Cornets and their supporters rode at the Common Riding. When the two parties met at the racecourse, there was reported to have been 'some disorder'. Incidents of this kind illustrated the strength of local attachment to the ridings and the readiness of people to defend traditional practices in these events. Whatever their motives, the authorities did not have a blank canvass to alter the ridings as and when they wished.

The Language of the Ridings

This section will examine the language of the eighteenth-century ridings, meaning the conventional symbols that were used to express certain ideas and values in the course of these events. Describing urban ritual and ceremony in English provincial towns between 1600 and 1800, Peter Borsay has observed:

> *All rituals and ceremonies were a piece of theatre in which the participants conjured a drama around themselves. Critical to the performance, and our interpretation of it, was the complex language and dramatic devices employed, which not only exploited words, but the full range of human sensations, appealing to the eye, the ear, the mouth and the body.*[47]

As well as burgh records, two sources about the eighteenth-century ridings deserve particular attention as they provide a fascinating insight into these events. *The Grand Procession of Musselburgh Fair or Marches Riding* is a mock epic poem that describes the Musselburgh riding

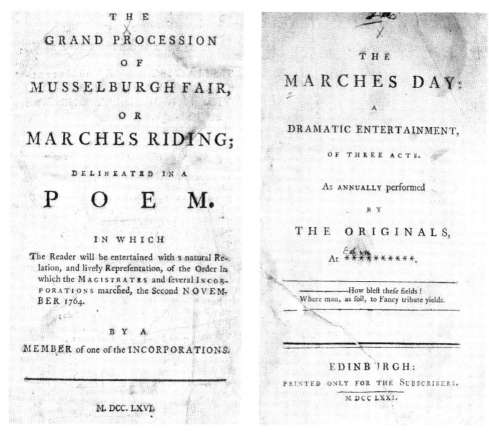

THE

GRAND PROCESSION

OF

MUSSELBURGH FAIR,

OR

MARCHES RIDING;

DELINEATED IN A

P O E M.

IN WHICH

The Reader will be entertained with a natural Relation, and lively Reprefentation, of the Order in which the MAGISTRATES and feveral INCORPORATIONS marched, the Second NOVEMBER 1764.

BY A

MEMBER of one of the INCORPORATIONS.

M. DCC. LXVI.

THE

MARCHES DAY:

A

DRAMATIC ENTERTAINMENT,

OF THREE ACTS.

As ANNUALLY performed

BY

THE ORIGINALS,

At ************.

———————How bleft thefe fields !
Where man, as foil, to Fancy tribute yields.

EDINBURGH:

PRINTED ONLY FOR THE SUBSCRIBERS.

MDCCLXXI.

Above left: The Grand Procession of Musselburgh Fair is a mock epic poem that describes the Musselburgh riding of 2 November 1764. (Trustees of the National Library of Scotland)

Above right: The Marches Day is a unique (and very funny) play about Linlithgow Marches, published in Edinburgh in 1771. (Trustees of the National Library of Scotland)

of 2 November 1764.[48] It was written by a 'Member of One of the Incorporations' and published in 1766. Of equal importance, *The Marches Day. A Dramatic Entertainment of Three Acts* is a play about Linlithgow Marches written by John Finlayson and published in Edinburgh in 1771.[49] It is not known when or where the play was performed, but it is likely that some of the characters, who have names such as Timothy Quotewell, Saunders Shrillpipe and Needy Strap, were based on real people.

Special clothing was one of the most important visual stage-props in the ridings. The main participants wore special costumes to enhance their status. In 1703, Hawick town council purchased new coats for the officers, piper and drummer. In 1726, the council bought a new pair of shoes for one of the officials and brightly coloured ribbons for the officers and drummer.[50] In Musselburgh, five musicians headed the procession, being described as, 'delightful to the eye/In red and scarlet shine'.[51] In Linlithgow, the town council issued special instructions before every Marches Day, 'to make ready the officers coats'. In 1706, the town purchased special coats for the officers, drummer and piper. Similarly, in 1800 the town hired a local tailor to make the 'Town's servants coats', including 3s 4d for 'trimming the hatts'.[52]

Council members were entitled to wear badges of office on formal occasions such as the ridings. The provost usually wore special robes or gowns and a chain of office. In 1764, the Musselburgh town officer attracted particular attention for his fine clothes:

White gloves he wore fringed fine,
With silk like to a crow,
Black boots with ancient spurs did shine,
No little pomp did show.[53]

Occasionally, burgh authorities could be parsimonious about buying new clothes for their officials, perhaps anxious to avoid charges of needless extravagance or out of genuine poverty. In 1712, Hawick town council ordered the treasurer to buy cloth to make coats for the officers, piper and drummer, but to make sure that he bought it 'as cheape as he can'.[54]

All participants were expected to dress smartly in their 'best apparel'. In 1727, the burgesses of Peebles were to be, 'in their best equipage for the riding the commonties'.[55] Finlayson's play about Linlithgow Marches opens with the characters preparing their clothes for the big day. One of the them, Tom Cockerwell, a shoemaker, declares: 'Weel faith, this is ae day o' the year, on which ev'ry body pits on their best.' He plans to wear a brown coat and trousers, a scarlet double-breasted waistcoat, and 'a weel-powder'd wig'. Another character wears a brightly-coloured vest, which he keeps only for funerals, fairs and weddings. Sawnuck, an apprentice hammerman, only has an old coat to wear and is afraid that everyone will laugh at him.[56] It is likely that other people, including women and children, made efforts to dress-up for ridings, perhaps saving money over long periods to buy fine clothing and other luxuries. Wearing new or special clothes enhanced an individual's experience, giving them the feeling of being important and in some cases powerful. It was an opportunity for personal display, to cut a figure, for indulgence and to make a temporary escape from customary dullness. For both men and women, personal appearance could win approval from the opposite sex, the first point of contact. In *The Marches Day*, Tom Cockerwell wears his best clothes to, 'keep the lasses een, and smile i' their faces'.[57]

The ridings also employed a wide range of moveable artefacts, the most important of which were flags and banners. In Musselburgh, the guilds had their craft banners bearing the symbols of their professions. The banner of the Fleshers bore the cross of St Andrew and a bullock's head whilst the Weaver's banner had a leopard's head with a shuttle in its mouth. Some members of the guilds carried the tools of their profession. One of the Bakers carried a sheath of wheat, the Tailors carried pairs of scissors and the Gardeners decked themselves in green leaves and foliage. All participants in the Musselburgh riding carried swords, which they held on high as they passed through the town:

A sword most clear at this Town-end,
Each from his scabbard drew,
And with it, naked in his hand,
The Town he marched through.[58]

Civic architecture might also be described as a stage-prop of the ridings. The tollbooth or town house provided an impressive background to the ridings, which usually began at the market cross.

The ridings exercised senses other than sight, especially hearing and taste. Music had an important role, and drums, pipes, trumpets, flutes and violins were used to draw attention to processions. Guilds had their own songs, which were used as they marched in procession, praising the craft and stressing its importance. At the Musselburgh riding in 1764, the Shoemakers Guild sang the following song:

This Trade is of great usefulness,
For none are cloth'd complete,
However richly they do dress,
Without shoes on their feet.[59]

Similarly, craft guilds used songs to show the antiquity of their trade. At Linlithgow Marches, part of the Hammermen's song drew the origins of the trade back to the earliest times:

> *When Adam first ate of the tree,*
> *And thence knew the good and the bad,*
> *Uncover'd himself he did see,*
> *Which caus'd him grow laguid and sad.*
> *But he soon found the secret of clothes,*
> *(Possessing an excellent head),*
> *With hammer to work then he goes,*
> *And – a needle is instantly made!*[a]

Oral stimulants also played their part. Most ridings concluded with some form of banquet or feast, and social intercourse was lubricated with plentiful supplies of strong drink. At the conclusion of the Musselburgh riding:

> *Then off the field did march, that they*
> *Might dine, and after spend,*
> *What time remained of the day,*
> *With pleasure to the end.*[b]

The ridings also engaged the minds of participants by using coded messages. Symbols and visual language, such as coloured ribbons, rosettes, certain foodstuffs, or plants and flowers, were used to express allegiances and group loyalties. In Musselburgh, the members of the guilds wore different coloured cockades on their hats to signify their guild. In 1815, Selkirk participants at the Carterhaugh ball game identified themselves by wearing fir twigs.[c] In the modern ridings, towns have adopted their own colours, often displayed in bunting or rosettes, and it is likely that these were derived from much older traditions whose original purpose is now forgotten or lost.

The Decline of the Ridings

The second half of the eighteenth century saw the gradual decline of the ridings. Many towns discontinued their ridings, although some would later revive them. Edinburgh, for example, held a riding in 1718 and did not stage another one until the Peace Riding of 1946. Likewise, Aberdeen held only two ridings in the eighteenth century, in 1754 and 1790, although the tradition lingered until 1889. Ridings were also discontinued at, amongst other places, Lauder, Peebles and Haddington. However, the ridings did not decline everywhere. They continued to take place annually in Hawick, Selkirk, Lanark and Linlithgow, whilst Musselburgh held a riding at regular intervals. The question is why did the ridings decline in some towns but survive in others?

   The decline of the ridings is closely linked with the agricultural changes in the eighteenth century and in particular the enclosure movement, which peaked in the 1760s and again around 1810. By its nature, enclosure involved building fences and walls, which meant that there were fewer incidents of encroachment or disputes about the sites of boundaries. Consequently, there was less need to ride the marches, freeing people from what had sometimes been an onerous responsibility. Moreover, accurate maps and plans were becoming more widely used. These could be copied and retained by authorities and other landowners, replacing the burden of making regular physical inspections of the ground.

Closely linked with these changes, there was mounting pressure on open spaces, which had been used for the ridings and their associated customs. Enclosure walls, hedges and regular field patterns restricted the movement of formal processions, either on foot or horseback. In 1764, Peebles racecourse was ploughed up and planted with crops, which ended the ancient Beltane races.[63] In Hawick, the 'greatest blow' to the Common Riding was the sale of the racecourse to a railway company to build a station (although in this case a new racecourse was established).[64] In addition, increasing urban development undermined customs that were essentially rural in nature. The ridings depended on participants having ready access to horses, something that was inconvenient in urbanised areas.

The survival of the ridings in some towns may reflect the close, homogeneous nature of these communities. R.W. Malcolmson has observed that: 'Custom is particularly the mark of the small, close-knit community, and it tends to lose its force in a larger, more mobile, and more impersonal world.'[65] Large urban areas were thus more impersonal and diverse than smaller isolated communities. It was harder to impose and to maintain traditional customs, given that there were more outlets for the exercise of individuality. However, whilst Hawick, Selkirk and Langholm (from 1816) continued to hold ridings, other Border towns were less enthusiastic. In Peebles, the town council had great difficulty persuading inhabitants to take part. In April 1702, the council observed that many burgesses were 'necessarily absent' because they were at fairs in Lanark and Dunblane. The council altered the timings of the local ridings away from these events, stating that the 'haill maisters of familyes' were to take part, 'under the paine of fyve merks'.[66] But this change doesn't seem to done much good. In May 1727, the town council admitted that the inhabitants found the new dates 'very inconvenient and troublesome ... being the time of labour and seed'.[67] The ridings were subsequently moved to the first Monday in June, but once again this was unsuccessful. In June 1774, the council admitted that the local people were lukewarm about the ridings because they 'created not only a good deal of trouble, beside expense to them, and many could not get horses on that occasion'. In future, the council decided to select only a few people to accompany the magistrates, 'and not put the bulk of the inhabitants to trouble and charges'.[68] In 1775, only fifteen 'ordinary' inhabitants took part with the magistrates. By the early 1800s, the riding had fallen into abeyance, only to be revived in 1897.

The survival of the ridings was also closely linked with a prevailing craft or guild culture, which remained very influential in some towns well into the nineteenth century. In the Borders, industrial development was in its infancy in 1800. The hosiery and tweed industries were slowly emerging, but towns such as Hawick and Selkirk were largely untouched by industrial developments. In 1791, less than 100 people in Hawick were involved in cloth and hosiery manufacture.[69] When the textile trade finally did take off, manufacture was concentrated in 'shop' units rather than factories, which encouraged the survival of traditional work habits. Trade and craft guilds had an intimate association with the ridings, arguably providing the backbone of events. Guild culture had many characteristics that were paralleled in the ridings. Both were centred on men, worlds to which women were rarely admitted. Strong drink underpinned many of the activities. Guild members loved to hear stories about the history of their institutions, to carry out traditions and maintain a sense of continuity with the past.

Guild culture was instinctively radical, stressing group identity and independence. This often led to conflict with manufacturers who were opposed to pre-industrial work habits. Moreover, because of its radical tendencies, guild culture was distrustful of social hierarchies. In 1777, Hawick lost around a third of its common land to the overbearing Dukes of Buccleuch, who claimed a share of the division of the local common. Thirty years later, the loss of the common still rankled in Hawick and there was resentment that an ancient privilege had been taken away. James Hogg, a stocking-maker and political radical, used his *Common Riding Song* to attack the Buccleuchs:

Magistrates! Be faithful trustees,
Equal poise the scales of justice,
See our Common rightly guidit,
Quirky lairds nae mair divide it.

Finally, it is clear that in some towns the ridings had very firm roots and inhabitants wanted them to continue, even when the original purpose had been lost or diluted. In May 1794, the town council of Hawick debated the Common Riding, deciding 'by a majority to have none in future'.[70] Within two days, a petition was laid before the council, 'praying that there should be a common riding this year'. Special meetings had been called of the trade and craft guilds, 'and they are of the opinion that the Common Riding should be continued'.[71] In the face of public opinion, the council quickly backed down and the Common Riding went on as usual. But the struggle for the future of the ridings was only just beginning. The next chapter will show that in the nineteenth century the ridings had to adapt to a rapidly changing world, which in turn led to many arguments and much controversy.

5

'The Devil's Annual Pandemonium': Change and Continuity, c.1800-c.1880

By 1800, the future of the ridings was by no means certain. Many had died out and only a few, such as Selkirk, Hawick, Lanark and Linlithgow, continued to take place annually. The story of the ridings in the nineteenth century is one of change and continuity. Everybody lives in changing times, but occasionally there is a clear division from one kind of society to another. People are aware that theirs is an age of transition. From the mid-eighteenth century, Britain underwent unprecedented change in the wake of rapid industrialisation, population growth and the development of towns and cities. Popular customs like the ridings were not isolated from these changes and contemporaries recognised that many of the old ways were under threat. In the 1860s, William Henderson, a collector of folklore in the north of England and the Scottish Borders, observed:

> *The age we live in is remarkable, as in other points of view, so in this, that old habits and customs, old laws and sayings, old beliefs and superstitions, which have held their ground in the universal mind from the remotest antiquity, are fast fading away and perishing.*[1]

Until recently, historians generally accepted this view. R.W. Malcolmson, for one, has argued that between 1750 and 1850 the foundations of many traditional customs were swept away, leaving only a vacuum which was later filled by sport and organised leisure.[2] But this notion of a sharp break with the past has now been challenged. Whilst some popular customs did decline, especially in rural areas, many traditional events survived. Gradually, the older world of pre-industrial customs, which often had an undercurrent of violence, became more controlled, orderly and less threatening. These changes did not take place smoothly or without controversy, and the history of the ridings reflects these often bumpy transformations. By 1900, the ridings had developed many new roles and functions. This chapter traces the history of the ridings in the nineteenth century. First, there is an account of various social changes and the effects of these, and the reasons why some people were opposed to the ridings and tried to abolish them. The chapter then looks at different attempts to undermine the ridings, why these were unsuccessful and why the ridings continued to attract widespread popular support. Finally, there is a description of how the ridings adapted to wider social changes.

Social Change and the Ridings

Popular customs like the ridings have always had their critics. In chapter two, it was shown that the behaviour of 'mock kings' in the sixteenth century sometimes incurred the wrath of burgh authorities. Occasionally, the ridings were attacked for the heavy drinking that accompanied them, but in general the critics were isolated and most local people took part, irrespective of their social status. As the editor of the *Hawick Advertiser* wistfully recalled in 1868:

> *that sympathy and confidence between the classes which tends to soften the inequalities of social position, and develop the kindly side of human nature, used to exist at the Common Riding to a very marked extent.*[3]

In the first half of the nineteenth century, as the editor was only too aware, this situation had changed. Many people had withdrawn from the ridings and no longer took part in them. As the *Hawick Monthly Advertiser* commented in 1847:

> *For some years back, the Common Riding has considerably fallen off, partly owing to the higher classes not taking the interest that they used to do.*[4]

What had caused this shift in attitudes towards the ridings? In the Borders, they were rooted in dynamic social and economic changes, especially with the rise of the hosiery (later knitwear) industry. Nowhere were these changes more apparent than in Hawick, which in a few decades grew from an insignificant village to the largest manufacturing town in the Borders. Commercial frame-knitting is believed to have started in Hawick in 1771 when Bailie John Hardy, a local merchant, bought four knitting 'frames' and began to manufacture stockings.[5] Hardy gave up the trade soon afterwards, but he influenced others to set up similar schemes. Initially, the fledgling industry made slow progress. In 1791, there were only eight frames in Hawick and in 1800 hosiery manufacture was still insignificant. However, there then followed a period of rapid expansion. By 1812, about 500 of Scotland's estimated 1,450 knitting frames were located in Hawick and the surrounding area. By 1816, the annual production of frame-made stockings in the town had risen to about 328,000 pairs.[6] By the mid-1840s, out of 2,605 frames in Scotland, 1,200 were located in Hawick.[7] Hawick had become such a hive of industry that Robert Chambers, the famous publisher, described it as 'a sort of Glasgow in miniature'.[8]

The success of the hosiery and textile industry in Hawick and other Border towns made the Borders an attractive location for economic migrants, who came from other parts of Scotland, Ireland and the textile districts of England. Many of the early pioneers in the industry had relatively humble origins, often learning their trade on the knitting frame itself. Some of them were eager supporters of the ridings. John Nixon came from Hexham and had an important role in setting up the textile trade. His son, William, was Cornet of Hawick in 1813. Similarly, William Beck, another Englishman, settled in Hawick and became a successful hosiery manufacturer. His son, William, was Cornet in 1808. However, the early enthusiasm of manufacturers and entrepreneurs for the ridings quickly fell away. The new industry created great personal wealth for some individuals (although there were also some bankrupts), and this in turn intensified social divisions between manufacturers and labour. The former built large mansion houses on the outskirts of the towns to fence themselves off from the unsanitary conditions of their workforce.

Living in more restricted social spheres, manufacturers and others began to adopt strict codes of behaviour and refine their social attitudes. They were influenced by a long-term shift in habits and manners, a phenomenon that has been termed 'the civilising process'.[9]

The process spanned several centuries, beginning in the later Middle Ages among the social élite and then spreading slowly through the rest of society. It dealt with a whole host of changes about what is now called 'decent' behaviour, such as using a knife and fork when eating food or not picking one's nose or urinating in public. The rise of a powerful and expanding group of commercial and professional people was central to this process. By the beginning of the nineteenth century, they had become the leaders of this social reformation.

Attitudes were further hardened by the rise of evangelicalism, which had a profound impact in Scotland, especially in the first third of the nineteenth century. The core of evangelical faith was the conviction of personal salvation through Jesus Christ. Many evangelicals looked back to the Scottish Covenanters of the seventeenth century, attracted by the fervent and puritanical nature of their belief. Like the Covenanters, evangelicals wanted to see their ideals adopted in wider society, especially the values of thrift, sobriety, moderation and self-help. It was their duty to dedicate themselves to the service of others, especially the working classes, in the hope of reforming them and bringing them to God. Some of the founders of the hosiery and textile industries had strong evangelical sympathies. A travelling preacher called James Haldane set up one of the earliest frame 'shops' in Hawick, which was known as the Tabernacle because of his religious beliefs. Similarly, William Wilson and William Watson, the co-founders of one of the most successful of the early firms, were both fervent Quakers. During the nineteenth century, many evangelical attitudes became common currency and infiltrated popular thinking. Often, evangelicals preached to a converted audience. It must be remembered that in the nineteenth century religion was a major leisure pursuit for millions of people, far more so than today. In 1866, Selkirk had a population of only about 3,700 people, but it had six churches and branches of the National Bible Society, the Evangelical Alliance and the YMCA ('for the purpose of spiritually improving the mind by biblical research and discussing religious topics').

These social and cultural changes had an important influence on the nature of the ridings. In 1868, the editor of the liberal-leaning *Hawick Advertiser* perceptively wrote:

> *The gradual withdrawal by the middle class from any participation in the festival has lowered the status of the Common Riding and its supporters … with the rise of a new generation, accustomed from their youth to move in a more restricted circle, this feeling* [of social equality] *is rapidly disappearing, and this is the real cause of that falling off in respectability which is used as an argument for withholding support for this ancient custom.*[10]

It is clear that in the first half of the nineteenth century attitudes towards the ridings had changed. Many people withdrew their support and some went one step further and argued that the ridings should be abolished. But what was it about the ridings that they found objectionable and offensive?

Respectable Fears and the Ridings

One of the major fears about the ridings was that they were potentially uncontrollable. Crowds of excited people were on the streets, many of whom had been drinking heavily, and normal rules of behaviour were temporarily relaxed. 'The public houses enjoyed very fair patronage,' said one report of the Hawick Fair in 1857, 'and there was a good deal of noise in the streets during the night, a little fighting and rather more swearing and blustering.'[11] There was an element of personal risk about taking part in the ridings. Fights and drunken brawls could easily break out and there was lots of shouting and boisterous behaviour. An additional danger in some events was that horses were galloped wildly through the streets. There were no attempts at crowd control, which led to a risk of collisions and serious injuries. Twice, this was to have fatal consequences at Hawick Common Riding.

For most people however, the greatest injury that they were likely to suffer was an assault on their dignity. Popular customs like the ridings had plenty of rough and tumble about them. Part of the experience was about the loosening of inhibitions and mucking in. Riders regularly got soaking wet, plastered in mud and grime or thrown off their mounts. Similarly, some of the ridings involved mock fights or battles, when coins or food were thrown into the crowd, usually at places that marked an important boundary position. In Lanark, hot rolls or cakes were thrown from the roof of the Provost's house, 'in the scramble for which there is often much of the ludicrous'.[12] In Hawick, there were unruly scrimmages for small packets of snuff. The ridings might also involve some form of ritual humiliation or induction. In Lanark, people were ducked in the river near the site of a march stone. As William Davidson observed in 1828, there was no respect for an individual's social status:

> Those who for the first time have enrolled themselves under the banners of the procession, must wade in, and grope for the stone, during which act they are tumbled over and immersed. There is no distinction of rank, – and were the greatest potentate to appear, he would share the fate of the most humble plebeian.[13]

Likewise, at some ridings, newcomers were ignominiously swung against special dumping stones, which was designed to impress upon them the site of a boundary. In Aberdeen, new burgesses had to endure a special 'doupin' ceremony:

> Two of the company, who are already 'doup-free burgesses', will then take the novice by the shoulders, and two others will lay hold of his legs, lifting him breast-high above the point of a rock, to which they will return his posteriors with a velocity proportioned to their respect for his character.[14]

There were two ways of seeing these kinds of customs. For some people, they were just high-spirits, part of the fun, something to be experienced and then laughed about, and in time to inflict on others. But for others, they represented a serious affront to their dignity and self-respect.

The ridings created further disapproval because they were thought to attract undesirables into the towns. Describing the build-up to Hawick Common Riding in 1858, the *Border Advertiser* noted: 'Tawdry-looking women and convict-looking men are pouring into the town from all quarters.' These included blind and lame beggars, 'a swarm of vagrants and blacklegs [and] a large sprinkling of that wandering class who gain a precarious existence in attending such occasions as this'.[15] The ridings were ideal hunting grounds for the unscrupulous and the unabashed. Normal circumstances were reversed and money was liberally exchanged, almost given away. Local people spent on almost anything, regardless of quality, and few of them worried about it until afterwards. It was feared that criminals were drawn to the ridings because people were temporarily off their guard. Pickpockets and thieves preferred to operate amongst crowds, which gave them perfect cover, and racecourses offered them rich pickings.

Workers in the travelling fairground attracted great suspicion, mainly because of their itinerant lifestyle. The fairground itself was seen as a frivolous distraction. One of the principal attractions was gambling and games of chance, albeit on a small scale and for limited prizes. Describing the Common Riding fair in 1856, the *Hawick Advertiser* noted: 'Dice men and knaves of every description reaped an abundant harvest, the cardsharpers as usual getting their livelihoods out of the pockets of the shrewdest.'[16] The problem was that people were wasting their money, allowing themselves be taken in, and therefore rewarding dishonesty.

The fairground was also thought to contain attractions that were lewd and sinful. Women, often the stallholders themselves, were used to lure potential customers and encourage them to spend. In 1875, the *Hawick Express* reported that: 'Shooting saloons mustered strongly, in charge of which young ladies whose bewitching smiles induced many to try a shot.'[17] Even worse, in 1883 there were raised eyebrows at the 'gaudily attired dancing girls of all ages'.[18] Until the advent of large, mechanical rides in the 1880s, the fairground was essentially a collection of tents and booths, each competing against the other. Some of these booths were completely enclosed, like small theatres, and customers had to be drawn in. 'Parade girls', dressed in circus leotards and tights, were used to attract public attention and give male customers the come-on with the promise of seeing more inside. For some critics, this display was indecent and dangerously close to prostitution. Later in the century, the fairground would also be attacked for its titillating film shows and 'What the Butler Saw' stereoscopic views.

Nineteenth-century fairgrounds were certainly no place for the serious-minded or the squeamish. Fortune-tellers and astrologers, who had always occupied an ambiguous social role, were a common feature, and their presence upset both evangelicals and scientific rationalists. There were also displays of human curiosities, described in 1858 as 'specimens of nature's freaks in caravans'.[19] Whilst some of these 'freak shows' were fairly innocent, such as displays of indigenous peoples, others were base and repellent by modern standards. In 1871, the Hawick Fair had amputees and people who had been deformed in industrial accidents, 'one with his arm burned to the bone by the latest colliery explosion'.[20] Fairs were also shameless about displaying people with birth defects, missing or extra limbs, and other disfigurements. Respectable opinion regarded this kind of entertainment as highly distasteful and degrading, although it might be argued that it provided some sort of a living for people who might otherwise have been forced to beg. Freak shows gradually declined, thanks to improved social provision and a change in public sensibilities. However, it was still possible to see giants, dwarves and bearded ladies until the 1970s.

The boxing booth was another objectionable feature of the fairground. Companies of boxers toured around fairs and markets, issuing challenges to local men to try to beat one of the professionals. Describing the Common Riding fair in 1858, the *Hawick Advertiser* reported:

> *Mr Mickey Bent, a professor of the true British art of self-defence, accompanied by a staff of assistants, juvenile and adult, issued most pressing invitations to the public and offered free admission and a glass of brandy to any gentleman who would make a choice of and vanquish any member of his company.*[21]

Until the early 1800s, bare-knuckle fighting was a common feature of fairs, although regulated contests with gloves were introduced later. Contests were often extremely violent, more like wrestling than pugilism. The professional staff, which sometimes included female boxers, knew that their livelihoods were at stake and were ready to resort to any 'mean tricks' to win. Boxing, even at this level, was a popular spectator sport. Crowds gathered to watch a match, especially when a local favourite took on one of the travellers. Tempered by drink and violent excitement, it was easy to imagine the crowd getting out of control.

There was also concern about the use of animals in the fairground. Animal welfare was one of the great causes of the nineteenth century and its development shows the civilising process in action. For centuries, cruelty to animals was commonplace and unremarkable. All levels of society, including royalty, accepted and took pleasure in it. Animals, it was once thought, had been created to serve human beings, and any suffering that they might experience as a result was largely irrelevant. Gradually however, attitudes began to change. Scientific advances in the eighteenth century showed that humans were only a small part of natural creation. The next logical step was that all creatures had an equal right to exist and live their lives free from pain and cruelty. By the late eighteenth century, concern for animal welfare was a distinctive feature of middle-class life. The Society for the Prevention of Cruelty to Animals (SPCA) was formed in 1824, and its Scottish equivalent (SSPCA) in 1839. Inspired by a strong evangelical ethos, the aim of the Society was not only to protect animals but also to reform the behaviour of those who treated them cruelly, especially amongst the lower orders. By encouraging them to treat animals kindly, they would become considerate towards other people and eventually be drawn to religion.

The use and abuse of animals was an ancient feature of popular customs. Most fairs and markets had some animal entertainments and often these were extremely vicious in character. Cockfights and dogfights attracted large crowds, who bet feverishly on the outcome as the animals tore each other apart. The problem was not just that dumb animals were made to suffer, but events excited the bloodlust of the crowd. Numerous efforts were made to stamp out animal sports, but they were popular and very persistent. According to the *Hawick Express*, cockfights 'witnessed by 4–500 people' took place on the common as late as the 1860s.[22] In addition, there were no reservations about using animals as performers. Most fairs had exhibitions of creatures that were supposedly intelligent, such as dogs, cats and farm animals that appeared to tell the time, know different colours or count by pawing the ground. 'Toby the Learned Pig', who was claimed to know arithmetic, was a feature at Hawick and Selkirk Common Ridings in the 1850s. Fairs also had displays of dancing bears and other performing animals, often dressed in human clothes for comic effect. Performing animals of this kind could be seen in two ways. For some people, they were just a harmless amusement, but for others they were a serious abuse of God's creation.

The animals that seemed to suffer most in the ridings were, of course, horses. Some riders lacked basic skills and caused great distress to their mounts, whipping them and drawing blood or pushing them to the point of exhaustion. Often during the ridings, horses were injured and had to be put down. Another concern was the intimate link between the ridings and horse racing. By the nineteenth century, it was argued that the ridings had lost their original purpose and had become an excuse to hold a race meeting. In 1871, the *Hawick Express*, although broadly sympathetic towards the Common Riding, admitted that the racing had become more important than the ceremonial events:

> *The want of sympathy and support which used to be given by the authorities and wealthier citizens to the Cornet, together with the great influx of strangers, have all combined to render the Common Riding less the centre of attraction and less participated in by the bulk of the inhabitants and make the occasion more of a turf speculation.*[23]

Other critics went further. In 1872, in a grim lecture called 'Abominations: Local and General', Reverend James McEwan claimed that the horse racing 'and all its sordid accompaniments' were a serious blight on Hawick Common Riding. It was his firm belief that the Common Riding, 'would die out in three years were it not for these horse races, and the horse racing would die out throughout the country were it not for gambling and drinking.'[24] Similarly, when the town council subscribed £20 to the races, 'Minster' thundered in the press that the Common Riding was, 'a relict of a semi-barbarous age, degrading to those who engage in it, and demoralising to the general community.'[25]

Horse racing was thought to be incompatible with animal welfare. In 1802, James Hogg, the Ettrick Shepherd, went to see the famous races at Leith. As a sheep farmer, Hogg was no stranger to animal suffering, but he was greatly disturbed at the brutal treatment of the horses: 'The only sensations I felt were rather unpleasant. I pitied the poor animals that were strained at such a rate and trembled for the riders, who were cleaving the atmosphere with a velocity I had never before witnessed.'[26]

The Common Riding races were also criticised because they were very localised and the level of sport was poor, especially when compared with the more famous national meetings. The jockeys were generally local amateurs. In 1858, only three riders took part in the Farmers' Steeplechase at Hawick, during which the horses refused to jump a stone wall until spectators lowered it.[27] Local racecourses were crude and makeshift. Tracks were only roughly marked out and there were no barriers or fences to protect the public from the galloping horses. During Leith races in 1802, James Hogg saw a 'poor boy' being run over and seriously injured by a horse. Hogg wrote: 'I saw him carried by me in the greatest agony and, as I believed, on the borders of eternity; I felt extremely for him and wished for his sake that there had been no races that day.'[28] In 1858, the *Hawick Advertiser* reported that children and 'foolish people' had wandered over the course during the races, 'and the inevitable dogs appearing at a critical moment'.[29] Spectators (and dogs) were not the only ones in danger. For some reason, the old racecourse at Hawick was shaped in a figure '8', which meant that there was a high risk of collisions between horses. Criticisms were also made of the athletic events ('the gymnastics'), which accompanied the races. In 1859, people took part in the wrestling competitions at Hawick 'only to get themselves laughed at', whilst the sack race was described as 'an absurdity'.[30]

Like modern football matches, race meetings were believed to present a latent threat to public order. Crowd trouble sometimes erupted, especially when bookmakers absconded or 'welshed' on their debts. However, the main objection to racing was that it appealed to the decadent rich and idle poor, breaking the cardinal rule that recreation should be serious, not sensual. The primary purpose of racing was, of course, betting and gambling. It was blatant and could not be ignored. In 1883, a description of the Hawick races noted: 'bookmakers had fantastic dresses and powerful lungs and kept bawling and shouting to the terror and alarm of those who were not betting inclined'.[31] There was an enormous social gulf over betting and gambling. To some people, the whole culture of betting, with its ill-gotten gains, hopeless addictions and material lusts, summed up human folly and sinfulness. The sight of the working class betting was particularly offensive. In 1855, the *Hawick Advertiser*, although friendly towards the Common Riding, loftily observed:

> That festivals like the Common Riding are calculated to bring out and show off in their native colour the worst and most degraded of our species is but true. Of the many strange sights that met the eye of the observer at our annual festival, that of tossing for money was the worst.[32]

There was no question that gambling led to cheating and dishonesty, and hence to the moral corruption of the soul. George Lewis, the owner, editor and printer of the *Southern Reporter*, embodied many of these attitudes. Lewis was an ardent moralist and in the 1850s and 1860s he used his newspaper to run a personal crusade against the Selkirk races and all their 'attendant vices'. Reporting the races of 1856, he observed:

> The promoters of the races had, contrary to general expectations, succeeded in raising more than the usual amount of funds for their sport, and the great proportion of the people of the town, set free from their employment, proceeded to the Gala Rig to witness the races. From all that we have heard they did not afford anything like satisfaction, and a good part of the funds was pocketed by the gentlemen of the turf without giving the subscribers anything like fun for their money.[33]

Lewis served on Selkirk town council and every year he proposed that the council withdraw the £5 that was given to the races, usually without much success. In 1859, the editorial of the *Southern Reporter* condemned the races for their 'low, and debasing influences, and their attendant jugglery, debauchery, and profanity [that] had long been looked upon by many as a nuisance'.[34]

There were also suspicions, perhaps partly justified, that many of the horse racing and athletic events were rigged. Reporting the athletics at Hawick in 1858, the *Hawick Advertiser* noted: 'The footraces were well contested but there was a most shameful attempt to deprive one of the winners of his place by knocking him down as he was nearing the post.'[35] But for many people, especially amongst the working classes, betting and gambling was a way of life. It was, in George Orwell's phrase, 'the cheapest of luxuries'[36], offering the chance of instant enrichment and escape, hope for the desperate.

At the heart of all of the problems with the ridings there was drink. Drink was the great social demon of the nineteenth century. It was, in Christopher Smout's words, 'an ubiquitous permeation of Scottish society'.[37] Drink was consumed in enormous quantities by all social classes in Scotland and there were no legal restrictions on who might buy it. In the eighteenth century, the Scots were renowned as drinkers of claret, but later there was a switch to drinking whisky, which was cheap, readily available and associated with courtesy and hospitality. Any occasion was used as an excuse to drink and drinking to the point of intoxication was common at fairs, holidays and funerals. Recalling the eighteenth century of his youth, the Reverend Thomas Somerville of Jedburgh wrote: 'Intemperance in drinking was frequent ... At public festive meetings, there was indeed a wanton rivalry in drinking to excess, and a species of merit ascribed to the person who held out longest.'[38] Drinking was central to leisure and for working men in particular the public house, the inn or the tavern was at the heart of their cultural and social life. In the Scottish Borders, workers in the early textile industry were notorious for their drinking habits, partly because they worked in terribly damp and airless conditions. Overcrowding also encouraged men and women to turn to drink as an escape route. Indeed, in many ways it was very difficult for a working man not to drink. Drinking was seen as manly and it was thought very insulting to refuse the offer of a drink. Abstinence, in Somerville's words, was 'censured as a certain indication of a sullen and niggardly disposition'.[39]

Drink has always been an essential part of the ridings and regularly brought them into conflict with the authorities. Huge quantities of drink were consumed during the ridings. Riders were plied with alcohol when they went out to ride the marches and also on their return. Regular refreshment stops and stirrup-cups were taken during rides. In 1815, over half of James Henderson's expenditure as Cornet of Hawick went on drink. Out of a grand total of £138 9s 10d, Henderson spent over £81 on whisky, wine, ale, rum and 'shrub' (sweetened wine).[40] In 1884, the Spread Eagle Hotel in Kelso was contracted to supply drink to the Hawick Common Riding races. Two wagons were loaded with 'fully 1000 bottles of beer and aerated waters' and a steam traction engine was used to pull the wagons, which weighed 14 tons, to the racecourse.[41] Strong drink literally lubricated and financed some of the ridings. Until 1865, the Hawick Cornet covered most of his expenses by selling drink. From his election until the Common Riding, the Cornet had the right to sell spirits from his house without a licence.[42] It was hardly a coincidence that when Hawick town council withdrew their support from the Common Riding, the bussing of the flag took place in the Cornet's favourite pub.

It is easy to find humour in the excesses of the ridings, but it should be remembered that heavy drinking bred sporadic, casual violence and was the cause of great suffering and distress, often to the innocent. Heavy drinking could lead to social misery, especially to married women, who were often the victims of indulgence and lack of control. Isolated and vulnerable, most of these women had little choice but to suffer in silence. Domestic abuse, to use the modern term, was a social taboo at this time and its existence was rarely admitted. In a sermon about Hawick Common Riding given in 1894, Reverend J.W. Shannon, perhaps drawing on his own experience, pointed to the link between the ridings, strong drink and the abuse of women and families:

> *Some women in the town looked back upon that festival as one of the most dreadful experiences of their lives. At that time their husbands seemed to be unlike themselves. It seemed utterly wicked that women were almost maddened by the want and difficulties they had to suffer. To those who wished the real good of the town, it might be a good thing to stop the observation of the Common Riding.*[43]

Drinking habits in nineteenth-century Scotland were a mirror of social change. Traditionally, heavy drinking had been the mark of privilege. 'In pre-industrial Scotland,' writes Daniel Patton, 'wealth, leisure and education removed constraints on drunkenness rather than strengthened them. In the nineteenth century, the reverse came to be true.'[44] The leaders of society gradually became more restrained and indulgence was largely identified with the working classes. This does not mean that wealthy people stopped consuming alcohol, but they were less willing to get drunk in public and more likely to drink in private and at mealtimes. By the 1850s, few respectable gentlemen, and certainly no women, went into public houses. There were still, of course, plenty of middle- and upper-class drunks. The difference was that working-class drunkenness was open and highly visual, whilst that of the better-off was less conspicuous and more easily hidden. Popular festivals, fairs and holiday occasions, which largely took place in the open air, only made matters worse. Reporting the Common Riding of 1877, the *Hawick Advertiser* noted that the beer tents at the races did a 'roaring trade', adding that 'the evidences unfortunately were not far to seek'.[45] The sight of inebriated men and women could be ignored or laughed off, but for some it was deeply offensive, insulting their strongly held beliefs about human dignity and responsibility. The ridings only encouraged heavy drinking and all the problems that went with it.

The Abolitionists

These then were the principal reasons why, from about 1800 to 1880, many people withdrew from the ridings and refused to support them. The ridings brought upheaval and encouraged drunkenness, gambling and other irresponsible behaviour. They were seen as a threat to public morality and good order, and therefore it was right to abolish them. Of course, many of these fears were exaggerated and were based on ignorance and class prejudice. The next section will examine some of the attempts to curtail the ridings and why these were unsuccessful. Particular reference is made here to Hawick Common Riding, largely because of the existence of a detailed local press, which gave extensive coverage to various Common Riding controversies. The debate was only one example of a much wider argument about the future direction of popular customs.

During the first half of the nineteenth century, Hawick Common Riding had attracted much criticism from the town authorities. In 1817, the town council declared that the Common Riding, 'has been very hurtful to the morals of the young people in the town'.[46] Similarly, in 1833 the council described the event as 'corrupt to the morals of youth'.[47] Increasingly, the town council tried to distance itself from the Common Riding, hoping that without its support the event would wither away. By the 1850s, council support of the Common Riding had largely ceased. It had been customary for the council to elect twelve burleymen to accompany the bailies at the Common Riding, but in 1857 this practice was abandoned. Similarly, the flag had traditionally been bussed in the home of one of the magistrates, but between 1862 and 1887 it was carried out in a pub or a hotel chosen by the Cornet.

The exception to the withdrawal of civic countenance by the town council was the annual election of the Cornet. Between 1856 and 1878, this was the subject of great controversy, encapsulating the debate about the ridings at this time. Traditionally, the town council had chosen the Cornet from a shortlist provided by the Cornet's lads. In 1856, the Cornet-elect, David Patterson, decided not to take up his post because it was too expensive. This was the opportunity that some members of the town council had been waiting for. They refused to elect a replacement, preferring to wash their hands of the whole affair. By electing a Cornet, the council argued that they were encouraging the excesses of the Common Riding.

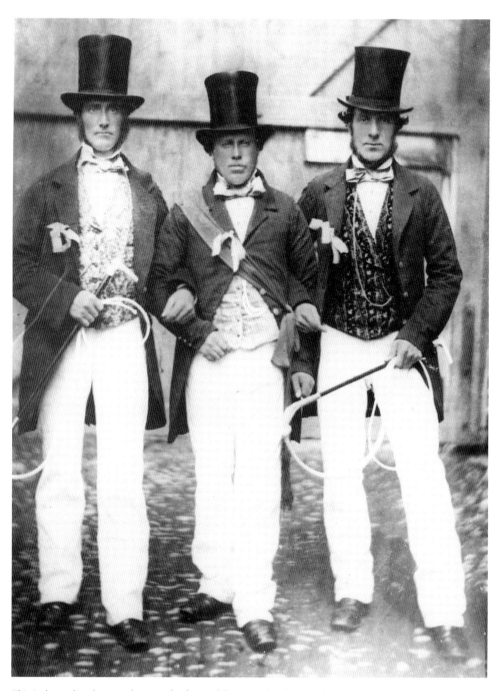

This is the earliest known photograph of any of the Scottish ridings. It shows the Hawick principals in 1857, Cornet Andrew Leyden supported by his Right-Hand Man Andrew Knox and Left-Hand Man John Elliot. *(Scottish Borders Museum and Gallery Service (Hawick Museum Collection))*

In future, it was up to the lads to make their own decisions. Significantly, there was an immediate response from local people. A new Cornet, Adam Knox, was chosen at a public meeting and the Common Riding went ahead as usual. But the incident left a bad taste. It was believed that the town council had failed in one of its most important public duties.

When the issue resurfaced in 1857, public pressure forced the council to grudgingly change its position and elect a Cornet as normal.

However, the question was not allowed to rest. In 1860, Bailie Thomas Purdom, a solicitor, refused to take part in the Cornet's election, 'as he considered the acceptance of the office was the worst thing that a young man could do'.[48] This represented a remarkable turnaround for the Purdom family because Thomas's father, Robert, had been Cornet in 1803. A Cornet was eventually chosen, but the majority of the council members refused to vote. In 1862, the issue was raised again. At a stormy public meeting, the newly reformed council was sharply divided over the election. Speaking against, Peter Laidlaw, a hosiery manufacturer, made it clear that the debate was really about the future, if any, of the Common Riding:

> *It was no good reason that a custom should continue simply because it had hitherto been observed, and there was no benefit accruing to the public from its observation. Besides, the Common Riding was the remnant of a barbarous age, a custom verging into dotage, a mere shadow of what it once was, a mere burlesque, a mock pageantry. The election to the Cornetship had been the means of bringing many young men to a premature grave.*[49]

But not everyone agreed with this opinion. Taking a forward-looking paternalist approach, Walter Laing, also a hosiery manufacturer, argued that the council should take over the running of the Common Riding rather than turning a blind eye:

> *The more countenance given to* [the Common Riding] *by the authorities, the more likely* [it] *would be conducted in an orderly and decorous manner. It was quite proper that there should be a certain number of holidays in the year for the working classes, and working men should have the opportunity of enjoying their holidays in a proper and reasonable manner.*[50]

Significantly, Walter Laing's company, Dicksons and Laings, was at the forefront of new developments in the hosiery trade. The company had introduced steam-driven machinery, which meant that most of the workforce was based in a factory unit and subject to new legislation and controls.[51] The final outcome of the dispute was that the town council decided by a single vote to continue to elect a Cornet. It was reported that the result, 'was received with much applause by a large number of the public who had been present at the meeting and who had followed the discussion with keen and lively interest.'[52] In 1876, the council once again had reservations about electing a Cornet. In a letter to the *Hawick Express*, 'Progress' said that if the council elected a Cornet, 'they are giving their countenance to a great deal of drinking, promiscuous dancing, late hours and all their concomitant evils.'[53] The previous year, 'Per Contra' had argued that the council was to blame for electing a Cornet and then leaving the event in the hands of 'a few boys, many of whom never recovered from the drinking and other customs incident to the occasion, but [who] go from bad to worse until they become confirmed drunkards'.[54] In 1877, the council finally refused to elect a Cornet and the duty fell to a public meeting.

In Hawick and Selkirk, other more subtle attempts were made to undermine the ridings and to draw people, especially children, away from them. Using the newly developed railways, churches and religious groups organised excursions as wholesome alternatives. In 1859, George Lewis, the religiose proprietor of the *Southern Reporter*, argued that the railways were a godsend and could be used to provide 'rational entertainment' for the people, taking them away from temptation. 'The idea of large excursion trips at once commended itself to those who were anxious to establish a better order of things.'[55] The Selkirk Sabbath Schools organised a special excursion by train to Kelso on the Common Riding Friday, which according to George Lewis had been an enormous success:

It has already secured the approval and support of the right thinking and better portion of the community; and we do not think ourselves over sanguine in predicting that it will ultimately entirely supplant those ancient sports and usages from which the public have hitherto had few inducements to withdraw themselves.[56]

Similarly, in 1874 Hawick Sabbath Schools organised an outing to a local farm. Shortly after the Cornet and his supporters had passed along the High Street, a huge procession of adults and children, some carrying religious banners, marched the opposite way to the railway station.[57] The choice between salvation and damnation could not have been made more explicit. Excursions of this kind were very popular. In 1875, over 2,000 adults and children were estimated to have taken part in the Hawick Sabbath Schools trip to Langholm. At a time of limited horizons, outings of this kind were a rare opportunity for pleasure, even if in the circumstances some of it was rather forced. Participants saw new places, played games, listened to music and took part in singsongs, and had lots of fun. In 1875, the *Hawick Advertiser* reported: 'music [was not] wanting, one fellow performing with rare skill on a coffee-pot made into an instrument played like a flute, while violin and banjo gave harmonious accompaniment.'[58] However, the main attraction was usually a picnic. Lemonade and sweets were a rare treat and were consumed more eagerly than religious messages. Occasionally, religious groups tried to tackle the ridings head on. At Hawick in 1873, a group of evangelicals from Carlisle, assisted by 'several townspeople', distributed religious tracts to people going to the racecourse, warning them that they were on 'the way to Hell'. There were, however, no converts.[59]

The Supporters

The failure of these evangelicals was, in many ways, symbolic. It has been shown that the ridings attracted much criticism during the nineteenth century. It was believed that the ridings harmed public morality and that they should be abandoned. But the abolitionists and opponents were unsuccessful in their aims. Tradition was firmly established and the ridings continued, although they did not survive unaltered. As we will see, change and adaptation were necessary for these events to endure. The next section will examine why the ridings continued, despite many pressures trying to bring them to an end.

There is no doubt that criticisms of the ridings were often counter-productive. Reviewing the Common Riding of 1872, the *Hawick Express* noted that there had been an unusually large number of riders, adding that the opponents of the Common Riding, 'more than all the other considerations combined have helped to revive the festival. Opposition is sometimes productive of remits not quite in keeping with the objects aimed at.'[60] Similarly, as James Edgar observed in his history of Hawick Common Riding in 1886:

Of late years attempts have occasionally been made to throw discredit upon the proceedings and uproot the time-honoured institution, but instead of having the desired effect, they have only served to demonstrate the tenacious hold it has in the hearts of the people.[61]

Supporters of the ridings were always ready to defend them and to highlight their many good points. As the *Hawick Advertiser* put it in 1858, there was 'something excellent' about an event that, 'drives care and sadness away to give place to merry making and gaiety and joy'.[62] It was acknowledged that there were some problems with the ridings, but these should not be allowed to obscure the more positive aspects. Supporters argued that it was only a small number of irresponsible people who caused trouble and gave events a bad name. In 1862, the *Hawick Advertiser* commented: 'It is wrong to deprive the many of the means of enjoyment because a few worthless, thoughtless people choose to abuse them.'[63] In 1865, the *Border Advertiser* echoed: 'Such occasions are sadly abused by some, but they are enjoyed in a rational way by many more.'[64] Any problems had been highly exaggerated and there was very little to worry about. Reporting the dinner at Hawick Common Riding in 1848, the *Border Advertiser* noted approvingly that the occasion had passed off with great dignity and self-control, despite a large number of toasts that were drunk with 'rapturous enthusiasm':

> *We would solicit to those sentimentalists who are hostile to our annual festival to take a glance at the dinner party who annually assemble at Mr Fenwick's and say if they can decry anything at variance with the rule of etiquette or morality. The meetings are quite as decorous and well-conducted as a soiree.*[65]

Clearly, the ridings had many supporters as well as opponents. Some features of the ridings might have been disagreeable to some people, but they were appealing to others. Horse racing, for example, had a wide range of enthusiasts and followers. Part of the attraction of racing was that it was very popular with royalty and the aristocracy, and gave people lower down the social scale an opportunity to imitate their social superiors. There was a degree of snobbery at the races, even at minor meetings. In Hawick, entry to the course was free, but the socially pretentious could pay to sit in a special grandstand, which kept the gentle safely

Andrew Kennedy's painting of 1846 shows the horse racing at the Hawick Common Riding. Note the temporary grandstand, which was erected by Mrs Hay, the enterprising landlady of the Crown Inn. Underneath the stand was an exclusive refreshment bar for paying customers, one of whom is being helped home across the river. Note also the Cornet and his Right- and Left-Hand Men in the bottom left corner, seemingly rather out of things. *(Allan Turnbull)*

Horse racing was enormously popular and attracted great interest thanks to the prizes on offer. *(Author's collection)*

apart from the unwashed. In 1848, the *Border Advertiser* reported that the stand was 'well filled with the paragons of excellence', who had exclusive access to their own refreshment bar, something like corporate hospitality at modern sporting events.[66] In Hawick and Selkirk, the races also attracted some aristocratic patronage. Racing was an important feature of upper-class life and aristocrats were usually keen to support their local meetings. In 1848, the family of the late MP, Andrew Pringle, gave the principals at Selkirk Common Riding a 'generous donation' for the local race meeting.[67] In 1857, the *Hawick Advertiser* went into raptures when Lord Hay, brother of the Duchess of Wellington, was spotted in the paddock.[68] Upper-class visitors leant race meetings an air of respectability and in theory they also had lots of money to spread around. However, there was wariness that they might try to exert too much influence on the ridings, using them for their own devices and excluding local people. In 1877, the *Hawick Express* commented:

Many attempts to destroy the local part of the amusements are to make the meeting more aristocratic. Those imbued with aristocratic notions desire no exhibition of common persons contesting on horseback for whips. The idea of weavers and stocking-makers indulging in the exhilarating pastime of horsemanship is painful to their notions of dignity.[69]

Undoubtedly, anyone who attempted to influence or divert the ridings encountered strong resistance. Earlier, it was shown that in 1857 Hawick town council refused to undertake their traditional duty of electing a Cornet. Local people were outraged and within one week 'an immense number of the inhabitants' had signed a petition demanding that the council reverse its decision. As the petition stated, the Common Riding had been, 'the delight of the people of Hawick for a long series of years, and is still welcomed with pleasure and enthusiasm by the present generation.'[70] The Cornet was 'the keystone of the arch' and had a 'vast amount of romantic associations'. The weight of public opinion was effective because in 1858 the council elected a Cornet without argument. What mattered here was not the ability to trace deep historical roots for traditions, but the sense that they were natural and right, that the ridings provided a fixed reference point in a changing world. Traditions linked one generation to another, gave a familiar rhythm to the year, and created strong feelings of continuity.

The principal reason why many people supported the ridings was that they brought temporary relief from the monotony and drudgery of everyday life. They were something to look forward to each year, events to be remembered with great fondness. In a description that could have applied to any of the ridings, the *New Statistical Account* of 1845 stated that Hawick Common Riding:

is considered by more than the youthful portion of the population as one of the most important days of the year ... [It] is kept up with much spirit by the great body of the people, as well from the influence of ancient associations, as from the holiday amusements with which it is invariably attended.[71]

In an era before television, cinema and the Internet, there were limited opportunities for spectacle and the ridings provided a welcome splash of colour. This was especially the case with the travelling fairground, which was bright, gaudy, loud and full of strange and wonderful things. How could anyone resist the fair described by the *Hawick Advertiser* in 1857? Two wizards unblushingly advertised themselves as practicers of necromancy. There was a panorama of the famed siege of Sebastapol. More than one opportunity of perfecting oneself for the Rifle Brigade was offered in the shape of patent safety shooting galleries; boxing rings and caravans where clowns rehearsed the stale jokes of long ago.[72]

The caravans of the travellers were often brightly painted with scenes from legends, myths, history and the Bible. The fair, like Christmas, held a particular appeal for children, providing them with deeply ingrained memories that would last a lifetime. In 1858, Hawick children would have been wide-eyed when they saw displays of 'tempting teetotal liquors of all hues of the rainbow' and 'gingerbread and confectionery enough to keep all the children on the Border sick for twelve months'.[73] Every year, people made great efforts to ensure that the Common Riding was set apart and special. One method of doing so, which almost everyone could indulge in, was by wearing new clothes. Writing in the 1820s, Robert Wilson, an ex-Cornet of Hawick, said that the Common Riding races attracted, 'perhaps five sixths of the inhabitants for several miles around, male and female, perambulating the green, all with their new Sunday suits on.'[74] Describing the scene in 1858, the *Hawick Advertiser* observed: 'The hill-side never presented a more animated or a gayer appearance, all were clad in their best, and many ladies scarcely required the finishing touch to enter a ball-room.'[75] As was shown in the previous chapter, dressing-up was a way for men and women to feel good about themselves and to put on a display, in part to appeal to the opposite sex. For young people and adolescents, this was (and is) much of the appeal of popular customs and festivals. The usual

Right: Douglas 'The Brave' cast the flag of the Selkirk Incorporation of Hammermen from the early 1830s to 1887 – his life's work. *(Robert D. Clapperton Photographic Trust)*

Opposite above: The fairground 'shows' brought colour to life, as pictured here at Hawick, *c.*1900. Note the roundabout in the background. *(Scottish Borders Museum and Gallery Service (Hawick Museum Collection))*

Opposite below: The ridings were a good place to meet the opposite sex. Dancing at the Hawick races, *c.*1900. *(Scottish Borders Museum and Gallery Service (Hawick Museum Collection))*

close controls on their behaviour were temporarily suspended, leaving ample opportunity for encounters – innocent or otherwise – between the sexes. This was an important factor in the survival of the ridings. Looking back from the 1870s, the *Hawick Express* recalled that this was once the most important aspect of the Common Riding for young people:

> *When the racing was at the Haugh, on both days the lads and lasses enjoyed themselves in promenading arm in arm in long processions. To secure a partner to 'link' at the Common Riding was indispensable, and called for earnest attention weeks before the time, and who can describe the 'bliss beyond compare' which filled the minds of both sexes in anticipation of sharing the pleasures with the favoured one. This method of enjoyment was much more attractive to the parties engaged than whether the black or the brown horse would win.*[76]

Clearly, for many people, the local riding was one of the highlights of their lives. Indeed, for some individuals, it was their life. Every riding had (and has) its stalwarts who existed for nothing else. Take, for example, Walter Ballantyne of Hawick. 'Wat the Drummer', as he was known, joined the Common Riding band in 1822. His father and his grandfather had been members before him and his nephew, Andrew, would follow him. Ballantyne played the drum at the Common Riding for fifty-nine years in a row, his last being in 1881 when he was eighty-one years old.[77] Similarly, in Selkirk, John Douglas or 'Douglas the Brave' cast the flag of the Corporation of Hammermen every Common Riding for fifty-five years. Langholm also had its share of Common Riding worthies, such as Willie Dick, who carried the heather-decked spade for half a century and was famous for dashing through the Ewes Water 'in reckless mosstrooper style'.[78] Family traditions contributed to the survival of the ridings because they provided an essential link with the past.

The Reform of the Ridings

It has been shown that between about 1800 to 1880 the ridings were under stress. Some people, for various reasons, were opposed to them and tried to get them abolished. But these events were very tenacious and had many enthusiastic supporters, who were determined that the ridings should continue. However, this does not mean that the ridings were impervious to change. This was a period of great social and cultural upheaval, and the ridings were influenced by the wider transformations in British society, which in turn gave them new purposes and functions. The remainder of this chapter will examine the changing nature of the ridings in the nineteenth century.

For most people in Britain, life was becoming more civilised, ordered and safe. For instance, new standards of behaviour were reducing much of the casual violence of everyday life. Likewise, as was shown earlier, there was growing intolerance of cruelty to animals. As John Mason remarked on his tour of the Borders in 1825: 'It is gratifying to remark, how much rural sports are now divested of that cruelty, which, in former times, seems to have given them all their piquancy.'[79] The nineteenth century also saw the unmistakable growth of an intellectual culture, especially amongst the skilled working classes and artisans. Writing in the 1820s, Robert Wilson commented on, 'the changes that are in progress on the habits and enjoyments of the people, by the steady operation of education'.[80] A comparison between the old and new *Statistical Accounts* shows that in 1790 there were only two lending libraries in Roxburghshire, but by 1830 this number had leapt to thirty-eight.[81] In 1866, Hawick had a population of about 10,500 people, but it could boast a thriving intellectual life, including numerous charities and sports clubs, three agricultural societies, clubs for archaeology, horticulture, music and ornithology, two subscription libraries and something called an 'Eclectic Book Club'.[82]

Similarly, drinking habits were changing and more people were exercising control in their use of alcohol. In the 1820s, the temperance movement began in Scotland. The first wave of temperance, which was specifically anti-spirits, was short-lived and made little impact, but in the 1830s a new movement for 'total abstinence' swept the country. Between 1838 and 1840, the movement attracted widespread support, especially amongst skilled labour. In 1838–39, almost one third of the total population of Hawick signed 'the pledge', although many later withdrew or were expelled.[83] In its early years, total abstinence had strong links with radical politics and it was only later that it became associated with religion. Many of the leading figures in the early temperance movement were working men and artisans. Abstinence, they believed, was one of the keys to the social and moral improvement of the working class. Many Temperance supporters were also Chartists, a movement that had strong support in Borders towns. Scotland's first Chartist Provision Store was opened in Hawick in 1839. One of the founding principles was a ban on the sale of alcohol.[84] Some people were strong supporters of both the temperance cause and the ridings, recognising that reformed drinking habits could secure the future of these events. In Hawick, Robert Hunter, a life-long abstainer, wrote several Common Riding songs and also many temperance ditties, such as *Alcohol* and *Hoo Tamie Turned Teetotal*.

Contemporary observers were aware that attitudes and public behaviour were changing, and that these changes were reflected in the ridings. Reporting the Common Riding of 1863, the *Hawick Advertiser* noted that:

> *The occasion passed off on the whole most creditably. There were few brawls of any kind, and none resulting in serious or permanent injury and the good conduct of the people was generally never surpassed.*[85]

There was also growing intolerance of excessive drinking at the ridings. Reporting the Common Riding of 1883, the *Hawick News* stated:

> *It was a noteworthy circumstance that very few people were observed the worse for liquor; and we understand both the burgh and county superintendents of the police concur in stating that they never on any similar occasion had less reason to interfere.*[86]

Another important factor in the changing nature of the ridings, and of social behaviour generally, was the development of the police force. Police were first introduced into the Borders in the 1840s. Originally, the force carried out its duties 'in a very easy and perfunctory manner', but they became an increasingly effective deterrent to crime and anti-social activities.

None of this is to argue that the ridings lost their rougher aspects overnight. In 1868 and again in 1876, the worst fears of the critics were realised when fatalities occurred at Hawick Common Riding. In 1868, a horse knocked over and killed a nine-year-old boy called George Marriot. In 1876 a man named Edward Dearden was fatally injured when a horse bolted into the crowd. In the latter case, the Cornet and some of his supporters were arrested on a charge of furious and reckless riding, although they were later released.[87] Both cases seem to have been tragic accidents. Marriot, like a typical over-excited little boy, ran out in front of the horses. Dearden's relatives wrote to the Cornet absolving him of any blame. Two facts are worthy of note here. First, nobody tried to use these incidents as evidence against the Common Riding or as proof of the need to abolish it. The general view was expressed by one town councillor who wrote that it was 'very hackneyed' to see the event as a threat to public order.[88] Second, there was widespread agreement that urgent changes had to be taken to prevent similar accidents from happening in future. Galloping in the streets was an old feature of the Common Riding, but when it was banned in 1877 few people claimed that this was an attack on ancient liberties. As the *Hawick Express* observed:

> *The dangerous riding on the public streets of a few headstrong youths, the nocturnal abominations attending the Ball, and some of the other proceedings were disgraceful … [But] this year there is a wonderful change for the better.*[89]

As the nineteenth century progressed, organisation and control were increasingly manifest in many popular customs and leisure activities. A good example in the Borders was the development of rugby football, which by 1890 had become a standard feature of local culture. Some kind of ball game had been played in the Borders for many centuries, perhaps since Roman times. These games may have had some ritual significance, but to most neutrals they seemed little more than gangs of boys and ruffians fighting with each other and generally running amok. In the 1870s, this changed when a new game called 'football' was introduced, often by ex-public schoolboys working in the textile trade. Whilst the old street football continued, the new game quickly gained a cult following. Football had standardised rules, an all-powerful referee, organised teams and, through time, formal leagues and competitions. Unlike the old game, football took place on a designated playing area, and there was no danger of play spilling over into the streets and damaging property. Matches were also carefully timed, both in duration of play and also by mainly taking place on Saturday afternoons, to fit with new patterns of work and leisure.

This process can also be seen in the ridings. Although continuing to rely on precedent, there was a move towards greater organisation and formality. Timetables and programmes of events were drawn up and issued in the local newspapers (although they were not always adhered to). In Hawick, the town council restored their patronage to the Common Riding in 1885, which included taking part in a formal procession on Common Riding morning. In 1887, a 'Ceremonial Committee' was formed to organise and administer the Common Riding. The bussing of the flag, which had previously taken place in a pub or a hotel, was transferred to the council chambers, where it was performed in front of the provost, magistrates 'and a very large company of leading citizens'.[90] In 1896, the Colour Bussing was switched to the town hall, becoming a public event with a programme, tickets for seats, and distinguished guests. The involvement of the town council was welcomed because it gave an official stamp of approval for the Common Riding. Paternalists also argued that the council encouraged greater order and restraint amongst the general population. As the *Hawick Advertiser* put it in 1890: 'They acted as a dignifying and restraining presence. Their personal attendance among the masses proving certainly a definite source of control amongst them.'[91]

It was also around this time that the ridings began to incorporate some formal religious features. The 'Kirkin of the Cornet' was instituted in Hawick in 1887, where the principals attended a local church, either just before or after the Common Riding. The presiding clergyman was appointed as the 'Cornet's chaplain', giving spiritual guidance to the principals and stressing their responsibilities to the wider community. The principals were not only leaders of the riding, but were also expected to act as role models and to demonstrate high standards of personal behaviour and restraint. In a sermon given in 1906, one minister in Hawick argued that the Cornet was a kind of Christian warrior, battling against strong drink, gambling and other social evils:

> The enemy of today was not Lord Dacre or the Earl of Surrey. The call today was not to lay down their lives, but to live and stand firm against those social forces of the Devil which broke hearts and destroyed the peace of homes. Young men were counselled to band together around their Cornet on these lines, and let every man be true to the best that was in him.[92]

By 1890, a new form of the ridings had emerged. They had become more structured and orderly, and as a result they began to attract wider support. As the next chapter will show, from the 1880s the ridings enjoyed a golden age and were used to promote various social values and ideals. However, this does not mean that the debate about the ridings was finished. They continued to attract controversy well into the twentieth century. But the attitude of the critics had undergone a subtle shift. Until the 1850s, most opponents simply argued that the ridings were out of date and that they should be abandoned. Gradually, there was less emphasis on repressing the ridings and more on reforming them. Heavy drinking, gambling and other social problems had corrupted the ridings, but nothing was beyond redemption and they could be sanitised and saved. The solution was that right-thinking people, the guardians of public morality, had to put pressure on the authorities to take a firm grip. In Hawick, the Reverend William Johnman, a firebrand of the Free Church, described the Common Riding as 'a dead oak upheld in the embrace of parasitic ivy'.[93] The blame, he argued, lay firmly with the town council who gave their patronage to the horse races, and by implication other social evils:

> Gambling in my judgement is more widespread than ever. If the Christian community has the honest desire to give it a severe blow it will never rest till the Magistrates and the Town Council are interdicted from patronising it, at the annual horse races on the Moor. I ask the church of Christ to treat the Common Riding as the devil's annual pandemonium until the Council separates it from the horse races and gambling and other filth which are the habitual concomitants.[94]

Significantly, Johnman, and other critics of this time, did not argue for the abolition of the Common Riding, but rather that it should be reformed and purified:

> With heart and soul I would like to rescue the Common Riding, to keep it worthy as an annual attraction … as a restful delight to be enjoyed by poor and rich, and to be looked back upon without compunction and without regret.[95]

This attitude was typical of the new approach to popular customs and leisure in the late nineteenth century. Few people now argued for the suppression of the ridings, although there

By the beginning of the twentieth century, the Common Ridings attracted huge crowds, as seen here at The Toll in Selkirk, c.1900 (above) and the Snuffing at Hawick in 1912 (below).

(Above: Scottish Borders Museum and Gallery Service (Selkirk Collection))
(Below: Scottish Borders Museum and Gallery Service (Hawick Museum Collection))

were still plenty of concerns about some aspects of them. In general, the ridings had become compatible with existing social values and standards of behaviour. As the Hawick Cornet observed in 1890: 'It is the God-loving, church-going, religious people who are today the bulwark of our carnival.'[96]

The ridings had undergone many developments in the nineteenth century. Changing patterns of behaviour and social attitudes meant that the old style of the ridings were increasingly at odds with a society undergoing rapid transformation. Some people withdrew their support and wanted to see the ridings abolished. But the tradition was very resilient and many others continued to take part, even when the approval of town authorities had been withdrawn. Gradually however, a new form of the ridings emerged, reflecting wider social changes. Criticisms continued to be made, but there was less to find objectionable. By 1893, the *Hawick Express* argued that, 'the order, sobriety, and general tone of the whole proceedings, as now carried out, have stopped to a very large extent the pulpit tirades which used to be so frequent at this season of the year.'[97] Two years later, a minister in Hawick summarised the history of the nineteenth-century ridings: 'Several years ago, the Common Riding was often spoken of in an apologetic manner. It was a matter of sincere congratulation that these troubles had almost entirely passed away.'[98]

6

'Follow the Flag!':
The Twentieth-Century Ridings

So now, when'er the Teri heart there sounds high honours call
Of duty for the town we love, and cherish over all.
We'll lift our spears of service, where'er our feet may roam,
To the vision of the Pennon on the dear old hills of home.
Follow the Flag! – John Y. Hunter

On the surface, the subject of John Hunter's Common Riding poem *Follow the Flag!* was the Hawick tradition of 1514, but for any Edwardian reader the real message was clear.[1] Written in the early 1900s, the underlying theme of the poem was the importance of duty and service, suggesting that these attributes were part and parcel of the Common Riding. Hunter's poem shows the remarkable transformation that had taken place in the status of the ridings in the nineteenth century. Like other popular customs in Britain at this time, the older style of ridings had gradually become more formal and restrained, reflecting the influence of deep cultural changes taking place in British society.[2] By the 1880s, the ridings had been largely remodelled. The period between 1880 and 1914 was something of a golden age for the event. As one writer remarked about Lanark Lanimer Day in 1910: 'at no time has it been more vigorously conducted, more picturesquely and tastefully arranged, and more numerously attended by interested spectators than within the last ten years.'[3] This chapter examines the history of the ridings from 1880 to the 1950s. First, it looks at the various factors behind the popularity of the ridings, such as social and cultural values, the impact of the railways, business and commercial interests, the rise of a music culture and the influence of emigration. The chapter then considers the age of invented traditions, which had a profound influence on the ridings, and the effect of the two world wars, which led to the development of many new events. The chapter concludes by looking at the work of the poet Hugh MacDiarmid and his enthusiasm for Langholm Common Riding.

The Ridings Become Respectable

The previous chapter demonstrated that important changes had taken place in the ridings in the nineteenth century. By the 1880s, it was increasingly difficult for anyone to object to the ridings or to argue for their abolition. This does not mean that criticism of the ridings suddenly ceased: high-minded men and women continued to find fault with them well into the twentieth century. But the critics of the ridings were a decreasing minority, although sometimes a vociferous one. In 1890, Robert Milligan, the Provost of Hawick and a man noted for his 'outspoken utterances', dismissed critics of the Common Riding as a 'narrow-minded section of the officious parson element'.[4] The following year, the *Hawick Express* argued that most local people supported the Common Riding and that anyone who attacked it risked ridicule and censure:

> *The more 'goody-goody' section of the powers that be, who can see nothing but evil in the ancient festival and its associations, have … either to pocket their pride … or decide to sacrifice their popularity as public personages, and make arrangements for a speedy retiral to the obscurity of private life.*[5]

Of course, old habits sometimes died hard. Heavy drinking persisted, despite the presence of temperance booths, and drunkenness was always present at the ridings. Similarly, gambling and betting went hand-in-hand with the horse racing and the games. Nevertheless, by 1890 it was generally agreed that the ridings had much to recommend them and that it was only a matter of time before progress would eliminate anything that was disagreeable or unrefined. 'Efforts are made year by year to have the celebrations purified in a rational way,' observed the *Hawick Express* in 1891. 'The best friends of the fine old festival are those who aim to have it carried through with the maximum of enjoyment and the minimum of excess.'[6]

There are several reasons for the popularity of the ridings in the late nineteenth century. The ridings benefited greatly from a new form of civic pride, the origins of which lay with a new business class whose wealth and status were rooted in the local community. The economist John Kenneth Galbraith has written that, 'there was something seemingly distinctive about the new industrial capitalists. As compared with the ancient landed classes or the merchants, they were parvenus – new to the scene, economically committed, socially crude.'[7] Galbraith points out that until 1914 national government was firmly in the hands of the old landed classes and that it was a serious social and political disadvantage to be 'in trade'. Consequently, the business community was drawn to local politics, something which the nobility, and also eminent individuals, usually preferred to ignore. Urban government fell under the control of local business interests and men whose political horizons did not stretch much beyond the limits of their town or city.

The town and city fathers of late Victorian Britain were wealthy and confident, and local government became an instrument of vision and progress. There was great emphasis on community projects, such as ambitious schemes for civic buildings, town halls and public libraries. Accompanying these buildings, there was a parallel enthusiasm for civic pageantry and display. Every opportunity was taken to exhibit local power, to enhance the new men of local government and promote their achievements in the community. Of course, to some extent this was nothing new: the exercise of local power had long made use of display and ritual. But in late Victorian Britain, the display was very elaborate and taken very seriously. All over the country, colourful processions and pageants were staged to impress upon the general public the legitimacy of the law and local government.

Popular customs like the ridings were an ideal vehicle to promote local power and influence. In 1840, the Aberdeen riding began with a formal procession of the burgh authorities, which, in the words of the official booklet, was designed, 'in all respects, to impress the Town's vassals with a feeling of reverence and awe'.[8] In the late nineteenth century, the ridings became a great entertainment and display. Towns were decorated with bunting and flags, with special prominence given to the Union Flag on town halls and other public buildings and also on private dwellings. Local bands played and huge processions were organised to represent local life. In 1899, the procession at Lanark Lanimer Day featured,

Right: Houses and streets are decorated for the duration of the riding, as shown here in Hawick around 1910. Note the prominence given to the Union Jack and the slogan 'Safe Oot, Safe In'. *(Scottish Borders Museum and Gallery Service (Hawick Museum Collection))*

Below: The figure of Britannia loomed large at the early Beltane Festivals in Peebles. *(Scottish Borders Museum and Gallery Service (Tweedale Museum Collection))*

Above and below: Aberdeen last held a riding of the marches in 1889. This booklet was a humorous skit on the event at the expense of the city council. *(Trustees of the National Library of Scotland)*

amongst others, local friendly societies, the Burns Club, a comic cycle parade, a troupe of morris dancers, and hundreds of 'daintily dressed children, attired to represent flowers and fairies'.[9] In 1893, the procession at the Musselburgh riding was reported to have been a mile and a half in length.[10] 'Dramatic tableaux' were a popular feature of many processions, involving children and adults dressed in costume and modelling different scenes from history or the contemporary world. In 1914, Peebles Beltane Festival marked the 600th anniversary of the battle of Bannockburn with a tableau, 'which was at once pleasing to the eye of the native and inoffensive to the visitor from across the Border'.[11] Tableaux were often used to promote imperial themes, when children, some with blackened faces, represented various peoples of the Empire. Likewise, it was a pre-requisite that one float would feature a young woman dressed up as the figure of Britannia.

There were many signs of the growing involvement of the professional and commercial classes in the ridings, the kind of people who would have shied away in the previous generation. For example, in Hawick, the Cornet of 1891, Andrew Haddon, was a solicitor and 'a rising man of good standing'.[12] His successor in 1893, William Scott, was the son of a hosiery manufacturer. In 1896, Robert Mair was a doctor. The late nineteenth century saw the first stirrings of the movement for the political and social emancipation of women, something that was firmly rooted in middle-class society. In the 1890s, women started to take part in the ridings for the first time as mounted supporters. In 1893, Miss Craig-Brown, daughter of Thomas Craig-Brown, manufacturer and provost of Selkirk, became the first woman ever to ride at Selkirk Common Riding. Male riders were very impressed, and probably slightly put out, when she reached the Three Brethren cairns ahead of them all.[13] Likewise, at least one woman took part in Hawick Common Riding before the First World War. However, anyone, male or female, who took part in the ridings always ran the risk of losing their dignity. Enhanced social status could not hide an inadequate rider or a frisky mount. Describing the Aberdeen riding of 1889, the pseudonymous 'DOT' remarked that the ordinary citizens of the town thoroughly enjoyed seeing the great and the good falling from grace:

Oh, what a motley crew they were –
The fat, the small, the tall,
And here and there a woefall wail,
Told truly when a Councillor fell,
And the people raised a joyful yell
To see the Bailies fall.

For they ne'er had been on horseback
In all their lives, 'twas plain,
And from the tears which dimmed their eyes,
One truely could right well surmise
They'd never do't again.[14]

Occasionally, high spirits and horseplay could go too far. It was in the same riding that a local doctor sustained fatal injuries after he had been swung against the 'doupin' stone.[15]

Another sign of the changing status of the ridings in the late nineteenth century was the presence of distinguished visitors at some events. In 1897, Keir Hardie, 'the celebrated socialist', who admittedly was considered a public nuisance in some quarters, attended the Hawick Colour Bussing.[16] Of course, many of these visits were thinly disguised attempts at making political capital, what would now be described as a 'photo opportunity'. The Reform Acts of 1868 and 1884–85 had widened the franchise and anyone with political ambitions had to ingratiate themselves with the electorate. By taking part in the ridings, national figures could promote themselves locally whilst local politicians could rub shoulders with the famous. In 1904, Arthur Conan Doyle was Parliamentary Unionist candidate for the Border Burghs constituency. He took part in Hawick Common Riding, which as he later admitted, was 'an endeavour to get into comradeship with the people'. Unfortunately for Doyle, whose candidature was unsuccessful, his involvement in the Common Riding backfired, as he recalled in his autobiography:

an interminable ballad was recited with a sort of jingling chorus, to which all who are near the reciter keep time with their feet. As it would seem unsympathetic not to join in, I also kept time with the rhythm, and was amused and annoyed when I got back to London to see in the papers that I had danced a hornpipe in public before the electors. Altogether, I had no desire to face another Hawick common riding.[17]

Being largely unfamiliar with the ridings, visitors were sometimes guilty of offending local sensibilities, especially when they tried to push themselves to the front. In 1888, Austen Chamberlain, the future Chancellor of the Exchequer, was Parliamentary candidate for the Border Burghs. Like Conan Doyle, he took part in Hawick Common Riding, but his attempt to manipulate the event for his own benefit was not very popular. To make matters worse, Chamberlain committed a serious indiscretion when he rode in front of the Cornet during the Cornet's Chase, breaking the tradition that the Cornet always led. Unsurprisingly, Chamberlain's candidature was not successful.

Railways and Business Interests

Another important factor in the survival of the ridings in the second half of the nineteenth century was the development of the railway system. Built between 1847 and 1864, the Waverley Line ran from Edinburgh and Carlisle through the heart of the Scottish Borders, bringing to an end an ancient history of isolation and self-dependence for many Border communities. Gradually, as the railway system developed, it was possible to travel almost anywhere in Britain relatively cheaply and quickly. Railways dazzled the early Victorians. On 1 September 1855, 1,100 people made one of the first public railway journeys from Hawick to Galashiels, a distance of eighteen miles. They were greeted on their arrival by a group of civic dignitaries, cheering spectators and a brass band.[18] The effect of the railways on the ridings was double-edged. The availability of cheap travel meant that some people took advantage of the annual holiday at the ridings to visit other places. It was shown in the previous chapter that some religious groups used the railways for special outings to draw people away from the ridings and from the racecourse. But the railway also made it easier for people to travel to the ridings, whether as casual visitors or to return to their native town. The railway brought in a captive audience and the ridings were an ideal opportunity for towns to show off. In the 1890s, Selkirk town council made an annual request to the local railway company to run special trains from Galashiels for the Common Riding.

The influx of people for the ridings was welcomed by local businesses that were able to cater for their needs. The second half of the nineteenth century was a period of rising living standards in Britain. Deprivation continued to exist but in general people had more consumer power than ever before. Festivals and holidays were traditional periods of heavy consumption. Local businesses were keen to encourage the ridings because they provided a reliable annual windfall. The following advertisement appeared in the *Hawick News* in June 1906 and it is typical of many which appeared in local newspapers around this time:

For the COMMON RIDING!
A Special show is now being made in all the latest Novelties in MEN'S WEAR for the ANCIENT FESTIVAL. A TRUE TERI should be at the Front at this time, and T. SWINTON IS SECOND TO NONE in his excellent display of COMMON-RIDING TIES, CAPS, HATS, etc.
T. Swinton, Cap and Scarf Emporium, 6 Howegate.[19]

With the exception of publicans and bookmakers, local businesses made their money in the run-up to the riding rather than at the event itself, when most shops and stores closed down. Others business groups who supported the ridings were people working in the travelling fairground, whose livelihoods partly depended on the ridings. The later nineteenth century saw a significant change in the fairground with the introduction of large mechanised rides, driven by steam and later by electricity. Roundabouts and other rides made their first appearance around 1800. Originally driven by animal or human power, mechanically powered rides were introduced in the 1860s and soon became the main attraction of the fairground. As the *Hawick Express* observed in 1875: 'The old "hobby-horse", driven by willing hands, has given place to the latest novelty of steam-driven hunters and gilded omnibuses.'[20] It was during this period that the fairground took on its modern appearance. The older and basic 'shows' were pushed to the side (hence the 'side-stalls') and the new mechanical rides took over the centre ground. The point about these new rides was that they were a big capital investment and the owners wanted to maximise their returns. Here then was another business group that wanted to keep the ridings alive.

Another technological development in the fairground that is worth mentioning was the introduction of photography and moving films. At the beginning of the nineteenth century, the fairground had an arrangement called 'umbries', whereby an operator used the light of a candle or a lamp to cast shadows on a screen with his or her hands. This was later replaced by the 'magic lantern', which projected images painted on glass. The moving film was introduced at the end of the nineteenth century and proved an immediate sensation. Occasionally, new technology raised old problems. In 1898, there were angry letters in the *Hawick Advertiser* about various attractions at the fair that were 'vulgar or obscene in character', including 'stereoscopic photographs calculated to excite the basest passions'.[21] More innocently, the fairground also had instant photographic booths, where customers could have their picture taken, perhaps for the first time in their lives. By the early twentieth century, most towns had at least one semi-permanent cinema or 'picture house'. Proprietors sometimes hired equipment to make short films about the ridings and other local events, and these were a great attraction for local people, who went along to see themselves and their friends on the big screen. Similarly, local photographers, such as the Clapperton family in Selkirk, took dozens of shots of crowd scenes at the ridings and displayed these for sale in their shop windows.

Patriotism and the Influence of Chivalry

It is clear that many people supported the ridings because it was in their interests to do so. There was money to be made at the ridings, both for local and travelling businesses, and this was an important factor in the survival of the ridings. However, it would be misleading to explain their survival only in material terms. The ridings also flourished because they were the vehicles for expressing important social values and ideals.

Patriotism, the devotion to one's own country and the concern for its defence, was an important strand of the nineteenth-century ridings. Patriotic feeling was, of course, nothing new: it had been a feature of British life for centuries. In its early forms, patriotism was often linked with political radicalism and appeals to ancient British liberties. However, from the 1870s, patriotism was increasingly identified with right-wing politics, partly because loyalty to the state was seen as a means of reducing tensions between the social classes. Nineteenth-century Scotland has been described as a melting pot of different identities. As Michael Lynch has observed: 'The concentric loyalties of Victorian Scotland – a new Scottishness, a new Britishness and a revived sense of local pride – were held together by a phenomenon bigger than all of them – a Greater Britain whose prosperity and stability rested on the Empire.'[22] Most people saw no contradiction between belonging to a town or village, being Scottish, British and a member of the world's greatest Empire.

Patriotism, like charity, was thought to begin at home. Local attachments were strongly encouraged because they were seen as the building blocks out of which a wider patriotic sentiment was made. During the ridings, local and national identities regularly overlapped and reinforced each other. In a prophetic piece about Hawick Common Riding in June 1914, *The Border Magazine* observed:

> There are great cities which would almost sell their souls – if souls they have – to have a chain
> of sentiment or home love that could weld their segregated units into a homogeneous whole in
> such a link as Hawick has – and Selkirk – and create a local patriotism that would form a
> feeder to the greater patriotism which is today demanded, and tomorrow may be needed.[23]

The period between 1870 and 1918 has been described as 'the age of imperialism', meaning the era when nations tried to extend their rule over other territories, usually through aggressive expansionism. The British, especially the upper and middle classes, believed that they were a morally superior race and therefore fit to rule over those who could not rule themselves. To do so, there was a pressing need to send Britons overseas to inhabit new lands and to help build an Empire based on justice and the rule of law. The ridings were seen as part of the common British inheritance and as an inspiration to future endeavours. At the Hawick Colour Bussing in 1897, having made a long speech about Queen Victoria's Diamond Jubilee, Andrew Haddon, an ex-Cornet, stated:

> *I think it is very proper that Hawick should talk about patriotism. We are members of a great and magnificent Empire, of which we all feel very proud. It has been built up by the various deeds of our ancestors, and as the Common Riding comes round, we meet together and one of our purposes is to commemorate the valorous deeds of our ancestors.*[24]

At this time, many people made the connection between the tradition of the ridings and the great imperial mission. The ridings, it was believed, were about protecting freedom and upholding community, and these values were also the cement that held the Empire together. Addressing an audience of exiles at Hawick in June 1914, the Reverend J. Rudge Wilson, a local minister, stated:

> *The links of the Empire are not fleets and armies, not laws, and treaties, and statues, but the affections and the inspirations which cluster round the home. (Cheers.) They go out from us to Vancouver, to South Africa, to Australia, and wherever they go they carry with them the ideas of just government, and religious freedom, and happy family life, which they have inherited here. The true Teri [native of Hawick] is thus bound to be an Empire builder.*[25]

Closely associated with patriotism, another influence on the ridings was the revival of medieval chivalry. In his book *The Return to Camelot*, Mark Girouard has examined the popularity of chivalry from the late eighteenth century to the First World War.[26] At its simplest, chivalry is defined as the code of behaviour evolved for the knights of the Middle Ages. Girouard suggests that a revival of chivalry began in the eighteenth century when new methods were developed for the study of history. This created a fashionable interest in the Middle Ages and led to a widespread sympathy for chivalric ideals. The revival was further encouraged by chaos and upheaval of the French Revolution, which presented a stark contrast to the safe, ordered loyalties of the past. The Scottish Borders played an important part in the chivalric revival, having nurtured Sir Walter Scott. Scott, more than anyone, encouraged and popularised the chivalric movement, his best-selling works being full of chivalric imagery and romance. Not everyone shared Scott's enthusiasm for the past. Robert Wilson, a Cornet of Hawick, attacked Scott, arguing that cruder times were best forgotten and that writers should concentrate on the present. In fact, Scott saw chivalry as a medieval phenomenon that had evolved, although many of his followers saw no such development. The world, they believed, was still a battleground between good and evil. By the second half of the nineteenth century, chivalric ideals and imagery were a significant part of national culture. As Girouard's book illustrates, chivalric imagery was omnipresent, appearing in paintings, literature, drama, poetry and songs. Chivalric ideals provided a basic code of behaviour for many men, especially from the upper and middle classes.

The tradition of ridings, especially the emphasis on horses, seemed to have links with the old chivalric world. In Musselburgh, the Town Champion, played by a prominent local man, wore an antique suit of armour at the riding. Several riders at the Aberdeen riding in 1889 wore armour. The ridings also provided some excellent chivalric role models. Fortunately one might add, because Saint George, the patron saint of chivalry, was strongly associated with England. In Lanark, the statue of Sir William Wallace, which was erected in 1822 on the wall of the old parish church, provided an impressive backdrop for the Lanimer Day celebrations. In the Borders, people enjoyed stories of the Border Reivers, albeit the sanitised and romantic

The Town Champion at Musselburgh Riding of the Marches still wears an antique suit of armour, as shown in this photograph of William Caird in 1956. *(Author's collection)*

versions of Sir Walter Scott and John Mackay Wilson, whose *Tales of the Borders* was first published in book form in 1840 and delighted a huge audience.[27] Romantic traditions about the battle of Flodden also had a strong appeal, especially after Sir Walter Scott had popularised the battle in his epic poem *Marmion*, which was first published in 1808. The dead of Flodden epitomised some important chivalric ideals: honour, bravery, truthfulness, self-sacrifice and loyalty to one's superiors, even when it led to disaster.

Popular enthusiasm for chivalry had some tangible effects on the ridings. In June 1913, Selkirk unveiled a statue to mark the 400th anniversary of the battle of Flodden. The suggestion to commemorate the battle in this way had come from the Selkirk Colonial Society. As one contemporary writer put it, this showed, 'that the same old feeling that sent the Souters to Flodden in support of their King still survives in a wider imperialism than Scotland ever dreamt of four hundred years ago'.[28] The statue was based on the tradition that a lone soldier had returned from the battle bearing a captured English banner. Designed by Thomas Clapperton, the statue bore the simple legend 'O Flodden Field!' from the poem *Selkirk After Flodden* by J.B. Selkirk. Archibald, 5th Earl of Rosebury, unveiled the statue before a huge crowd and he was made an honorary burgess of Selkirk for his services. The 'Fletcher' statue was a commemorative artwork but it also expressed some of the values and ideals of the people who built it, in particular dignity and self-control in the face of defeat. Fletcher accepts his fate with stoicism, like any respectable gentlemen would do.

Similarly, in 1914 Hawick marked the 400th anniversary of the capture of the town flag with the unveiling of the 1514 Memorial. The original proposal for the monument was a Scottish mercat cross, but public opinion favoured a horse and rider theme. Paid for by public subscription, the monument was unveiled on 4 June 1914, the highlight of a week of special 'Quater-Centenary' events, which included a Grand Historical Pageant and an Exiles' Homecoming. The new monument subtly captured emotional extremes. The rider is elated and triumphant but his mount is weary and resigned. The base of the monument bore the Latin legend, *Merses Profundo Pulchrior Evenit* ('From the depths, the Borders emerged more beautiful').

In June 1913, Lord Rosebery, the former Prime Minister, unveiled the Flodden memorial statue in Selkirk. *(Robert D. Clapperton Photographic Trust)*

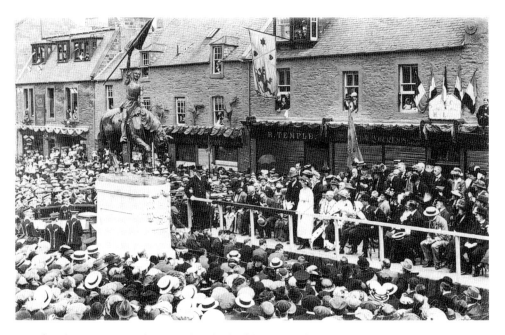

Unveiling the 1514 memorial at Hawick in the fateful summer of 1914. *(Hawick News)*

For an educated person, the message was clear. Struggle through and victory would come, even against the odds. Both of these statues would become doubly poignant after 1914.

Further evidence of the contemporary fashion for chivalry and its influence on the ridings can be found in the work of the Borders artist, Tom Scott. Scott was born in Selkirk on 12 October 1854, the eldest son of a tailor. After training in Edinburgh and making several trips abroad, Scott returned to the Borders, where he concentrated on paintings of the local countryside and scenes from Border legend. In 1897, Scott was commissioned by the Hawick town council to produce a painting commemorating the capture of the town flag in 1514. Financed by public subscription, the painting was unveiled at the Colour Bussing of 1898, where it was received with 'rapturous applause'. The painting depicted the young men of Hawick returning home in triumph with the flag and the townspeople coming out to meet them. It was full of fashionable chivalric imagery, including knights in armour, blonde-haired maidens, hunting horns, deerhounds and, in the midst of it all, the first Cornet carrying the captured banner. In 1898, one reviewer commented: 'Mr Scott has thrown over the scene an allowable glamour of historical romance', adding that the painting had been produced 'with all the patriotic fervour of a Border man'.[29] The painting was very popular and reproductions were sold in large numbers, many of which were sent overseas. Enough money was raised from the sale to allow for the building of a permanent memorial at the site of the flag's capture, two miles downriver from Hawick. At the unveiling ceremony on 1 June 1901, which was attended by hundreds of people, the provost said that the new monument 'would for ever keep green the heroic conduct of our ancestors'. The eleven-foot-high monument was in the form of a simple stone column and bore the inscription 'Lest We Forget'.

The phrase 'Lest We Forget' was taken from Rudyard Kipling's poem *Recessional*, which had been written for Queen Victoria's Diamond Jubilee in 1897. Kipling's poem achieved great popularity for its jingoistic overtones, although it was originally written as a warning against the arrogance of world power. The use of 'Lest We Forget' on the Hawick memorial pre-dated its appearance on many British memorials to the First World War. In his book *The Missing of the Somme*, Geoff Dyer has considered the meaning of the phrase in relation to memorial art. As Dyer asks: 'Lest we forget what? And what will befall us if we do forget?'[30] At the unveiling of the Hawick memorial in 1901, the answer was provided in a poem read by James Murray, the Acting Father. Murray argued that every right-thinking person had to see himself or herself as a modern warrior, a crusader, fighting to uphold certain values and ideals, both within themselves and throughout the world:

> *'Lest we forget' that they bequeathed*
> *The privilege of peace;*
> *'Lest we forget,' though sword be sheathed,*
> *The battling must not cease.*
>
> *Ours 'tis to tread the broader way,*
> *To live the sweeter life;*
> *Ours just as real in modern day*
> *The waging of the strife.*
>
> *'Gainst odds that grind the weak to earth*
> *'Gainst vice that wears the strong.*
> *'Gainst sland'rous speech that smirches worth,*
> *'Gainst every coward wrong.*[31]

The ridings were part of the wider struggle. Leading the community, the principals had to be Christian knights, battling against evil and injustice in whatever form they may take.

Organisation, Music and Emigration

Since the earliest times, the ridings had taken place largely by precedent. There were few written instructions or codes of practice. Events had taken place in a certain manner longer than anyone could remember and there was no reason to change them. Gradually however, attempts were made to bring more formal organisation to the ridings. The nineteenth century saw the introduction of printed timetables and songbooks, which in some cases included lists of previous principals. Official guests were invited to attend, and tickets and printed programmes were issued for some events. In addition, organising committees were established to oversee the running of the ridings, and clubs and societies were formed for those who took part.

A good example here was the Hawick 'Callants' Club, which was formed by a group of local businessmen and manufacturers in December 1903.[32] The club was established in response to the War Office's purchase of land near Hawick for a large training camp. It was feared that a large military presence would swamp the town and its native traditions. From its constitution, the objectives of the club included:

- *The cultivation of local sentiment;*
- *The preservation of the ancient customs and institutions of Hawick;*
- *The fostering of local art and literature;*
- *The commemoration of important local incidents;*
- *And the perpetuation of the memories of local townsmen.*

Left: The ridings became more organised and formal with printed timetables and programmes, such as the Hawick Colour Bussing in 1912. *(Scottish Borders Museum and Gallery Service (Hawick Museum Collection))*

Opposite above: Tom Scott's painting *Return from Hornshole 1514* captures the Victorian love affair with chivalry. *(Scottish Borders Museum and Gallery Service (Hawick Museum Collection))*

Opposite below: Unveiling the memorial at Hawick in June 1901 to commemorate the capture of the Common Riding flag. *(Scottish Borders Museum and Gallery Service (Hawick Museum Collection))*

The club membership was restricted to 100 members, who were expected to be active supporters of the Common Riding. Women were excluded, as was one of the original supporters, Martin Dechan. Dechan had been Acting Father in 1903, but in the words of the club history, he 'insisted that as a Roman Catholic and the son of an Irish father he was not the man to give the Club as good a start as some others'. The club was very active in promoting local identity, including buying a chain of office for the provost (who was usually one of their members) and building a memorial on the site where the burgess role was read at the Common Riding. The club also encouraged young people to take an interest in their local area by organising school competitions, awarding books with local themes as prizes. In June 1909, school pupils sat a formal examination to test their local knowledge. The senior (fifteen +) paper included the following questions:

– *Describe in the form of a letter to a Colonial friend the various places of interest you would pass in walking from Hawick to Teviothead.*

– *Mention the names of four historic residences not more than six miles from Hawick, telling briefly what you know about the famous men or women connected with them.*

The growing popularity of the ridings had other tangible results. The new sense of local pride created an interest in local history, which in turn led to several historical studies of the ridings. In 1898, Robert Craig and Adam Laing, two lawyers, published *The Hawick Tradition of 1514: The Town's Common, Flag and Seal*, which set out to examine the history of Common Riding. In Selkirk, Thomas Craig-Brown, a manufacturer, published his massive two-volume *History of Selkirkshire and Chronicles of Ettrick Forest* in 1886, which contained a great deal of material on Selkirk Common Riding. These men, and others like them, were great supporters of their local ridings, but their books were diligently researched and sometimes critical about accepted traditions.[33] Craig and Laing went to great efforts to trace early copies of the Hawick flag. As a result of their work, the design of the Hawick flag was changed from a red to a yellow cross on a blue background. Likewise, Craig-Brown expressed many doubts about the Flodden traditions of Selkirk, bravely commenting in his book's preface: 'tradition has been religiously set aside in favour of the truth, however destructive.'[34]

Among his other talents, Robert Craig was a prolific poet and songwriter, often taking inspiration from Border subjects. His work is typical of a large number of poetry collections and anthologies that were published in Britain at this time, which drew on local themes and which were designed to appeal to a local audience. The ridings were popular subjects for writers in the Scottish Borders. Whilst many of these poems and songs have now been largely forgotten, in some cases they became part of the ridings and still feature in the modern events. The riding songs were part of the growth in popular music in later nineteenth-century Britain. In his book *Popular Music in English Society*, Dave Russell observes that: 'Britain in the Victorian and Edwardian periods was an extraordinarily musical place.'[35] Throughout the country, people were coming together in unprecedented numbers to make music. In part, the growth of popular music was the result of key social and economic changes that were taking place in British society. As we have seen, from the 1870s, growing numbers of working-class people had more money and leisure time, and many of them turned to music for their leisure and entertainment. Popular music also benefited from the prevailing atmosphere of Victorian Britain. As Dave Russell states: 'Music, because of its association with religious ceremony and its supposed ability to civilise and humanise, was known to the Victorians as the "sacred art".'[36] The performance of music was encouraged because it was believed that music could elevate the human spirit and draw performers and listeners closer to God. The second half of the nineteenth century saw the steady development of a music industry in Britain. The manufacture of musical instruments expanded and growing numbers of people were able to purchase or hire their own instruments. For example, piano ownership gradually spread down the social scale. In 1840, the piano was a luxury item, but by 1910 there was one piano for every ten to twenty people.[37] By 1900, a piano had become a symbol of respectability in working-class homes, 'valued as an instrument but above all prized as the status symbol of the age'. The music industry was also able to supply all the basic requirements for making music, such as manuscript paper or music stands. Cheap music lessons were widely available from full-time teachers and part-timers.

One consequence of the growth of popular music was a huge expansion in the numbers of brass bands. It has been estimated that in 1856 there were only about six brass band contests in England but by 1896 there were over 240.[38] The brass band has been described as one of the most remarkable cultural achievements in working-class history. In 1855, Samuel Stainton, a local stocking-maker and staunch Tory, founded the Hawick Saxhorn Band, which was soon incorporated into the Common Riding.[39] Money was raised by public subscription and Stainton received a salary of £5 as bandmaster. In the 1870s, Selkirk town council used to hire the Hawick band to play at the Common Riding, giving rise to the local saying, 'It'll come again like the Hawick band'. Brass bands of this kind took themselves very seriously. In Hawick, forty hopefuls were given an audition to join the new band but only fourteen were eventually chosen. Despite their popularity, brass bands often experienced a precarious financial existence. Many performers could not afford to buy uniforms and had to wear their Sunday best. Regular inter-town contests took place and these attracted enthusiastic groups of followers. Occasionally, competitions threatened to get out of control. In May 1893, members of the Hawick Saxhorn Band were harassed by other musicians whilst preparing to take part in a contest at Linlithgow. One report stated: 'This unseemly conduct culminated in a cowardly and unprovoked attack on the judge and Mr Atkinson, the respected conductor of the Hawick Saxhorn Band. Stones were thrown and the police had to intervene. Undaunted, the Hawick band will play at Silloth tomorrow.'[40]

Brass bands featured in the ridings and they were used in processions and at other formal events. However, their involvement sometimes created resentment from traditional performers. Hearing that the Saxhorn Band was to take part in Hawick Common Riding, Walter Ballantyne, whose family had a long history of playing the drum at the event, angrily announced: 'A brass band tae play in front o' the Cornet wad never dae: yon's nae music for horses!'[41] The late nineteenth century also saw the emergence of bagpipe bands in some of the ridings. The British military had adopted the bagpipes when the first Highland regiments were raised in the early 1800s. Whilst some form of bagpipe had been played in lowland Scotland for many centuries, the formal bagpipe band was a Highland symbol whose popularity spread to the rest of the country. Regiments provided pipers and bands for some of the ridings although there were suspicions that they had an ulterior motive and were trying to use the ridings for recruitment. Choirs and choral societies were another popular musical form that featured in the ridings at this time. In 1887, to celebrate Queen Victoria's Golden Jubilee, Selkirk Choral Society sang the *Flo'ers o' the Forest* before the riders set off, and then *The Litin'* and *God Save the Queen* after the Casting of the Colours.

In this intense musical environment, songwriters and poets wrote about the things with which they were familiar. Until the invention of television, radio and the cinema, people relied largely on their own abilities and imaginations to entertain themselves. One of the most popular ways of passing an evening was by holding a family or neighbourhood singsong, perhaps accompanied by a piano or a fiddle. Songs about local subjects had great popular appeal and there was a huge market for local work. The growth of a musical publishing industry and the cheap printing of music scores further encouraged the production of local songs. By 1900, most towns in Britain had at least one entrepreneur who would publish local material in return for a fee. In Hawick, Adam Grant ran a music shop on the High Street from the early 1880s to his death in 1939. An outstanding organist and choirmaster, Grant published a host of Common Riding songs, including some that he had written himself.

Music has always been an important aspect of the ridings, as shown here with the Hawick Fife and Drum band in 1907 (above) and the Selkirk choir in 1884 (below).

(Above: Scottish Borders Museum and Gallery Service (Hawick Museum Collection))
(Below: Scottish Borders Museum and Gallery Service (Selkirk Collection))

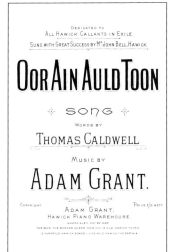

Adam Grant of Hawick was a typical publisher of local music, including many Common Riding songs. Note the dedication to 'All Hawick Callants in Exile'. (*Author's collection*)

One of the major themes of the songs was a longing to return home, something which struck a particular chord with the 'exiles', the people who had left their native towns to relocate either to other parts of Britain or to emigrate. It has often been said that Scotland's greatest export is people. For centuries, Scots of all levels of society and all regions have gone to other countries seeking greater opportunities. This process was accelerated in the nineteenth century by a sharp increase in population and the pressures of industrial change. Sydney and Olive Checkland have written that:

> in spite of her industrial and trading achievements, Scotland could not hold her natural increase in population at its prevailing growth rate. The peak emigration decade of the century was the 80s, with Scotland losing 41 per cent of natural increase or 218,274 persons. In all between 1861 and 1901 just under half a million Scots went abroad (including to England).[42]

Scottish emigrants had four main destinations: the United States, Canada, Australia and New Zealand. There was also a great deal of internal migration within Scotland. The bulk of the population steadily concentrated itself in the Central Belt, especially in and around Glasgow.

Naturally, moving into strange new environments, many emigrants experienced feelings of bewilderment and disorientation. Battling against homesickness and self-doubt, they sought comfort in what was familiar to them, the old world in the new. Writing about Robert Louis Stevenson, who was one of Scotland's most famous emigrants, Ian Bell observes, 'exile is a state of mind, as much a condition of the heart as a physical event. The exile is reminded, more often than the rest of us, to question who he is and what he is.'[43] Emigrants often tried to re-create something of their former lives, which led to a powerful bond between fellow emigrants drawn together with nostalgia and idealisation of their old home. This is not to say that they spent their time pining to be back home again, miserable in their isolation. Many emigrants went away quite willingly and were very successful in their new lives, often integrating into their adopted countries with great enthusiasm and confidence. Nevertheless, in the late nineteenth century Scottish (or 'Scotch') Border Clubs and Associations were formed in several cities in Britain and also in the Empire and the United States. Members organised special dinners, excursions, sports days and other events, all with a Border theme. In some cases, these organisations had a charitable ethos. One of the principles of the London Scotch Borderer's Association was to help young Border people who came to the capital 'and who perhaps got into straits'.[44]

Many emigrants had fond memories of their local riding and as the event came around each year they were reminded of the world and the life that they had left behind. Sometimes, emigrants organised imitation or 'little' ridings, which were loosely based on the original events. One of the earliest of these occurred in 1854 when a 'Hawick Common Riding' was held in Melbourne, Australia. The event included a Cornet, a copy of the flag, a procession and a grand dinner.[45] In Boston USA, an annual Hawick Common Riding was instituted in the late nineteenth century by John Scott, a wealthy tweed designer who had been the real Cornet in 1853. In June 1915, the Boston Common Riding included a dinner in honour of Hawick, the Borders and Scotland plus a colour bussing and a concert of Common Riding and Scottish songs. The next meeting in September 1915 was held in honour of Sir Walter Scott.[46] Through time, local affinities of this kind gradually weakened, particularly with the arrival of the second generation for whom the old country was just stories and songs. However, exiles' organisations were surprisingly persistent and survived well into the twentieth century. In the 1950s, an active Glasgow–Langholm Association existed, which was once addressed by the poet Hugh MacDiarmid.

Emigration and exile became one of the major themes of the ridings. Gwen Kennedy Neville has argued that emigration, like warfare, threatens the survival of a town and that when exiles return they represent the temporary victory of life over death.[47] Emigrants have special status in the ridings. In Selkirk, there is a Colonial Society for Selkirk emigrants, which was formed in Ontario in 1910. In June 1914, a special 'Exiles Homecoming' was organised at Hawick to mark the 400th anniversary of the capture of the town flag. The exiles were welcomed with a civic reception, where they were piped into a packed town hall. Around 160 people returned for the event, most of them from the United States and Canada.[48]

Emigration was a painful process, not just for those who went away but also for those who stayed behind. Recalling the mid-nineteenth century, James Turnbull of Hawick gave a moving description of emigrants leaving the Borders:

> When the emigrants were going away it was a special day, as they all had friends who wished 'to set them up the road a bit'. They all walked up the road 'cracking' away to each other; sometimes it was almost a crowd that went along with those who were leaving. When Martin's Bridge was reached the driver would stop the cart, and then the company lost grip of themselves, for they knew they had reached the parting of the ways. Too full for words, the emigrants would look up the river and all around them, and then shake hands with their friends. At this point I have known them try to sing Auld Lang Syne, but even that grand old anthem of human love and kindness, at such a time as this, was only a broken melody.[49]

Of course, many emigrants eagerly grasped the opportunity to start a new life, happy to escape the old constraints and hardships, and the pettiness of living in a small town. Some were never heard of again, once they had left their native land. However, others had a strong desire to maintain links between the 'mother town' and 'her sons and daughters across the seas'. This often led to the development of international communities of townspeople, where emigrants kept in contact both with each other and with the people at home. Letters and parcels flowed back and forth across the oceans, keeping emigrants in touch with local news, events and gossip. Reporting the Snuffing at Hawick in 1881, the *Border Advertiser* noted that as soon as the snuff had been distributed some of it was packaged up and sent to exiles in America.[50] As emigrants began to settle into their new lives and become more prosperous, there were often tangible benefits for the ridings. In Hawick, the Common Riding of 1854 was known as the 'Gold Nugget Year' because emigrants in Melbourne sent a gold nugget as a prize for the races.[51] In 1913, Peebles received a new Beltane Bell for the races, sent from exiles in the United States. After the First World War, Peebles also received a carved coronation chair from South Africa, crowning robes from New Zealand and an embroidered carpet from India.[52]

PROVOST

ROBERT SIM.

STANDARD-BEARER

GEORGE DOWNIE.

SELKIRK COMMON-RIDING, 1907.

O I wad be in Selkirk in the merry month o' June,
  When the Souters thrang thegither in the auld grey toon ;
An' the pride for fearless fathers an' the hame whaur they
  were born
    Thrills the heart o' ilka body on the Common-Riding morn.

Frae the auld stance in the Mercat, I wad stand an' see
  them ride,
  While the kindly sangs o' Selkirk wad gang pealin' on ilk
  side ;
An' my soul wad ride the mairches ower the hill an' by the
  corn,
    As my faithers rade before me on the Common-Riding morn.

An' I'd think o' waesome Flodden when I saw the colours cast,
  An' that time o dule and heart-break when brave Fletcher
  cam' at last ;
Standin' here before the people wi' the Flodden flag all torn,
  Snatched frae battle to wave proudly mony a Common-
  Riding morn.

O there's mony a hundred Souters in far lands across the faem,
  Wha's thochts turn aye in longing to their dear auld hame ;
An' to-day their hearts are hame-sick for the toon whaur they
  were born,
  An' their spirits follow wi' us on this Common-Riding morn

M. & M., SELKIRK.

Above and below: Postcards of this kind were specially prepared for local exiles. Note the sentiments of the Selkirk card (above) and a view of Hawick Common Riding (below).

(Above: Scottish Borders Museum and Gallery Service (Selkirk Collection))
(Below: Scottish Borders Museum and Gallery Service (Hawick Museum Collection))

An elephant and a camel trumpet the arrival of the travelling circus into Galashiels, a rare sight in the early 1900s. *(Author's collection)*

Improved links with other countries also benefited the fairground, as there were more opportunities to obtain exotic and original attractions. At this time, a person with a coloured skin was considered a great novelty in Scotland and there were no hesitations about putting them on display. Performances by indigenous peoples were a popular feature of the fairground, especially when they were dressed in their native costumes and carrying out traditional skills. Foreign countries were also an abundant source of strange and curious animals, and travelling menageries were a staple attraction. At Hawick Common Riding in 1903, there were tanks of live crocodiles, which locals found both repellent and strangely fascinating.[53] Unscrupulous entrepreneurs sometimes resorted to the old trick of displaying 'mystical' animals, such as horses disguised as unicorns. Similarly, there were displays of animals that had birth defects, such as double-headed lambs. In 1901, the fairground at Hawick and Selkirk featured a sheep with seven legs, 'and other monstrosities'.[54]

Another feature of the fairground that benefited from overseas contact were human performers who claimed to have special skills with animals, such as bareback riders, lion tamers or snake charmers. In 1863, the *Hawick Advertiser* reported that one of the most popular attractions at the Common Riding had been 'a showman who was on extremely familiar terms with a large serpent'.[55] Large animals were used to advertise the fairground and the arrival of the fair was often heralded with a street parade that featured an elephant, a camel or a giraffe, perhaps covered with promotional material. Crowds lined the streets to stare and marvel. From a modern perspective, these people might appear very easy to please, perhaps a bit soft in the head, turning out in droves just to see a wild animal or a person with a dark skin. But we should remember that they had virtually no other opportunities to see such things. The fairground, like the ridings, was a brilliant splash of colour in a world that was mostly grey.

The Invention of Tradition

The period between 1870 and 1914 has been described as the age of 'invented tradition'.[56] Commonly across Europe, 'traditions' were manufactured in response to rapid social changes, in particular the concentration of people in towns and cities, the development of industry and the decline of the old agrarian world. The invention of tradition fell into two broad categories. First, there was the invention of political traditions, where governments tried to establish new loyalties and social controls by creating 'traditional' activities. Second, there was the widespread invention of social traditions. A good example here was the invention of sporting traditions, such as Cup Final Day or annual International fixtures, which in football and rugby union date from the 1870s. The invention of tradition is important in the history of the ridings because much of what now appears to be very old is actually quite modern. In many cases, traditions that seem to have been handed down from time immemorial were often created quite recently, even within living memory.

Peebles Beltane Festival and March Riding, which was instituted in 1897, is an excellent example of this process. The Riding of the Marches had taken place in Peebles until the late eighteenth century, but died out because of agricultural changes and general disinterest. In 1897, a 'Citizens' Committee' decided to commemorate the Diamond Jubilee of Queen Victoria by holding a revival of the old riding. By this time, Victoria was very popular in Scotland, venerated as a symbol of permanence and national continuity. Eric Hobsbawm has observed that the Golden Jubilee in 1887 and Diamond Jubilee ten years later, 'were new insofar as [they were] directed at the public, unlike traditional royal ceremonials designed to symbolise the rulers' relation to the divinity and their position at the apex of the hierarchy of grandees.'[57] In other words, people throughout Britain and the Empire were encouraged to take part in the celebrations and to share in a sense of British achievement.

In Peebles, the new riding first took place on 22 June 1897. *The Scotsman* reported: 'Never in its history has the ancient and Royal burgh been so gaily or profusely decorated.'[58] W.H. Williamson, the town treasurer, acted as Cornet although he took part in a carriage rather than on horseback. Williamson led a procession that featured almost every aspect of burgh life, brought together as one to celebrate the great event. It included brass bands, the town council and officials, the police force, the fire brigade and engine, almost eighty horsemen and women, and representatives of all of the town's clubs and societies. The riding was so successful that it was decided that it should become an annual event. In 1899, it was renamed the 'Beltane Festival' after the ancient Celtic festival held on the first or third day of May. A pagan fire festival is believed to have taken place on these days, which in some parts of Scotland, including the Borders, survived until the late eighteenth century.[59] Whilst the pagan aspect of Beltane waned or adopted a Christian theme, it was a time of fairs, games and races. In the sixteenth century, Peebles Beltane Fair was an important social occasion, attracting royal visitors and inspiring the famous poem *Peebles to the Play*. In 1899, a prominent role was given to children, especially to a young girl who was chosen as the 'Beltane Queen'. Although she did not ride the marches, the Beltane Queen shared the symbolic leadership of the festival with the Peebles Cornet. The first Beltane Queen was Margaret Muir, dux girl of the 'English school'. In 1906, her successor, Nellie Louisa Dickman, was described as 'the cynosure of every eye ... elected to the proud position on account of her vivacity of spirit and intelligence of mind'.[60] The Beltane Queen was accompanied by a court of children, who were dressed up in a variety of exotic costumes. Imperial imagery was very prominent and children were dressed to represent the many different peoples and animals of the Empire.

The Beltane Festival probably owed some of its features to nearby Lanark, where the first 'Lanimer Queen' was appointed in 1893. In both towns, the 'tradition' of appointing a Summer Queen was quickly established, partly taking over from the Riding of the Marches.

Peebles Beltane Festival dates from 1899. Based on the old riding of the marches, it gave a special role to children. Here is the original Beltane Queen, Margaret Muir, with her Maids (above) and the crowning of the Queen at the Market Cross (below). *(Scottish Borders Museum and Gallery Service (Tweedale Museum Collection))*

The pre-Christian aspects of Beltane were tactfully ignored, apart from a large bonfire on one of the hills. Instead, the event concentrated on its principals, the colourful highlight being the crowning of the Beltane Queen on the steps of the Old Parish Kirk. From the outset, the Beltane had a strong patriotic theme and stressed that participants should take pride in their country as well as their town. One song written for the Jubilee Riding of 1897 concluded:

> *That the Peebles folk can do,*
> *Something worthy the occasion*
> *And that we are patriots true.*[61]

In its early years, the Beltane had a strong military presence. In 1906, a detachment of Scots Greys took part in the procession and staged a tattoo in the local park. The following year, 'a squad of lads' from HMS *Wellesley* put on a gun display. In an age of imperial expansion and international rivalry, the army and the navy were held in high esteem and it was reported that the visitors were received with great popular enthusiasm. In 1911, the Beltane was deliberately staged to coincide with the coronation of King George V (22 June). In a typical paternal gesture, the Provost of Peebles, Mr J.P. Ballantyne, and his wife presented each school child with a commemorative box of sweets, thus impressing on them the special significance of the day.

Other towns in the Borders invented traditions in this period. After a lapse of about eighty years, Lauder revived its Common Riding in 1911, also to commemorate the coronation of George V. The original Common Riding had been discontinued by the town council for reasons of public safety, probably because of widespread drunkenness and disorder. Having obtained advice from Selkirk, the new Common Riding featured the annual election of a Cornet, various ceremonies and a formal ride around the town and the marches. Lauder Common Riding was a great success and has taken place every year since 1911, apart from the war years. Similarly, towns that had no history of riding the marches used the original Common Ridings as a model for new events. Innerleithen created a riding around 'Saint Ronan's Border Games', which had been established in 1827 by, amongst others, Professor John Wilson and James Hogg, 'for the purpose of reviving the old Border spirit and to encourage the practice of athletic sports'. In August 1901, the Innerleithen 'Cleikum Ceremony' was introduced 'to familiarise the youth of the town with the legend of Saint Ronan'. Ronan was an early medieval monk who, according to local legend, caught or 'cleeked' the Devil and immersed him into a local well, giving the water a distinctive flavour. As the local song put it:

> *Doon where Leithen gurgled bricht,*
> *Centuries awa',*
> *Cam' St Ronan wi' his licht,*
> *Crook and cross and a';*
> *He shed it on us a',*
> *Oor forebears yin and a',*
> *By symbols rude and precepts good,*
> *He kept the de'il in awe!*

The dux boy at the local school was selected to play Saint Ronan and a kilted Standard Bearer was appointed to carry the town banner. There was also a torchlight procession of Freemasons, dressed in their full regalia. The week's events concluded with the spectacular burning of an effigy of the Devil on a nearby hill.[62] Other towns were more casual about the invention of tradition. Annan staged a Riding of the Marches only at irregular intervals. On 21 March 1871, a special riding was held to celebrate the marriage of the Marquis of Lorne and Princess Louise, both of whom had local associations. Twelve years later, on 20 September 1883, a riding was held to mark the completion of the paving of the Annan High Street.

The next riding was not held until September 1913. *The Border Magazine* described it as, 'another instance of the revival of pageantry throughout the land'. Annan Common Riding did not become an annual event until 1947.[63]

A pattern of ridings was firmly established in the Borders by 1914. The older Common Ridings at Hawick, Selkirk and Langholm continued annually and attracted widespread popular support. New or revived events now took place at Peebles, Lauder and Innerleithen, all of which were very successful. In a process that was mirrored throughout Europe, these latter events were soon thought of as traditional, even though they had been invented in the recent past.

The First World War

The First World War was the great test for the ridings. Speaking at the Hawick Colour Bussing in June 1914, less than two months before war broke out, Lord Dalkeith, the principal guest, asked his audience:

> *What did the flag stand for? Everything good in this country! Their flag was won by the sword, and sooner or later, it might have to be defended by the sword. He hoped that the Cornet would not be called upon to do anything of the sort, but if he were he had the faith that he would emulate the deeds of his forerunner 400 years ago.*[64]

There are stock images for every period. For August 1914, one thinks of cheering crowds greeting the outbreak of war with unbridled enthusiasm and patriotic fervour. Deep down, most people were probably apprehensive about the war and only supported it out of a sense of duty and a belief that the country was in danger. Despite early assurances that it would be over by Christmas, it was soon realised that the war would require an enormous national effort and resources. In late August 1914, Lord Kitchener, Secretary of State for War, appealed to civilians for the creation of a 'New Army' of 100,000 men. British regular regiments had long carried regional titles but until 1914 prolonged overseas service had made these connections tenuous. Kitchener's recruiting campaign emphasised locality and gave the army strong links with the local community. Kitchener intelligently recognised that local loyalties could be the building blocks of effective national mobilisation. Young (and not so young) men had many different reasons for joining up: out of instinct, realism, peer pressure or fear of invasion, but an important incentive for many was the promise that they would be able to serve alongside their friends, relatives, neighbours and work colleagues. This policy was destined to have disastrous consequences for many communities in Britain, including the Scottish Borders, as the war progressed.

The ridings were used to motivate people behind the war effort and in particular to inspire young men to do their duty and join up. Flute, brass and bagpipe bands, which had an important role in the ridings, were used to promote recruiting meetings and other military events. Knowing what their audience wanted to hear, orators and local firebrands exploited the heroic past for the needful present. At a recruiting meeting at Hawick in October 1915, 'prominent Borderers' warned young men not to dishonour their illustrious predecessors:

> *They were all proud of the way the Hawick young men had fought after Flodden; they were all very fond of the Common Riding and of singing 'Hawick was ever Independent', but that song and those great traditions were won by brave men who did brave deeds – they were not won by the slack young man who went slouching down the street with the cigarette in his*

mouth to the picture palace. The Hawick motto then and now was 'Independence', and how did they win it? They did not win it by talking, they won it by fighting![65]

Similarly, popular newspapers and magazines stressed that it was the duty of all Britons to uphold their traditions by joining in the war effort. The message was reinforced by patriotic songs and poems, which flowed from the presses in the early years of the war. Typical of the new mood was Pringle Thorburn's poem *Up Borderers Up*, which was published in Border newspapers and magazines in 1916:

> *You boast of Flodden, and are proud*
> *Of the blood that runs in you.*
> *You think of home and loved ones,*
> *Yet you must up and do.*
> *For courage comes indigenous*
> *In the hour of fiercest pain –*
> *No coward blood flows thick and slow*
> *Where runs the patriot vain.*
> *You are needed, you are needed.*
> *Up Borderers Up!*[66]

As the war dragged on into 1915, the question was whether the ridings should take place at a time of national emergency. The joyful pre-war celebrations were clearly inappropriate with the new mood of the country. They were also, of course, impractical because so many people (and horses) were now on military service. But what form, if any, should the wartime ridings take? The issue caused a great controversy, as locals had to consider making an unprecedented break with the past. For some, it appeared that the very future of the ridings was at stake.

Two of the oldest Common Riding towns, Hawick and Selkirk, handled the crisis very differently. In March 1915, the *Hawick Express* surveyed a selection of local worthies for their opinions on the form of that year's Common Riding. Most agreed that the Common Riding should take place, but on a restricted scale. It was argued that the town's senior magistrate rather than the Cornet should carry the flag, symbolising that the nation came before the town. However, the old campaigner Adam Laing wrote that not to appoint a Cornet would be 'an act of vandalism', a view which was supported by fifteen former Cornets who sent a petition to the town council requesting them to elect a Cornet as usual. They set out a strong patriotic case for the Common Riding, arguing that it might encourage local recruitment:

> *The annual flying of our flag by a selected youth is a commemoration of the patriotism of the past, and one of the strongest incentives to the patriotism of the present day and in the future. It appeals in a most picturesque way to all that is noblest and best in the spirit of our young manhood.*[67]

Other writers suggested that the Cornet should be chosen from local men serving in the army and that the event should take on a 'military air'. Adam Laing proposed that the calling of the burgess role should be revived as a Roll of Honour, meaning that there would be a reading of the list of local men who were on active service or those who had died. It was generally agreed that the horse racing, games and travelling funfair should not take place. Several writers saw the war as an opportunity to settle old scores. Reverend David Cathels wrote that he favoured a wartime riding but that the horse racing 'and all its swindling and sordid accompaniments' should be suspended, perhaps in the hope that this might kill off the races for good.

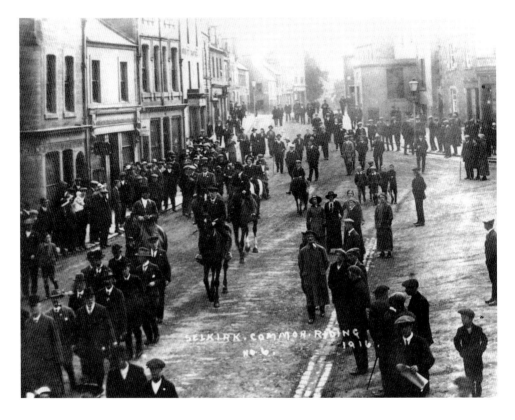

KEEP SMILING!

THE HAWICK

COMMON-RIDING FAIR

—— IS GOING ON ——

The Haugh.

MOTOR CARS, GALLOPING HORSES, HELTER-SKELTER, CIRCUS, CINEMATO-GRAPH, and SIDE SHOWS of all kinds.

NOW OPEN.

SO DON'T BE DOWNHEARTED. ☞ COME AND ENJOY YOURSELF.

Above: Keep smiling! Despite the First World War, the Hawick Common Riding shows went on as normal. (*Hawick News*)

Left: Trooper John Riddell was chosen from Selkirk men on active service to be Royal Burgh Standard Bearer in 1915. (*Scottish Borders Museum and Gallery Service (Selkirk Collection)*)

Below: In 1916, only six riders took part at Selkirk, the smallest number ever recorded. (*Robert D. Clapperton Photographic Trust*)

Ultimately, on 11 May 1915, the town council voted not to elect a Cornet or to grant a licence for the games or the races, which led to the abandonment of the Common Riding. The actual day of the riding (11 June) was observed as a local holiday. Many people left on special excursions, although children were encouraged to take part in special patriotic sports that were held in the afternoon.[68] In these circumstances, it is surprising that the funfair took place as normal. The 'shows' were largely outside the council's control, but it was recognised that the owners' livelihoods were at stake and that they had a right to carry on their trade. In fact, the fairground was not immune to the war and many men who worked in it had already left to join the forces. Those who remained tried their best to cheer everyone up, raise local morale and take people's minds off the war. However, most of their customers were soldiers from the nearby military camp, who appropriately excelled on the shooting galleries.

Selkirk faced a similar dilemma over its Common Riding. The same arguments were gone over, but unlike Hawick it was decided that the Common Riding should continue but on a restricted scale. This decision was not universally accepted: the Provost of Selkirk, Andrew L. Allan, actually resigned from the council in protest against it. A Standard Bearer was selected from Selkirk men serving in the armed forces and on 25 June 1915 the Common Riding took place 'in a manner befitting the times'. Only fourteen riders were involved in the 1915 riding as against 136 the previous year.[69] There was no bussing of the colours, horse racing or guilds, but the Casting of the Colours took place in Selkirk town square as usual. For those present, it must have been a doubly poignant moment. Thomas Craig-Brown encouraged locals to take pride in their sacrifice:

> *Children of the warrior race –*
> *In race, valour still confiding,*
> *While youth takes its honoured place,*
> *Age will keep your ancient Riding.*
> *Flodden and Flanders – hallowed pride –*
> *In the Border heart abiding,*
> *In days to come will, side by side,*
> *Be cherished with each Common Riding.[70]*

Later in the war, Selkirk Common Riding was even more restricted. In 1916, there were only six riders and the town standard was carried and cast by the senior burgh officer. A wreath was laid at the Flodden memorial. It said: 'In memory of Selkirk's sons who have fallen in this war. Common Riding morning, 16 June 1916.'[71]

For those at the sharp end of the war, the ridings could act as a comfort and a spiritual bond, as it had also done for the exiles. There is no doubt that the men of the New Army were dedicated to their cause, but essentially they were civilians in uniform and, unlike the regulars, they often lacked a strong sense of identity with the regiment. Consequently, group solidarities were expressed differently from those of professional soldiers. Impromptu concerts of Common Riding songs often took place between recruits on leave or when they were resting behind the lines. Similarly, there were many instances of men from the same town being brought together because one overheard the other whistling or singing a local song. Imitation ridings were sometimes organised amongst groups of soldiers. Writing from a camp in May 1918, Corporal John Dodds reported that a group of Hawick prisoners had staged their own Common Riding:

> *After choosing the Cornet and Right- and Left-Hand Men, we have only one supporter, we intend to issue complimentary tickets to natives of Gala and Selkirk* [who were also in the camp]. *We anticipate that it will be possible to provide donkeys for the occasion.[72]*

The terrible losses of the First World War had an enormous impact in Scotland and the Borders. The tradition and imagery of the ridings, which had been used to motivate people, were also used to express their feelings of sacrifice and loss. Contemporary writers were quick to draw a parallel between the dreadful battle of Flodden and the war. Poems such as Robert Craig's *A Dream of Flodden*, which was written in the 1890s, acquired a whole new meaning after 1914:

> *They came from lonely moorlands and far sequestered towers,*
> *And every hill and valley yielded its fairest flowers.*
> *From Liddel and Esk and Yarrow, from Teviot, Tweed and Jed,*
> *They were gallant hearts who followed, and a king himself who led,*
> *From Carter Fell and Cheviot to lone St Mary's Lake*
> *They failed not at the summons, who knew the black mistake.*
> *And they rode away to the eastward, and the land was still as night;*
> *And never a man that faltered, and never a thought of flight.*[73]

For the Scottish Borders, the blackest day of the First World War was 12 July 1915, when the territorial battalion of the King's Own Scottish Borderers (1/4 KOSB) was involved in heavy fighting at Gallipoli. The Battalion was ordered to charge the Turkish defences, but, as so often happened during the war, the attack ended in confusion and slaughter. Over 300 men were killed and over 200 were injured in a single action that wiped out over half the fighting strength of the Battalion. It was with good reason that 12 July 1915 became known as a 'second Flodden' for the Borders. John Buchan, a famous Borderer himself, wrote: 'The losses ... had been such that for the Scottish Lowlands it was a second Flodden. In large areas between the Tweed and the Forth scarcely a household but mourned a son.'[74] The image of Flodden was used to commemorate the disaster at Gallipoli. Every year on the anniversary of the famous charge, a special service for veterans was held at the 1514 Memorial in Hawick, when a large wreath was placed on the monument. In 1916, the inscription on the wreath stated: 'The ancient spirit of our fathers hath not gone.'[75]

The end of the war brought about the resumption of the ridings. Whilst partly overshadowed by a sense of loss, the sheer relief at the end of the war gave the ridings of 1919 a special poignancy, as they would also do in 1946. Everywhere, the ridings were celebrated with great enthusiasm, representing the victory of life over death. In the 1920s, the ridings were used as a focus for commemoration. In Hawick, it was proposed that the dates '1914–1918' be added to '1514' on the town flag.[76] It was also suggested that bronze plaques bearing the names of the fallen be added to the base of the 1514 Memorial. It was in the 1920s that ceremonial visits to local war memorials were incorporated into the ridings: the principal rider and others laying wreaths of remembrance on behalf of the community.

New Ridings and the Second World War

The inter-war period saw the development of more festivals based on the original Common Ridings. The war had heightened the sense of community in many towns and drawn people together in a common purpose and struggle. The new ridings were a positive response to the

Opposite: In the 1920s, a visit to the local war memorial was incorporated into all of the ridings. Here a wreath of remembrance is laid at Hawick, photographed in the 1990s. *(Scottish Borders Tourist Board)*

Galashiels Braw Lads' Gathering was instituted in 1930. These photographs are from the album of the first Braw Lad, Henry Poulson. Poulson and the Braw Lass Hazel Gardiner (above); crossing the River Tweed (above, left); an Act of Homage at the war memorial (left) and the Blending of the Roses ceremony (below). *(Scottish Borders Museum and Gallery Service (Selkirk Collection))*

war and reflected the strong desire to build a better future. In 1930, Galashiels instituted the 'Braw Lads' Gathering', which was an immediate success and became one of the most popular events in the annual Borders circuit.[77] (The term 'Braw Lad' came from the Robert Burns poem *Braw Lads o' Galla Water*.) The original proposal for the Gathering came from the provost, J.C. Dalgleish, although it was only agreed after lengthy consultation in the community. Galashiels did not possess common land so the Gathering was based on significant events in the town's history. These included the defeat of some English marauders in 1337; James IV's gift to Margaret Tudor of the lands of Ettrick forest; the granting of the town charter in 1599; and the commemoration of local loss in the war. The Gathering drew features from other ridings, including a civic reception for overseas visitors and exiles. It was the 'Galaleans' Society' of Lawrence, Massachusetts, that provided the sashes of office for the principals, Braw Lad Henry Polson and Braw Lass Hazel Gardiner. Significantly, the Braw Lass was appointed in her own right and not as the partner of the Braw Lad. On 28 June 1930, the first Gathering had a mounted cavalcade of 269 riders, including about fifty female riders and visiting principals from other towns. Ceremonies were held at the 'Raid Stane', the mercat cross, Abbotsford (the home of Sir Walter Scott, who probably didn't like the Common Ridings very much), and Old Gala House. The Gathering was described as 'a day of crowded joys', although the war cast a shadow over proceedings. The climax of events was an 'act of homage' at the war memorial. *The Scotsman* reported: 'As the strains of the *Flowers of the Forest* broke on the air, the Burgh Standard was slowly lowered, heads remained uncovered and a silence reigned.'[78] The Galashiels war memorial was an outstanding piece of work by the sculptor Thomas Clapperton. It showed a Border Reiver on horseback, capturing 'the spirit of the Border'. In the 1920s, H.V. Morton, the famous travel writer, described it as 'the most perfect town memorial in the British Isles'.[79]

In the 1930s, other towns followed the example of Galashiels and instituted their own ridings. In 1932, Dumfries revived the old local riding in the form of Guid Nychburris Day, the name being taken from sixteenth-century records that exhorted burgesses to be good neighbours to each other. The new event featured a Cornet and a Cornet's Lass, and there was also a Pursuivant, who symbolised royal authority, and a Queen of the South, another variation on the theme of a Summer Queen. In August 1935, Musselburgh staged a Riding of the Marches, the first since 1919, which was so successful that it was decided to hold an annual event. In July 1936, Musselburgh instituted the Honest Toun Festival, which was loosely based on the traditional ridings. Similarly, in 1937 Kelso instituted an annual Civic Week, featuring the Kelso Laddie and ride-outs to neighbouring villages and to Floors Castle, home of the Duke of Roxburghe. In 1938, Melrose introduced an annual Summer Festival, which was designed, 'with the idea of impressing on local people and in particular on the rising generation the rich heritage to which they were the heir'. The Melrose Festival had ceremonial visits to various historic sites in the neighbourhood, such as Trimontium Roman Fort, Darnick Tower, Abbotsford and Melrose Abbey. At some places, the Melrosian and the principals met local people dressed up in historical costumes and, judging by photographs, trying hard not to appear self-conscious.

The Second World War created new challenges for the ridings, although there was a precedent to follow and controversial decisions were largely avoided. Most towns suspended their ridings for the duration, although in some places an element of continuity was upheld when a former principal or a town officer rode the marches on their own. Selkirk, uniquely, continued to hold a Common Riding, although on a restricted scale. In 1946, the *Southern Reporter* justified this decision, stating that, 'the flags had been carried in procession at the Common Riding in defiance of Hunnish Nazism.'[80] The Second World War also produced a remarkable testament to the strength of local attachment to one of the ridings. In 1945, workers at the Pringle hosiery factory in Hawick made a replica of the town flag and sent it to local men serving in Germany with B Company, 4th Battalion of the King's Own Scottish Borderers.

Three cheers! Kelso Civic Week dates from 1937. Here, the Laddie and his supporters greet the crowd (above) and dance a reel in the Market Square (below). Both pictures date from 1950. *(Robert D. Clapperton Photographic Trust)*

Melrose Summer Festival was instituted in 1938. Pictured here in the late 1940s, the Melrosian and principals visit historical sites in the vicinity of the town, including Trimontium Camp (above) and Darnick Tower (below), complete with Roman soldier and medieval monk. *(Author's collection)*

Above: Casting the Colours at Selkirk on the roof of an air-raid shelter, June 1942. *(Robert D. Clapperton Photographic Trust)*

Right: In June 1945, a group of Hawick men on active service in Germany held their own Common Riding. This photograph, taken in the 1980s, shows the 'Cornet', Corporal Jim Reid, with the special flag sent by women from a Hawick factory. The flag, embroidered with battle honours, is now preserved in the Hawick museum. *(Pringle of Scotland)*

The battle honours of the company were embroidered on the flag, which became known as the 'Letzlingen flag' after the town where the company were stationed. 'Principals' were appointed from the company, including a Cornet, Acting Father and a Provost. On 8 June 1945, the day of the real Common Riding, the flag was carried in procession through the streets of Letzlingen and dipped in the River Elbe.

With victory won, the ridings of 1946 were particularly memorable, as they had also been in 1919. Everywhere, there was great relief at the end of the war and the promise that life would gradually get back to normal. In 1946, all of the ridings were revived and people made great efforts to be at home for these special occasions. In June 1946, the *Hawick Express* observed that local people were 'exceptionally enthusiastic' about that year's Common Riding, 'feeling the need to revive old memories after the lapse of celebrations during six years at war'.[81] The following week, the same paper claimed that the Common Riding of 1946 had been, 'the most jubilant Common Riding of the century and perhaps the best supported Common Riding of all time'.[82] The principals of 1946 were ex-servicemen who had done their bit. For instance, the Melrosian was Arthur Brown, who, in the words of the *Southern Reporter*, 'on the rugby fields and on the stern fields of war has proved his manhood. In him will be symbolised the Melrosians who shed their blood and all who served their country in the struggle for liberty.'[83] The restrictions and shortages of post-war Britain led to great difficulties for the organisers of the ridings and in many respects these ridings were make-do events. In Peebles, there were many problems in obtaining material to make the children's costumes and people had to make strenuous efforts to procure outfits. As in 1919, the ridings acquired new meanings and symbolism for the wartime generation. Reporting Selkirk Common Riding, the *Southern Reporter* stated: 'The old songs of Selkirk had a new significance when sung at the victory Common Riding. They were triumphant songs, declaring that the name and fame of the Royal Burgh had been upheld in the latest holocaust of war.'[84]

The emotional impact of the ridings was elevated as people drew parallels between their own experience and local tradition. In 1946, the *Southern Reporter* described the Casting of the Colours at Selkirk as:

> *A memorial to brave men who had fallen and to women who have sorrowed. The Burgh Standard Bearer made the Flag to tell with an eloquence and revenue more powerful than words the tragic and triumphant story of Flodden and of other fields right up to yesterday. As the flag of the Empire was dipped, the silence fell. The assembly remembered heroes of the past and more especially their own kith and kin who had not returned.*[85]

The invention of tradition continued in the post-war era when more ridings were instituted. Like the Edinburgh International Arts Festival, which was established in 1947, these ridings were a positive response to the universal degradation of the Second World War and a desire to maintain the strong feelings of community that the war had engendered. A special Riding of the Marches was held in Edinburgh on 8 June 1946 to celebrate peace, attracting seventy riders and a crowd that was described as 'approaching royal visit dimensions'. The Lord Provost of Edinburgh said that the riding had been 'a picturesque method of uniting the past with the present'.[86] In Jedburgh, the Jethart Callant's Festival was instituted in 1947, which included ride-outs to places of historic interest, notably to the site of the Raid of Redeswire, a sixteenth-century Border skirmish where the Jedburgh men saved the day. The first Callant was Charles McDonald, an ex-serviceman, who, in the words of the *Southern Reporter*, carried the flag as, 'the emblem of our past glories, and the symbol of our hope for future achievements'.[87] In 1949, Duns instituted the Reiver's Week, which had the Duns Reiver as principal and an open-air service on a local hill to commemorate the Scottish Covenantors. Likewise, in 1952, Coldstream introduced an annual Civic Week, which included a ride over the Border to the Flodden battlefield where there was a guest oration and a wreath-laying ceremony.

Above and left: Jedburgh (or Jethart) Callant's Festival dates from 1947. These photographs, taken in 1965, show the riders passing the ruined medieval abbey (above) and the oration at the Redeswire stone (below). *(Robert D. Clapperton Photographic Trust)*

Two Border villages also introduced horse festivals in the post-war era, although these events had rather tenuous links with the Riding of the Marches. In the far north of Tweeddale, West Linton revived the traditional Whipman Play in 1949. Whipman is an old Scots word for a carter, someone who drives a cart, but in this context it meant anyone working with horses. The Whipman Play is believed to have started in 1803 when local carters, ploughmen and others formed a benevolent society for members and their children. The annual outing of the society was marked with festivities and games, especially horse competitions and horsemanship. Over the years, the style of the day gradually changed and it was interrupted by the two world wars. In 1949, the principal riders at the new event were The Whipman and his Lass, and a schoolboy Barony Herald. Further south in the lea of the Cheviot Hills, the twin villages of Yetholm and Kirk Yetholm introduced an annual summer festival in the early 1960s. Kirk Yetholm was once the capital of the Scottish gypsies and travelling people, and appropriately the principals of the new festival reflected this gypsy heritage: the Bari Gadgi and the Bari Manushi, which were Romany names meaning Braw Lad and Bonnie Lass. The Yetholm Festival included sports and games, dances and a ride-out. Several towns in the south-west of Scotland also introduced ridings after the Second World War, including Kirkcudbright (1951), Wigtown (1953) and Lockerbie (1955), although these had mixed success and did not always become annual events. Another revival of the Riding of the Marches took place as recently as 1986 in the unlikely setting of Kirkwall in the Orkney Islands. There are records of a riding having taken place in Kirkwall on 24 July 1706, when the magistrates and council, 'with a great many of the respective burgesses and several others of the community,' met on horseback at the Tolbooth to view the town's marches. The event, which may not have taken place annually, seems to have petered out around 1800, but was revived in 1986 to mark the 500th anniversary of the granting of Kirkwall's charter.[88]

Langholm Common Riding and Hugh MacDiarmid

This chapter concludes by examining the relationship of the writer and poet Hugh MacDiarmid and Langholm Common Riding, the most idiosyncratic and eccentric of the Scottish ridings. Unlike the Common Ridings at Hawick, Selkirk and Lauder, the origins of which are lost in history, Langholm Common Riding can be shown to have begun at a specific date. In 1759, after a legal dispute about land ownership on the outskirts of the town, the Court of Session, the supreme court for civil cases in Scotland, ordered that boundary marks, cairns and beacons be set up to define the limits of the Langholm common. The burgesses were expected to maintain these markers and ensure that the boundaries were clear and in good order. Originally, the town drummer, a man called Archibald 'Bauldy' Beattie, carried out an annual inspection of the marches on foot, which he did for over fifty years, dressed each time in his official uniform and a three-cornered hat. It was Beattie's successors who instituted the Riding of the Marches, the first taking place in 1816.

Langholm Common Riding, which always takes place on the last Friday of July, has several unique and curious features. The day's events begin with the flute band leading the way to Whitta Hill, where there is a ten-mile race for foxhounds. Known as the 'Langholm Classic', the race is highly regarded by enthusiasts and followers, and there is great prestige in owning the winning dog. Back in the town, the street procession includes the 'Four Emblems', which are carried proudly by specially appointed bearers. First there is the Barley Bannock and the Salted Herring, nailed to a wooden platter and carried aloft on a pole, and signifying the Duke of Buccleuch's rights in local mills and fisheries. The next emblem is the spade, which is used for cutting sods of earth at various points on the common. Then come two mysterious emblems: a gigantic thistle, perhaps symbolising Scotland or just to give a prickly warning to potential troublemakers, and also a large floral crown, which may be a symbol of royalty, although nobody really knows its true purpose. Langholm Common Riding also has the Crying of the Fair. The Langholm Fair pre-dates the Common Riding and the two events seem to have become confused because it was another of Bauldy Beattie's responsibilities to Cry the Fair. Unusually for an official announcement, even in Scotland, the Fair Crying is given in broad Scots, a language that Hugh MacDiarmid grew up with and later used to great effect in his poetry. In a bizarre ceremony, the official Fair Crier, having first demanded 'Seelence', delivers the oration standing on the back end of a stout horse, propped up by its rider. The first Crying of the Fair and the Common Riding actually proclaims the riding only.

> *Now, gentlemen, we are gaun frae the Toun,*
> *And first o' a' the Kilngreen we gan' roun';*
> *It is an auncient place where clay is got,*
> *And it belangs tae us by Right and Lot;*
> *And then frae there the Lang-wood we gang throu'*
> *Whar every ane may breckans cut and pou;*
> *And last o' a' we to the Moss do steer*
> *To see gif a' our Marches - they be clear;*
> *And when unto the Castle Craigs we come,*
> *A'll cry the Langholm Fair – and then we'll beat the drum.*[89]

The second Fair Crying takes place in a hemmed-in market place once the Cornet and the riders have returned to the town. Full of archaic Scots words and phrases, the second Crying proclaims the eight-day fair and has the following wonderful admonition:

> *… and ony hustrin, custrin, land-louper or dub scouper or gae-by-the-gate swinger, wha comes*
> *here to breed ony hurdum or durdum, huliments or bruliments, hagglements or bragglements or*

Above and middle: Langholm Common Riding is the most eccentric of the Scottish ridings. These photographs were taken in 1930 and show three of the Emblems (above) and the Crying of the Fair in the Market Square (below). *(Scottish Borders Museum and Gallery Service (Selkirk Collection))*

Left: Langholm Common Riding, *c.*1912. Just visible between the poles supporting the Crown of Roses and the Barley Bannock is the young Christopher Grieve, later known as the author Hugh MacDiarmid. *(Edinburgh University Library)*

squabblements, or to molest this public Fair, shall be ta'en by order of the Bailie and the Toun Cooncil, and his lugs be nailed to the Tron wi' a twalpenny nail, until he sit doon on his hob-shanks and pray nine times for the King and thrice for the muckle Laird o' Ralton, and pay a groat to me …[90]

It will be clear from all of this that Langholm Common Riding has a special atmosphere of its own, having much in common with medieval fairs and the original style of the ridings. As F. Marian McNeill observed in the 1960s: 'Compared with the ordered pageantry of, say, Hawick or Lanark, the celebrations are robust and somewhat easy-going.'[91]

Hugh MacDiarmid, whose real name was Christopher Murray Grieve, was one of the intellectual and artistic giants of twentieth-century Scotland. MacDiarmid was born in Langholm on 11 August 1892, the son of a postman, and lived in the town until he was sixteen years old. Langholm left an indelible mark on MacDiarmid, as it does for most natives. His prose and poetry are rich in topographical references to the town and the surrounding countryside, and he constantly drew inspiration from his early life in the 'Muckle Toon', as locals affectionately call their town. On his seventy-ninth birthday, Valda Trevlyn, MacDiarmid's second wife, wrote in tribute:

> *Over the years you've dreamed your dreams*
> *And as always*
> *You go back to your past*
> *In Langholm — your tap-root.*[92]

Langholm now promotes itself to tourists as the 'Birthplace of Hugh MacDiarmid', but it is well known that MacDiarmid was rather unpopular in the town during his lifetime, partly as a result of his intellectual left-wing politics and support for radical Scottish Nationalism. When he was buried in Langholm in September 1978, many local people, including the town's provost, pointedly stayed away.

The Common Riding was, and is, the traditional focus of community life in Langholm. MacDiarmid loved the event and later in life he made every effort to return for the Common Riding, coming back as a proud exile and not as a famous literary figure. The language and imagery of Langholm Common Riding is a recurring theme in MacDiarmid's work. His short story *The Common Riding* was first published in the *Glasgow Herald* on 12 March 1927.[93] The story is based in Langholm and is about a Common Riding obsessive called 'Yiddy Bally', who was 'Common-Riding daft' and might have been based on a real person:

> *He seemed to leeve for naething else. This year's was nae suner owre than he begood talkin' aboot next year's. He was like that memory man in the papers — only the Common Riding was Yiddy's a'e subject … He'd the names o' a' the Cornets aff by hert frae A to Z, and no' only the Cornets, but the dogs that wun the hound trail; the horses that wun the races; the men that wun the wrestlin' and wha' cairried the Croon o' Roses and the Thistle and the Bannock and the Saut Herrin' … He was a fair miracle.*[94]

MacDiarmid's enthusiasm for the Common Riding is apparent throughout the story but there are also some sly criticisms, probably based on his observations of the real event. An exclusive clique controlled the Common Riding, excluding all others:

> *Ye ken what a Committee is in a place like this. It's aye in the haunds o' a certain few, and if ye dinna belang to their cleek ye've nae mair chance o' gettin' on to't than a rich man has o' gaen' through the e'e o' a needle.*[95]

MacDiarmid also noted that it was only wealthy or well-connected individuals that had a chance of becoming Cornet:

The Cornets are aye drawn frae the sprigs o' the gentry or young bluids o' fairmers – no' factory haun's. It tak's a bonny penny to be a Cornet.[96]

In the conclusion, Yiddy, like a true native, gives his life to uphold the dignity of the Common Riding.

Hugh MacDiarmid's undisputed masterpiece was his epic poem *A Drunk Man Looks at the Thistle*, which was first published in 1926. The poem has been described as, 'not only the most revolutionary work in Scots literature, but also one of the most powerfully imaginative achievements in twentieth-century poetry.'[97] The poem is informed at a deep level by memories of Langholm and of the Common Riding in particular. The most obvious image is that of the thistle itself. A thistle is one of the Four Emblems that are carried at the Common Riding procession, a monster specimen eight foot in height and specially grown for the purpose. In the poem, the thistle is not only a symbol of Scotland but is used to investigate the divided nature of humanity. It becomes all things, including bagpipe music, a pair of bellows, a skeleton, parts of the human anatomy and a flash of lighting.[98] *A Drunk Man* has specific reference to Langholm Common Riding and MacDiarmid used the poem to record some of his earliest memories of the event:

> *Drums in the Walligate, pipes in the air,*
> *Come and hear the cryin' o' the Fair.*
>
> *A' as it used to be, when I was a loon*
> *On Common-Ridin' Day in the Muckle Toon.*
>
> *The bearer twirls the Bannock-and-Saut-Herrin',*
> *The Croon o' Roses through the lift is farin',*
>
> *The aucht-fit thistle wallops on hie;*
> *In the heather besoms a' the hills gang by.*[99]

MacDiarmid retained fond memories of Langholm Common Riding, believing that it reaffirmed community, basic human decency and optimism, an event that was uniquely Scottish but which had a universal relevance. His feelings are best summed up in this short excerpt from his 1967 poem *The Borders*, which also captures many people's love of the ridings:

> *O dinna fear the auld spirit's deid,*
> *Gang to Selkirk or Hawick or Langholm yet*
> *At Common-Riding time – like a tidal wave*
> *It boils up again, and carries a' afore it.*[100]

Final Canter

This book has traced the history of the Riding of the Marches in Scotland from the early sixteenth century to the present, focusing on general trends and developments. There is no doubt that the modern ridings, such as Hawick and Selkirk Common Ridings, are remarkable historical survivals, the key to which has been the ability to adapt to different social environments. The original purpose of the event has become largely obsolete, but the ridings have not become anachronistic because they have been used to express various social values and ideals. In other words, the ridings have survived because they have meant different things to different people at different times. Predictably, the evolution of the ridings has not been smooth or easy. It was shown in chapter five that the ridings faced a major challenge in the nineteenth century when new standards of behaviour became increasingly influential. Similarly, in the late twentieth century, the changing role of women in society has produced deep antagonisms and controversy, especially at Hawick Common Riding but also at other events. These arguments have shown that popular customs like the ridings, which are rooted in older, more traditional societies, do not always fit easily or conveniently into existing social conventions.

The modern ridings have a very complex history, having gone through several distinct stages of development, all of which are discernible in the modern events. First, there is the original Riding of the Marches, which began when common lands were granted to the burghs, and the inhabitants had to make regular inspections of the boundaries to check any encroachments. These ancient ridings survive in the form of the towns 'riding-out' around their lands, although this now takes place only in a symbolic way. They are also reflected in the prominent role given to town flags, the craft and trade guilds, and youth groups, especially to a young, unmarried man who is chosen to lead the riding. In addition, Hawick and Selkirk have strong local traditions about the battle of Flodden, which may be contemporary with the battle, although these have also developed more general meanings about patriotism and sacrifice.

The next phase of the history of the ridings begins in the eighteenth century. Many ridings were discontinued at this time because of dynamic social and economic changes, in particular agricultural improvements and urban expansion. The surviving ridings acquired new meanings and functions, as the original purpose of the event became less important or urgent. In the later eighteenth century, the ridings began to reflect powerful national trends and to some extent they were politicised. There was, for instance, the steady growth of national patriotic sentiment, beginning in the reign of George III and reaching its zenith in the late Victorian period. The ridings were local events, but national allegiances were not ignored.

Dancing the Cornet's Reel at Hawick in 1913. *(Scottish Borders Museum and Gallery Service (Hawick Museum Collection))*

The ridings also benefited greatly from the national mania for horse racing, without which it is likely that most of these events would have disappeared.

The nineteenth century was a period of great change in Britain, which presented new challenges for the ridings. Long-term shifts in standards of behaviour and taste gradually led to new levels of control and organisation in the ridings. Events became more ordered and formal, which in turn encouraged greater participation and involvement from wealthier social groups. Similarly, large-scale emigration threatened to undermine communities by draining many of the youngest and best away from the towns. The ridings were an opportunity to reverse this trend and reaffirm family and social links. Even today, the 'exiles' make a special effort to return for the ridings, where they are warmly welcomed and given special status for the duration of the events. Another important legacy from the nineteenth century was the invention of a strong local song culture, which continues to flourish in the modern ridings. These songs were concerned with local themes, but many of them also stressed national and patriotic values. During the two world wars, the ridings acquired another layer of meaning and symbolism. They were used to express communal solidarity in the face of terrible sacrifice and loss, whilst the local traditions about Flodden acquired special poignancy. In addition, the period from about 1890 to 1960 has been the era of invented traditions for the ridings. Many new ridings have been created, often with striking original features, whilst older events have been revived or remodelled.

Finally, there are the modern events, which combine all of these previous stages. The ridings are built into busy schedules and modern patterns of living, where mental horizons are much less restricted and many locals travel regularly away from their town for work, leisure, holidays or shopping. Several of the ridings now have their own websites on the Internet, where it is possible to read reports and see pictures of events, and to check on the dates of forthcoming events. It is fair to say that most locals are only vaguely aware of the original purpose of the ridings and of the complex historical development of these events.

Riders at Jedburgh Callants Festival ford the river. *(Scottish Borders Tourist Board)*

Nevertheless, they eagerly anticipate the ridings each year and take part with great enthusiasm and enjoyment.

Whilst the ridings have gone through several distinct phases of development, they have also retained some consistent features and themes. One of these is the close relationship between human beings and horses. It is easy to forget the crucial role that horses have played in the development of human society and culture, having been used in work, leisure and in warfare. Countless human activities have only been possible by the use of horses, such as travelling around the marches in a single day. Horses have always been a symbol of political or social power, and they have been used in the ridings to enhance local authority and status. Throughout the history of the ridings, processions have been stage-managed to display the social hierarchy that existed in the towns, with prominence given to the authorities, members of the craft and trade guilds, anyone who was rich and powerful. Other people, such as women, children and the poor, have been deliberately excluded, thus being reminded of their lowly status.

The history of the ridings also suggests that the festival or carnival aspect has always been an important feature. The ridings had the serious purpose of defining the burgh lands, but they were also occasions where there was some licence, where normal inhibitions were relaxed. Riders and other participants were fortified with food and strong drinks, and events usually ended with some kind of corporate feast. Enjoyment was also extended to non–riders, who could visit the horse racing and the fairground, and hold small celebrations of their own. Another feature of the ridings emerges here: the reinforcement of social harmony. In some respects the ridings were divisive, but they were also events that drew people together in a common purpose and outlook, a solid piece of social cement.

The ridings encouraged communal identity because they drew boundaries between people in the towns and the outside world. The ridings, old and new, have a strong sense of inside and outside, of belonging to a town and of being an outsider. Boundaries imply the existence of an external threat and groups of people who feel themselves threatened will be drawn closer together for mutual support, as happens during wartime. This has been a vital factor in the survival of the ridings, although the threats have changed though time. One threat came from neighbouring landowners and the local aristocracy, such as the Dukes of Buccleuch, whose power and influence threatened to wrestle control of the commons away from the towns. Similarly, towns have had to deal with dynamic social and economic changes, such as rapid population growth, which threatened to swamp the native culture. In the twentieth century, mass emigration and warfare have threatened to undermine communities, drawing many of the brightest and best away from the towns, often never to return. More recently, there has been the loss of the old town councils to the regions and overbearing presence of national government and, increasingly, of a centralised Europe. The ridings have provided comfort and reassurance in times of great uncertainty and change. By undertaking the ritual each year, local people have created a sense of renewal and confidence in themselves and their community.

Arguably, the presence of an external threat can also be seen in the controversy over women's involvement, especially at Hawick. Since the 1970s, the textile industry in Hawick and the Borders, once the major employer, has been through severe depression. In contrast, the Common Riding has been a reliable beacon amongst the economic gloom. In their attempt to take part, women have called into question its accustomed hierarchy and also threatened to change the fundamental nature of the event, creating doubt over its future. Change always carries with it an element of risk. Nobody really knew what shape the Common Riding would take if women were allowed to take part in it. Most people know that they have no power over economic or social forces, having little choice but to go along them. Some critics dismissed the Hawick case as nothing more than provincial backwardness, but they missed the point that there were no objections when a woman became honorary provost. In the era of Mrs Thatcher, it was unremarkable to have women who were prominent in public or political life. But the Common Riding was different; something that local people had control over. Traditionalists argued that there were enough problems in the world without upsetting the tried-and-tested formula of the Common Riding. It may be true that some people were uncomfortable with recent changes that have questioned traditional gender roles. Privately, they might think that these changes have gone far enough and that some things should be left as they are. If women were to take part in the Common Riding, then who was going to make the sandwiches or look after the children?

One of the surprising features of the modern ridings is that they are so little known outside of the places where they are staged, even in the rest of Scotland. These events are intensely local and private, a sub-culture that is accessible only to members of particular communities. The ridings have their own songs, music, language, customs and traditions, and knowledge of these can only be gained by living in the towns and regularly taking part in the ridings. The experience of taking part in the ridings, whether on horseback or otherwise, differentiates local people from others. But, whilst the culture of the ridings is localised, it provides a healthy alternative to the 'tartanism' that characterises much of the modern Scottish identity (although pipe bands, kilts and other Highland symbols do feature in some of the ridings). A unique and independent lowland culture has survived in Scotland, and continues to flourish. It remains to be seen how the ridings will adapt to the new Scottish Parliament and a country with a growing sense of identity and self-confidence. This book has, I trust, been wide-ranging and comprehensive, but it is by no means the last word on the ridings. Valuable accounts could be written of individual events, such as Selkirk Common Riding, Lanark Lanimer Day and Linlithgow Marches. Likewise, a detailed study could be made of the new or revived ridings, showing how the original purpose of riding the marches took on new meanings and functions.

And what about the future? What is the state of the ridings as they enter a new century? The pessimistic argument is that there are many things that threaten to undermine the ridings and to destroy much of what makes them unique. Increasingly, we live in a global culture where everyone seems to consume the same goods, entertainment and experiences, irrespective of where they live. Global culture is immensely seductive to those who have the means to buy into it. It is glamorous and it can make local events like the ridings seem small and amateurish. But it would be easy to take this argument too far. It is fairer to say that people have a pluralist culture, meaning that local tradition successfully co-exists with modern influences. Observe any gathering at the ridings and this process is clear. People might wear the replica shirts of distant football teams such as Glasgow Rangers or Manchester United, but they might also wear the colours of their local rugby team. Similarly, they take pride in having the latest styles of clothes, but decorate them with Common Riding ribbons and rosettes. An impromptu singsong is likely to be a mixture of local songs and commercial pop music. Even drinks are adapted locally. At Hawick, rum and milk are mixed together to produce the traditional Common Riding drink.

There is, however, a danger that, in the wake of incessant social and cultural change, some of the traditions of the ridings might turn stale. To take one example, many of the riding songs were written before the First World War. There is no doubt about their current popularity, but in future they may become anachronistic and obsolete, a problem that some traditional churches now face. Likewise, how long will the tradition of the travelling fairground survive in the twenty-first century? The ridings are also challenged by economic problems. The running costs increase every year, although amateur enthusiasts carry out the organisation and administration. A partial solution may lie in sponsorship and some events have attracted financial support from outside agencies. In the 1990s, the Colour Bussing at Hawick received money from a national bank whilst the games were sponsored by a local knitwear company. But sponsorship of this kind can be double-edged. Organisers have to be wary that they do not surrender too much control of their riding and repeat the mistakes made by some sports, such as rugby union, where sponsors have influenced rule changes to make the game more attractive. There are fears that 'big business' is taking over and sucking the life out of communities. In 1993, a new Safeway supermarket was opened in Hawick; ironically, the Cornet and his Lass performed the opening ceremony. There were concerns that it would erode local identity and force smaller traders out of business. A song was written about the arrival of the new store, which captured the sense of powerlessness in the face of commercial pressures (to be sung, incidentally, to the tune of Frank Sinatra's *My Way*):

> *Last night, I had a dream,*
> *And wi' this I end my ditty.*
> *It was twenty year frae now*
> *Hawick had been renamed Safeway City.*
> *And such was the extent*
> *They'd ta'en owre the town we bide in,*
> *They'd even come to run the Common-Riding.*
> *There were nae horses at the Chase,*
> *Safeway trolleys hed ta'en their place,*
> *And on the Cornet's flag quite clear,*
> *This altered slogan did appear,*
> *Withoot a doobt, it said*
> *Safe Oot, Safe In and Safeway.*[1]

One of the biggest threats to local identity is population mobility and the large numbers of incomers coming into the towns. The Scottish Borders offers an alternative to the busy cities, especially for families with young children or retired people. This has attracted many people

Young people are encouraged to take part in the ridings and perhaps one day some might become principals. *(Scottish Borders Tourist Board)*

into the region, who threaten to undermine the basic homogeneity of communities. In her book on Selkirk Common Riding, Gwen Kennedy Neville quotes a Selkirk man whose family had run a business on the High Street for several generations. Recalling his boyhood before the Second World War, he said: 'Back in those days ... everyone knew everyone else. 80 per cent of the town was Selkirk. Now only about 20 per cent is Selkirk.'[2] Modern incomers have a slightly ambiguous status. They are made welcome, but it is feared that the arrival of too many of them will swamp a distinctive way of life. The presence of non-natives often acts as a benefit to the ridings. Incomers are usually anxious to shed the label of being an outsider and become actively involved in the community, taking on administrative roles and other voluntary duties. In many cases, it is incomers who are amongst the staunchest supporters of the ridings.

Conversely, another threat to the ridings is the steady drain of young people away from the towns. This problem has been exacerbated recently because of greater educational opportunities and from the need for employment flexibility and mobility. One consequence for the ridings has been that there are fewer young people to take on the role of principals. Indeed, whilst there is intense competition in some of the older Common Ridings, some towns have had difficulties in finding young people, especially young men, to come forward and fill the roles. In 1996, the festival committee at Duns could not find a local man to take on the mantle of Duns Reiver. In this case, the problem was solved in a novel way by creating the new post of 'Reiver Lass', nineteen-year-old Vicki Rybowska, who carried the flag on the day of the riding. In future, female Standard Bearers of this kind may become increasingly common (though probably not in Hawick).

So it is clear that the ridings cannot afford to become complacent. As in the past, innovation and imagination will be required for them to survive. And yet there is much to be confident about. The various threats to local identity have, paradoxically, encouraged a growing sense of individuality and the need to protect local institutions. In many communities, the local riding is seen as one of the pillars that make the town unique and special, the badge of local identity and belonging. It might be argued that the ridings are now more popular than they have ever been. There are so many horses taking part in some events that landowners and farmers have been unhappy at the damage that they are causing to valuable land. There are other factors working in favour of the ridings. Increasing standards of personal wealth mean that more people are now able to own or to hire horses. Since the 1960s, horses have become associated with leisure rather than work, somehow symbolising a lost Arcadian past. Likewise, as a result of improved transport, it is easier and quicker for exiles and others living away from the towns to return for the ridings. For many local businesses, the ridings, like Christmas, have become a vital part of the annual economic cycle, the reason why many of the principals have strong links with local business communities.

The ridings have also attracted some national interest. In part, this may be a reaction to the blandness of much of modern culture and the desire to return to more innocent events that foster community and a sense of belonging. Undeniably, there are also feelings of envy from the outside world. As the ridings draw round each year, national newspapers such as *The Scotsman* and *The Herald*, and some London-based titles, often have photographs and articles about the ridings. In 1991 and 1992, colour photographs of Hawick Common Riding were given pride of place on the front cover of *The Scotsman*. The ridings have also been featured on television and radio. In 1991, Selkirk Common Riding was broadcast live across the United Kingdom on breakfast-time television (when the presenter, Ulrika Jonsson, committed something of a *faux pas* by referring to Selkirk as 'the village'). Locals are flattered by outside media attention, but they do not actively court it. In this the ridings are dissimilar to events devised for the tourist industry. They have very little promotion simply because they do not require it. Local people know about them and when they take place, and that is enough. However, with the growing importance of tourism in the local economy, this attitude may have to change and force the ridings to become more tourist-friendly.

Face of the Future? In 1996, the festival committee at Duns selected Vicki Rybowska to be 'Reiver Lass' because of a lack of male candidates. *(Peter Kemp)*

Since the end of the Second World War, there have been huge changes to urban life in Britain. Standards of living have risen and most people are wealthier than ever before. Material prosperity has many benefits, but it has also had the unfortunate effect of undermining community life. People live much more privately than they once did, partly because they are economically independent and tend to rely far less on one another for support. Many of the economic functions traditionally undertaken by family, friends and neighbours are now the responsibility of the state. Families have changed. People have fewer children than before, perhaps none, and there are not so many celebrations and 'get-togethers'. Young adults have to move away for work and education, meaning that families see a lot less of each other. Small aspects of life have also contributed, such as changing shopping patterns. Until the 1960s, married women often went shopping every day, as much to catch up on the news and gossip as to buy groceries. Today, shopping is much more likely to be done weekly, or even monthly, in a superstore and the little corner shop is fast becoming a thing of the past. The influence of the Church, another focus of community life, has been eroded with the growing secularisation of society. In short, there are far fewer opportunities for human contact and people live more in isolation. A common complaint is that society is not so civil as it once was: that towns used to be much friendlier places, but increasingly seem full of strangers.

Community festivals like the ridings offer a counter-balance to the isolation of modern life. They are an opportunity, if only for a moment, for people to be together and recapture a feeling of belonging. The ridings stress simplicity, altruism and friendship in a world that is bedevilled by materialism, selfishness and lack of contact. They encourage the humanist ideal that people have an intrinsic worth in themselves, irrelevant of their social status or personal wealth. Local people rarely articulate these thoughts. Ask them why they take part in their riding, and why it is important to them and they will struggle to give you an answer. The riding is part of them and that is good enough. The following passage about Selkirk Common Riding sums it all up:

> *They* know *what the Common Riding is: it isn't really something to be described at all, but something to be experienced – something they live through together and in a sense re-create anew each year. As much as anything it is a celebration of communal identity: a declaration of attachment to each other and to the place that bore them: an assertion by the people of this town of what they feel and know themselves to be. They do it each year because they have always done it: they do it because of what they are.*[3]

Notes

Introduction

1. Barclay, H.B., *The Role of the Horse in Man's Culture* (London and New York, 1980), p. 1.
2. Edwards, E.H., *Horses. Their Role in the History of Man* (London, 1987), p. 14.

Chapter One

1. *Cornet's Official Time-Table 1995* (Hawick, 1995), p. 2.
2. *Hawick Express*, 11 June 1881, p. 2.
3. *Southern Reporter*, 1 May 1986, p. 3.
4. *Border Telegraph*, 17 June 2003, p. 18.
5. The same can also be said of sports and games. See Malcolmson, R.W., *Popular Recreations in English Society 1700-1850* (Cambridge, 1979), pp. 85-6. Malcolmson says that through sports, 'the common people were able to create small-scale success systems of their own.' Sport provided an ideal (and for some the only) channel for gaining personal recognition. The same theme is echoed in Laurie Lee's essay *An Obstinate Exile*: 'City honours are not village honours. Like certain wines, they do not travel ... Village honours are still severely local. They include life-long success on the dart-board, sharp wits in the cattle market, skill at growing whopping but useless vegetable marrows, weight-lifting, spitting, ringing bells, ... Outside things don't count – and why should they?' Lee, L., *I Can't Stay Long* (London, 1975), p. 44.
6. Mosspaul is a hotel on the county border of Roxburghshire and Dumfriesshire. Traditionally, a hostelry has existed on the site for hundreds of years and is supposed to have been founded by monks from Melrose Abbey. Many famous travellers have broken their journey at Mosspaul, including Sir Walter Scott, the Wordsworths and the Liberal Prime Minister W.E. Gladstone. When the railway between Hawick and Carlisle was opened in 1861, the hotel lost most of its passing trade and quickly fell into disrepair. In 1900, a company of local gentlemen, many of whom were Common Riding stalwarts, rebuilt the hotel to cater for the then modern craze of cycling.
7. *Hawick Advertiser*, 19 June 1858, p. 4.
8. *Southern Reporter*, 7 July 1994, p. 16.
9. Neville, G.K., *The Mother Town* (New York, 1994), pp. 61-2.
10. *The Scotsman*, 3 June 1985, p. 8. See also Liston, J.A., 'Phoney Festivals. Where are all the Women?', *Harpies and Quines.* (October/November 1992), pp. 40-3.
11. Quoted in *Border Life Then and Now* (June 1996), p. 21.
12. *Southern Reporter*, 16 June 1994, p. 7.
13. Haynes, D.K., 'The Lanimer Spirit', *The Scots Magazine*, new series, vol. 87, no. 6 (1967), p. 515.
14. Mavor, R., *Dr Mavor and Mr Bridie* (Edinburgh, 1988), p. 146.

15. Muir, G., 'The Landemeers. A Burlesque Poem', quoted in Reid, T., *Lanimer Day. Lanark 1570 to 1913*, 2nd edition (Lanark, 1921), p. 28.

16. Oak is associated with the Norse thunder gods, Thor and Odin. There may also be a Flodden connection. In March 1906, the *Hawick News* noted 'a Common Riding heroine' called Jenny Smith, who 'about 80 years ago' went to Flodden Field and gathered twigs for the Cornet's coat. *Hawick News*, 2 March 1906, p. 4. In England, 29 May is known as Oak Apple Day, a date that marks the anniversary of the Restoration of 1660. Traditionally, wearing oak apples or oak leaves was a sign of commemorating the Restoration. Popular legend states that after the battle of Worcester on 6 September 1651, Charles Stuart escaped the Parliamentarian forces by hiding in the branches of an oak tree.

17. Quoted in Neat, T., 'It's Common Riding Day!', *The Scots Magazine*, new series, vol. 115, no. 4 (1981), pp. 362-3.

18. Curds and cream are mentioned in William Langland's *Piers the Ploughman* of 1362: 'Twey grene cheeses and a fewe curddes and crayme' (A text: passus vii, lines 265-6). Also in William Shakespeare's *The Winter's Tale*: 'Good sooth she is The Queen of Curds and Crème' (act 4, sc. 4, line 161).

19. For example, in the 1995 Selkirk Common Riding, BBC television presenter, Jenni Falconner, who was making a film about the Common Riding for the adventure activities programme *The Big Country*, fell from her horse and broke her thumb. *Southern Reporter*, 22 June 1995, p. 15.

20. *Southern Reporter*, 23 June 1994, p. 16.

21. *Ibid*, 12 June 2003, p. 32.

22. Quoted in Neat, 'It's Common Riding Day!', p. 366.

23. *Hawick Express*, 26 April 1895, p. 3.

24. From *Hawick in Song and Poetry* (Hawick, 1978), p. 52.

25. Hunter, R., 'Hawick Common Riding'; *Ibid*, p. 21.

26. *Common Ridings and Festivals. The Pageantry of the Horse* (Newtown St Boswells, 1980), p. 1.

27. *Southern Reporter*, 11 April 1996, p. 5.

28. 'J.A.D.'; 'Selkirk Common Riding After Twenty Years', *The Border Magazine*, vol. xxvii (1922), p. 101.

29. *TSAS*, vol. xxiv, p. 360.

30. 'J.A.D.'; 'Selkirk Common Riding', p. 101.

31. *The Scotsman*, 22 June 1991, p. 1.

32. *Hawick Quater-Centenary Souvenir Programme* (Hawick, 1914), p. 63.

33. Quoted in *Hawick News*, 3 June 1955, p. 4.

34. *Scotland on Sunday*, 10 June 1990, p. 5.

35. *The Scotsman*, 11 June 1994, p. 3.

36. *Ibid*, 1 June 1996, p. 4.

37. *Southern Reporter*, 23 May 1996, p. 4.

38. *The Scotsman*, 4 June 1996, p. 7.

39. *Ibid*.

40. *Ibid*, 31 May 1996, p. 3.

41. *The Herald*, 8 June 1996, p. 7.

42. Petre, J., *By Sex Divided. The Church of England and Women Priests* (London, 1994), pp. 11-12.

Chapter Two

1. Beresford, M., *History on the Ground*, revised edition (Stroud, 1998), p. 28.

2. *Peebles Records*, vol. i, p. 16. Symms, P., 'Selkirk at the Time of Flodden and the Charters', *Flower of the Forest. Selkirk: A New History*, ed. Gilbert, J.M. (Selkirk, 1985), p. 48.

3. Barrow, G.W.S., *Kingship and Unity: Scotland 1000-1306* (London, 1981), p. 123.

4. Dickinson, W.C. (ed.), *Early Records of the Burgh of Aberdeen 1317, 1398-1407*, (Scottish History Society, Edinburgh, 1957), p. 238.

5. Ewan, E., *Townlife in Fourteenth-Century Scotland* (Edinburgh, 1990), p. 51.

6. *Selkirk Burgh Court Book*, vol. ii, p. 165.

7. Symms, P., 'Social Control in a Sixteenth-Century Burgh: A Study of the Burgh Court Book of Selkirk 1503-1545' (Unpublished Ph.D thesis, University of Edinburgh, 1986), p. 79.

8. *Selkirk Burgh Court Book*, vol. ii, p. 168.

9. *Glasgow Records*, vol. ii, p. 13.

10. *Selkirk Burgh Court Book*, vol. i, pp. 72-3.

11. *Ibid*, vol. ii, p. 208.

12. *Ibid*, vol. i, pp. 101-2.

13. *Ibid*, vol. ii, pp. 207-8.

14. These details taken from Symms, 'Selkirk at the Time of Flodden', pp. 44-5.

15. *Selkirk Burgh Court Book*, vol. ii, p. 168.

16. In June 1796, the burgh council of Hawick appointed twelve burgesses, 'to ride the whole marches of the town. Part of them being old and acquainted with the marches and others of them being young in order that they may be acquainted with the marches.' Hawick Records, 7 June 1796.

17. Thomson, J., 'The Border Queen', *Hawick in Song and Poetry* (Hawick, 1945), p. 67. Thomson's song was written in 1887.

18. Hawick Records, 1 June 1706.

19. Stone, L., *The Family, Sex and Marriage in England 1500-1800* (London, 1977), p. 50.

20. In *The History of Hawick*, Robert Wilson, an ex-Cornet, described a traditional local football match played annually between young men living on either side of the River Slitrig. 'This amusement had a bad tendency in keeping up, and promoting, time out of mind, between people of the East and West divisions of the town. This feud, in which the boys below sixteen were the chief combatants, was fostered by their seniors; and even parents and masters have been known to encourage their apprentices and children to join in the scene of contention. The youngsters of that period, too, formed themselves into regiments; had drums, standards, and halberds, and were armed also with stones, clubs, and even swords. These battles were sometimes carried to such a height that adults were induced to mingle in them.' Wilson, R., *The History of Hawick*, 2nd edition (Hawick, 1841), pp. 178-9.

21. Turner, V.W., *The Ritual Process* (London, 1969), p. 167.

22. *Aberdeen Records*, vol. i, pp. 439-40.

23. Holt, J.C., *Robin Hood* (London, 1982).

24. Paul, J.B. (ed.), *Accounts of the Lord High Treasurer of Scotland*, vol. ii (1500-1504), (Edinburgh, 1900), p. 377.

25. *Aberdeen Records*, vol. i, p. 140.

26. *Peebles Records*, vol. i, p. 212.

27. *Aberdeen Records*, vol. i, p. 280.

28. *Ibid*, p. 435.

29. *Ibid*, p. 14.

30. *Ibid*, pp. 279-80.

31. Stuart, J. (ed.), *Extracts from the Council Register of Aberdeen 1643-1747*, (Scottish Burgh Records Society, Edinburgh, 1872), p. 203.

32. Watson, G., 'Annual Border Ball Games', *Transactions of the Hawick Archaeological Society* [THAS] (1922), p. 7.

33. Ure, D., *The History of Rutherglen and East Kilbride* (Glasgow, 1793), p. 93. *Scottish Notes and Queries*, 2nd series, vol. viii, no. 1 (July 1906), p. 14.

34. For an example of a sixteenth-century banner: in the aftermath of battle of Pinkie, 10 September 1547, English soldiers found, 'a banner of whyte sarcenet, whereupon was paynted a woman with her hair about her shoulders, knelynge before a crucifix, and on her right hande a churche.' Patten, W., 'The Expedicion into Scotlande of the Most Woorthely Fortunate Prince, Edward Duke of Somerset', *Fragments of Scottish History*, ed. Dalyell, J.G. (Edinburgh, 1798), p. 73.

35. *Selkirk Burgh Court Book*, vol. ii, p. 151.

36. *Aberdeen Records*, vol. ii, p. 27, 179, 388.

37. *Edinburgh Records*, vol. iv, p. 124.

38. *Stirling Records*, vol. i, p. 127, 206.

39. *Edinburgh Records*, vol. iv, p. 310, 341.

40. *Aberdeen Records*, vol. ii, p. 179.

41. *Peebles Records*, vol. i, p. 344.

42. *Glasgow Records*, vol. ii, p. 69.

43. *Edinburgh Records*, vol. iv, p. 341.

44. Hawick Records, 4 January 1640.

45. Quoted in McDowall, W., *History of Dumfries* (Edinburgh, 1867), p. 358.

46. *Aberdeen Records*, vol. ii, p. 345.

47. *Glasgow Records*, vol. ii, p. 353.

48. *Peebles Records*, vol. ii, p. 200.

49. *Aberdeen Records*, vol. ii, p. 179.

50. *Selkirk Burgh Court Book*, vol. ii, p. 124.

51. On 29 October 1459, a woman named Meg Woodhall was made a burgess of Peebles, and there are records of other women being appointed. Marshall, R.K., *Virgins and Viragos. A History of Women in Scotland 1080-1980* (London, 1983), p. 51.

52. *Lanark Records*, p. 90.

53. *Selkirk Burgh Court Book*, vol. i, p. 73.

54. *Aberdeen Records*, vol. ii, p. 27.

55. *Edinburgh Records*, vol. iv, p. 124.

56. Leslie, John, *The Historie of Scotland*, vol. i, ed. Cody, E.G. (Scottish Text Society, Edinburgh and London, 1888), p. 102.

57. *Edinburgh Records*, vol. iv, p. 341.

58. *Lanark Records*, p. 92.

59. Bain, J. (ed.), *Calendar of Border Papers*, vol. i, 1560-1594, (Edinburgh, 1894), p. 189.

60. Sempill, Robert, 'The Life and Death of Habbie Simson, the Piper of Kilbarchan', *The Oxford Book of Scottish Verse*, 2nd edition, eds

MacQueen, J. and Scott, T. (Oxford, 1981), pp. 305-8.

61. *Edinburgh Records*, vol. i, p. 52

62. *Aberdeen Records*, vol. i, p. 105.

63. *Ibid*, pp. 166-7.

64. *Lanark Records*, p. 70, 79

65. *Peebles Records*, vol. ii, p. 201.

66. *Dundee Records*, p. 184.

67. *Stirling Records*, vol. i, p. 118, 156.

68. *Linlithgow Records*, 4 May 1706.

69. *Selkirk Burgh Court Book*, vol. ii, p. 168.

70. *Peebles Records*, vol. i, p. 230.

71. *Selkirk Burgh Court Book*, vol. ii, p. 168.

72. *Lanark Records*, p. 104.

73. *Peebles Records*, vol. i, p. 230.

74. Wilson, J., *Hawick and its Old Memories,* (Edinburgh, 1858), pp. 38-9.

75. Elliot, W. and Maley, T. (eds), *Selkirk Protocol Books 1511-1547*, (Stair Society, Edinburgh, 1993), p. 128.

76. *Stirling Records*, vol. ii, p. 13, 29.

77. *Glasgow Records*, vol. ii, p. 13, 137.

78. *Peebles Records*, vol. i, p. 230.

79. Maxwell, A., *The History of Old Dundee* (Dundee and Edinburgh, 1884), p. 243.

80. Ure, *History of Rutherglen*, p. 93.

81. *Aberdeen Records*, vol. ii, pp. 322-6. Following the Aberdeen riding of 1861, it was commented: 'It's few places that hae a wassail cup on ilka march stane, to fill wi' wine, if they hae a mind, an' the watchword o' "*Bon Accord*", that won a hail countryside, for the friendly pledge o' the drinkers.' *The Rydin' o' the Landimyres 12 October 1861* (Aberdeen, 1861), p. 3.

82. Quoted in Bruce, J., Duncan, W. and Robertson, J., *The Riding of the Landymyrs of the City of Aberdeen* (Aberdeen, 1840), p. 6.

83. Wilkie, T., 'Old Rites, Ceremonies and Customs of the Inhabitants of the Southern Counties of Scotland', NLS Adv. Ms. 121, p. 147.

84. Kennedy, J.W., 'Wilton Common', *THAS* (1916), pp. 4-6.

85. *Peebles Records*, vol. ii, p. 13, 55, 71.

86. *Ibid*, p. 201.

87. *Ibid*, p. 204.

Chapter Three

1. Instituted in 1952, Coldstream Civic Week has a strong Flodden link. Thursday of Civic Week features a ride-out to the battlefield of Flodden where the Coldstreamer lays a wreath at the Flodden memorial to commemorate the dead of 1513, followed by a short service at Branxton and the oration delivered by a guest speaker. In 1991, the guest speaker was the 27th Earl of Surrey, a descendant of a Flodden hero. Speaking of his invitation, the earl said, 'Maybe it is a sign that after almost 500 years the role of my predecessor at Flodden has been forgiven.' Brave words indeed. *The Scotsman,* 25 June 1991, p. 3.

2. Hodge, J., 'An Account of the Remarkable Places and Parish Churches in the Shire of Selkirke'; 'Geographical Collections Relating to Scotland. Containing a Particular Description of the Shires, Parishes, Burroughs, etc in that Kingdom', vol. i, comp. Macfarlane, W. NLS Adv. Ms. 35.3.12(i), pp. 466-8.

3. *OSAS*, vol. ii, p. 436. The Flodden battlefield is not 'plain' but hilly ground. This was an important factor in the course of the battle.

4. Scott, Sir Walter, *Minstrelsy of the Scottish Border*, vol. iii, ed. Henderson, T.F. (Edinburgh and London, 1902), p. 390.

5. Symms, P., 'Selkirk at the Time of Flodden and the Charters', *Flower of the Forest. Selkirk: a New History*, ed. Gilbert, J.M. (Galashiels, 1985), p. 49.

6. Rae, T.I., *The Administration of the Scottish Frontier 1513-1603* (Edinburgh, 1966), p. 11.

7. Symms, 'Selkirk at the Time of Flodden', p. 47. *Selkirk Burgh Court Book*, pt. 1, pp. 23-4.

8. MacDougall, N., *James IV* (Edinburgh, 1989), p. 273.

9. *Letters and Papers, Foreign and Domestic, of the Reign of Henry VIII* [*L. and P. Henry VIII*], vol. i, pt. ii, 2nd edition (London, 1920), no. 2283.

10. *Edinburgh Records*, vol. i, p. 143

11. MacDougall, *James IV*, p. 280. *Aberdeen Records*, vol. i, p. 85.

12. 'Articles of the Bataill bitwix the Kinge of Scottes and the erle of Surrey in Brankstone Feld, the 9 day of September' ['Articles of the Bataill'], *L. and P. Henry VIII*, vol. i, pt. ii, no. 2246. Full text given in *State Papers*, vol. iv, pt. iv (London, 1836), pp. 1-2.

13. Contamine, P., *War in the Middle Ages*, trans. Jones, M. (Oxford, 1984), p. 229.

14. Robert Lindsay of Pitscottie, *Historie and Chronicles of Scotland*, vol. i, ed. Mackay, A.E.J.G. (Scottish Text Society, Edinburgh and London, 1899), p. 270.

15. Buchanan, George, *The History of Scotland*, vol. ii, trans. Aikman, J. (Glasgow, 1827), p. 256.

16. *The Scots Peerage*, vol. iv, ed. J.B. Paul (Edinburgh, 1907), p. 455.

17. Symms, 'Selkirk at the Time of Flodden', p. 47.

18. This version from Johnson, J., *The Scots Musical Museum*, vol. v (Edinburgh, 1796), p. 450.

19. Craig-Brown, T., *The History of Selkirkshire or Chronicles of Ettrick Forest*, vol. ii (Edinburgh, 1886), p. 205. *Scots Peerage*, vol. iv, p. 464.

20. Crawford, T., *Society and the Lyric. A Study of the Song Culture of Eighteenth Century Scotland* (Edinburgh, 1979), p. 142. Crawford suggests that *The Souters o' Selkirk* is a work song, similar to weavers' songs. The purpose of a work song was to 'sweeten labour'.

21. Hall, Edward, *Chronicle*, ed. Ellis, H. (London, 1809), p. 562; 'A Contemporary Account of the battle of Flodden' ['Trewe Encountre'], *Proceedings of the Society of Antiquaries of Scotland* [*PSAS*], vol. vii, part. i (1866-7), p. 148; Buchanan, *History*, vol. ii, p. 256; Pitscottie, *History*, vol. i, p. 270.

22. *Scottish Historical Review*, vol. iv, no. 13 (October 1907), p. 89.

23. Hay, D. (ed. and trans.), *Trewe Encountre. Articles of the Bataill*. Polydore Vergil, *Anglica Historia*, (Camden Society, London, 1950), p. 217.

24. Hall, *Chronicle*, p. 564.

25. *L. and P. Henry VIII*, vol. i, pt. ii, no. 2394.

26. Vergil, *Anglica Historia*, pp. 241-3.

27. Patten, W., 'The Expedicion into Scotlande of the Most Woorthely Fortunate Prince, Edward Duke of Somerset', *Fragments of Scottish History*, ed. Dalyell, J.G. (Edinburgh, 1798), p. 77.

28. Hall, *Chronicle*, p. 563.

29. *OSAS*, vol. ii, p. 436.

30. *Selkirk Burgh Court Book*, pt. 1, p. 63.

31. 'The Flodden Death-Roll', *The Scottish Antiquary or Northern Notes and Queries*, vol. xiii, no. 51 (January 1899), pp. 101-11; 'The Flodden Death-Roll – Additions and Corrections'; *Ibid*, no. 52 (April 1899), pp. 168-72.

32. Craig-Brown, *History of Selkirkshire*, vol. ii, p. 22.

33. *Ibid*. See also Symms, 'Selkirk at the Time of Flodden', p. 47.

34. Symms, P., 'Social Control in a Sixteenth-Century Burgh: A Study of the Burgh Court Book of Selkirk 1503-1545' (Unpublished Ph.D thesis, University of Edinburgh, 1986), pp. 46-7.

35. Craig, R.S., and Laing, A., *The Hawick Tradition of 1514: The Town's Common, Flag, and Seal*, (Hawick, 1898), pp. 61-2.

36. Balbirnie, A., 'The Common Riding Song', *Hawick in Song and Poetry* (Hawick, 1945), pp. 72-3.

37. Wilson, R., *The History of Hawick*, 2nd edition, (Hawick, 1841), p. 388.

38. Mason, J., *The Border Tour* (Edinburgh, 1826), pp. 162-3.

39. *Hawick in Song and Poetry*, p. 78.

40. Elliot, F.W., *The Trustworthiness of the Border Ballads* (Edinburgh 1906), pp. 160-3.

41. Ingles, A.L., *Notes and Comments on the Songs of Hawick* (Hawick, 1992), p. 3.

42. Groome, F.H., *Ordnance Gazetteer of Scotland*, vol. iv (Edinburgh, 1883), p. 252

43. Leslie, John, *The Historie of Scotland*, vol. i, ed. Cody, E.G., trans. Dalrymple, J. (Scottish Text Society, Edinburgh and London, 1888), pp. 101-2.

44. Wilkie, T., 'Old Scots Songs, Collected in Roxburghshire, Selkirkshire, and Berwickshire'. NLS Adv. Ms. 123, pp. 102-5.

45. Landles, J.C.G., 'The Hawick Tradition', *Transactions of the Hawick Archaeological Society* (1951), p. 6.

46. Ridpath, G., *The Border History of England and Scotland* (London, 1810), p. 488.

47. Wilson, J., *Annals of Hawick 1214-1814* (Edinburgh, 1850), p. 17.

48. Oliver, J.R., *Upper Teviotdale and the Scotts of Buccleuch. A Local and Family History* (Hawick, 1887), p. 96.

49. *Hawick in Song and Poetry*, p. 77.

50. Elton, G.R., *Reform and Reformation. England 1509-1558* (London, 1977), p. 40.

51. Scarisbrick, J.J., *Henry VIII* (London, 1968), p. 54.

52. Mackie, J.D., 'The English Army at Flodden', *Miscellany of the Scottish History*

Society, third series, vol. viii (Edinburgh, 1951), pp. 35-85.

53. The point being, of course, that untreated water carried disease whereas alcohol was less likely to contain harmful bacteria. This recalls the ancient proverb of Saxony: 'Drink wine, and reap the benefits from it; drink ale, and become fat; drink water, and die.' The sixteenth-century English dietician Andrew Boorde wrote: 'Water is not wholesome sole by itself for an Englishman.' See Barr, A., *Drink. An Informal Social History* (London, 1995), p. 252 and 270.

54. *L. and P. Henry VIII*, vol. i, pt. ii, no. 2386.

55. *Ibid*, no. 2390.

56. *Ibid*, no. 2406.

57. *Ibid*.

58. *Ibid*, no. 2443.

59. *Ibid*, no. 2394.

60. Fraser, G.M., *The Steel Bonnets. The Story of the Anglo-Scottish Border Reivers* (London, 1971), p. 218.

61. *L. and P. Henry VIII*, vol. i, pt. ii, no. 2913.

62. Paul, J.B. (ed.), *Accounts of the Lord High Treasurer of Scotland*, vol. ii (1500-1504), (Edinburgh, 1900), p. 454.

63. 'Jamie Telfer of the Fair Dodhead', *The Oxford Book of Ballads*, ed. Kingsley, J. (Oxford, 1982), p. 550.

64. *L. and P. Henry VIII*, vol. i, pt. ii, no. 2382.

65. *Ibid*, vol. iii, pt. ii, no. 3364.

66. Harrison, S.M., *The Pilgrimage of Grace in the Lake Counties 1536-7* (London, 1981), p. 27.

67. *L. and P. Henry VIII*, vol. i, pt. ii, no. 2913

68. *Ibid*.

69. *Ibid*, no. 2443.

70. *Ibid*.

71. Major, John, *A History of Greater Britain*, ed. and trans. Constable, A. (Edinburgh, 1892), p. 29.

72. *L. and P. Henry VIII*, vol. i, pt. ii, no. 2913.

73. Moir, W.B., 'The Burgh Muir of Edinburgh', *Book of the Old Edinburgh Club*, vol. x (1918), pp. 78-9.

74. Hall, *Chronicle*, p. 557.

75. 'The lord Hume, lord Chamberlayne fled and his banner taken.' *Ibid*, p. 556.

76. *NSAS*, vol. iii, p. 14. Watson, G., 'The Pennons of Jedburgh', *The Border Magazine*, vol. xvii, no. 198 (June 1912), pp. 136-40.

77. The Earl of Southesk, 'Douglas, Percy and the Cavers Ensign', *PSAS*, vol. xxxvi (1901-2), pp. 246-7. Paul, J.B., 'Notes on Four Ancient Scottish Standards', *Ibid*, vol. lii (1917-18), pp. 49-60.

78. Hawick Records, 9 May 1707, 30 May 1707 and 7 April 1710.

Chapter Four

1. Peebles Minute Book, 21 June 1775.

2. Hawick Records, 2 July 1816.

3. *Ibid*, 25 May 1737.

4. Peebles Minute Book, 9 November 1776.

5. Hawick Records, 7 March 1713. Walter Patersone of Burnflat was the father of Robert Paterson, on whom Sir Walter Scott based the character of Old Mortality.

6. Peebles Minute Book, 31 August 1779.

7. Hawick Records, 17 May 1755.

8. *Ibid*, 16 May 1759.

9. *Caledonian Mercury*, 18 October 1732, p. 3.

10. Linlithgow Records, 11 April 1767.

11. Balbirnie, A., 'Common Riding Song', *Hawick in Song and Poetry* (Hawick, 1945), pp. 72-3.

12. Linlithgow Treasurer's Vouchers, 17 June 1800.

13. Accounts Book of the Souters of Selkirk 1788-1830. SRO GD1/13/5, p. 6.

14. Treasurer's Book of the Linlithgow Shoemakers 1825-62. NLS Adv. Ms. 19292, *passim.*

15. Quoted in Craig-Brown, T., *The History of Selkirkshire or Chronicles of Ettrick Forest*, vol. ii (Edinburgh, 1886), p. 185.

16. Hawick Records, 23 May 1725.

17. *Stirling Records*, vol. ii, p. 239.

18. Hawick Records, 14 May 1816.

19. Colley, L., *Britons. Forging the Nation 1707-1837* (New Haven and London, 1992), p. 378-81.

20. *Hawick News*, 11 June 1897, p. 4. In the late eighteenth century, the fifes or flutes seem to have replaced the traditional bagpipes in Hawick Common Riding. Arthur Balbirnie's *Common Riding Song*, which was written sometimes in the 1790s, states 'Now Teriodin blaws the chanter/As rank and file the town we enter', clearly referring to a bagpiper. In 1797, the town records mention a fifer at the Common Riding and the following year the town paid 7 shillings to buy the fifer a new

pair of shoes. On *Dumbarton's Drums*, see Kennedy, J.W., 'Our Common Riding Airs', *Transactions of the Hawick Archaeological Society* [*THAS*] (1915), p. 7.

21. Colley, *Britons*, p. 222.

22. Thomson, A., *Lauder and Lauderdale* (Galashiels, 1903), pp. 51-2.

23. Ferguson, W., *Scotland: 1689 to the Present* (Edinburgh, 1968), p. 288.

24. Wilson, R., *The History of Hawick*, 2nd edition (Hawick, 1841), p. 234.

25. This tradition continued in the twentieth century. In March 1965, David Steel won a famous by-election victory to take the Parliamentary seat of Roxburgh, Selkirk and Peebles. The result was announced in Jedburgh town hall, following which Mr Steel was carried shoulder-high down the High Street by supporters singing the Hawick Common Riding song *The Border Queen*. Steel, D., *Against Goliath* (London, 1989), p. 43.

26. Wilson, *History of Hawick*, pp. 377-80.

27. *Ibid*, p. 52.

28. Lockhart, J.G., *The Life of Sir Walter Scott*, vol. x, (Edinburgh, 1903), p. 64. Anderson, W.E.K. (ed.), *The Journal of Sir Walter Scott* (Oxford, 1972), p. 656.

29. Groves, D., *James Hogg. The Growth of a Writer* (Edinburgh, 1988), p. 140.

30. Malcolmson, R.W., *Popular Recreations in English Society 1700-1850* (Cambridge, 1973), p. 78.

31. Vamplew, W., *The Turf. A Social and Economic History of Horse Racing* (London, 1976), p. 18.

32. Peebles Minute Book, 10 March 1736.

33. Hawick Records, 14 May 1824.

34. Peebles Minute Book, 11 March 1728 and 31 January 1731.

35. Craig-Brown, *History of Selkirkshire*, vol. ii, p. 90.

36. Hogg also noted some of the carnival element of the races, including a circus, ballad singers, itinerant musicians and peddlers of pornography. Hogg, J., 'A Journal through the Highlands of Scotland, Continued', *The Scots Magazine* (December 1802), p. 962.

37. Wilson, *History of Hawick*, p. 38.

38. Peebles Minute Book, 10 March 1736.

39. *Stirling Records*, vol. ii, pp. 111-2.

40. Hogg, *op. cit.*, p. 958.

41. *Stirling Records*, vol. ii, pp. 111-2.

42. Robertson, A.D., *Lanark. The Burgh and Its Councils 1469-1880* (Lanark, 1974), p. 147.

43. Linlithgow Records, 29 April 1710 and *passim*.

44. Hawick Records, 1 June 1706.

45. *Ibid*, 6 June 1809.

46. Quoted in Edgar, J., *Hawick Common Riding* (Hawick, 1886), p. 18-19.

47. Borsay, P., '"All the Town's a Stage": Urban Ritual and Ceremony 1660-1800', *The Transformation of English Provincial Towns 1600-1800* ed. Clarke, P. (London, 1984), p. 237.

48. *The Grand Procession of the Musselburgh Fair or Marches Riding: Delineated in a Poem by a Member of One of the Incorporations* (Place of publication not given [Musselburgh?], 1766).

49. [John Finlayson], *The Marches Day: A Dramatic Entertainment of Three Acts. As Performed by the Originals at XXXXXXXXXX [Linlithgow]* (Edinburgh, 1771). A second edition of the play was published in Falkirk in 1814.

50. Hawick Records, 17 May 1703 and 7 May 1726.

51. *Musselburgh Fair*, p. 3.

52. Linlithgow Records, 4 May 1706. Linlithgow Treasurer's Vouchers, 3 June 1800.

53. *Musselburgh Fair*, p. 3.

54. Hawick Records, 13 May 1712.

55. Peebles Minute Book, 22 May 1727.

56. Finlayson, *Marches Day*, pp. 2-4 and 22.

57. *Ibid*, p. 4.

58. *Musselburgh Fair*, p. 10.

59. *Ibid*, p. 7.

60. Finlayson, *Marches Day*, p. 28-9.

61. *Musselburgh Fair*, p. 13.

62. Windram, W.J., 'The Carterhaugh Ba' Game – 1815', *THAS* (1975), p. 17.

63. Peebles Minute Book, 17 February 1764.

64. Edgar, J., *Hawick in the Early Sixties* (Hawick, 1913), p. 111.

65. Malcolmson, *Popular Recreations*, p. 116-7.

66. *Peebles Records*, vol. ii, p. 167.

67. Peebles Minute Book, 22 May 1727.

68. *Ibid*, 13 June 1774.

69. Gulvin, C., *The Scottish Hosiery and Knitwear Industry 1680-1980* (Edinburgh, 1984), p. 18.

70. Hawick Records, 17 May 1794.

71. *Ibid*, 19 May 1794.

Chapter Five

1. Henderson, W., *Notes on the Folk Lore of the*

Northern Counties of England and the Borders (London, 1866), p. vii.

2. Malcolmson, R.W., *Popular Recreations in English Society 1700-1850* (Cambridge, 1973), *passim.*

3. *Hawick Advertiser*, 2 May 1868, p. 3.

4. *Hawick Monthly Advertiser*, no. iii (June 1847), p. 5.

5. Gulvin, C., *The Scottish Hosiery and Knitwear Industry 1680-1980* (Edinburgh, 1984), p. 16.

6. Brewster, D., *The Edinburgh Encyclopedia*, vol. x (Edinburgh, 1830), p. 662.

7. Gulvin, *Scottish Hosiery*, p. 20.

8. Chambers, R., *Picture of Scotland*, vol. i (Edinburgh, 1836), p. 95-6.

9. Elias, N., *The Civilising Process* (Oxford, 1978).

10. *Hawick Advertiser*, 2 May 1868, p. 3.

11. *Ibid*, 23 May 1857, p. 2.

12. Davidson, W., *History of Lanark* (Lanark, 1828), p. 83.

13. *Ibid*, p. 82.

14. Bruce, J., Duncan, W. and Robertson, J., *The Riding of the Landymyrs of the City of Aberdeen on the Seventh Day of September 1840* (Aberdeen, 1840), p. 7.

15. *Border Advertiser*, 11 June 1858, p. 3.

16. *Hawick Avertiser*, 7 June 1856, p. 3.

17. *Hawick Express*, 12 June 1875, p. 3.

18. *Hawick News*, 9 June 1883, p. 3.

19. *Hawick Advertiser*, 19 June 1858, p. 3.

20. *Hawick Express*, 10 June 1871, p. 3.

21. *Hawick Advertiser*, 19 June 1858, p. 3.

22. *Hawick Express*, 12 June 1875, p. 3.

23. *Ibid*, 10 June 1871, p. 3.

24. *Ibid*, 18 May 1872, p. 3.

25. *Ibid*, 11 May 1872, p. 3.

26. Hogg, J., 'A Journal Through the Highlands of Scotland, Continued', *The Scots Magazine* (December 1802), p. 961.

27. *Hawick Advertiser*, 19 June 1858, p. 3.

28. Hogg, *op. cit.*, p. 961.

29. *Hawick Advertiser*, 19 June 1858, p. 3.

30. *Border Advertiser*, 17 June 1859, p. 3.

31. Quoted in Scott, F., 'The Tradesman's Handicap 1884-1984', *Transactions of the Hawick Archaeological Society* [*THAS*] (1984), p. 12.

32. *Hawick Advertiser*, 7 July 1855, p. 3.

33. *Southern Reporter*, 5 July 1856, p. 5.

34. *Ibid*, 23 June 1859, p. 2.

35. *Hawick Advertiser*, 19 June 1858, p. 3.

36. Orwell, G., *The Road to Wigan Pier* (London, 1937; Harmondsworth, 1962), p. 79.

37. Smout, T.C., *A Century of the Scottish People 1830-1950* (London, 1986), p. 136.

38. Somerville, T., *My Own Life and Times 1741-1814* (Edinburgh, 1861), pp. 371-2.

39. *Ibid.*

40. Winning, J.G., 'The Common Riding Statistically: How Old Time Cornets Met Their Expenses', *THAS* (1919), pp. 4-7.

41. Quoted in Scott, 'Tradesman's Handicap', p. 13

42. *Hawick Express*, 12 June 1875, p. 3.

43. *Hawick Advertiser*, 22 June 1894, p. 4.

44. Paton, D.C., 'Drink and the Temperance Movement in Nineteenth Century Scotland' (Unpublished Ph.D thesis, University of Edinburgh, 1977), p. 44.

45. *Hawick Advertiser*, 9 June 1877, p. 3.

46. Hawick Records, 17 May 1817.

47. *Ibid*, 15 May 1833.

48. *Hawick Advertiser*, 12 May 1860, p. 3.

49. *Ibid*, 17 May 1862, p. 3.

50. *Ibid.*

51. Walter Laing was also the founder of the Hawick Working Men's Building Society, a director of the Hawick dairy, instigator of the local hospital and free library, and a champion of free trade and Gladstonian liberalism. The introduction of power looms in the hosiery trade led to the increasing employment of girls and unmarried women, who were cheaper to employ. See Gulvin, C., 'The Rise and Fall of Dicksons and Laings, Hosiery and Tweed Manufacturers 1802-1908', *THAS* (1975), pp. 29-40.

52. Edgar, J., *Hawick in the Early Sixties* (Hawick, 1913), p. 120.

53. *Hawick Express*, 6 May 1876, p. 3.

54. *Ibid*, 5 June 1875, p. 3.

55. *Southern Reporter*, 23 June 1859, p. 2.

56. *Ibid.*

57. *Hawick Express*, 6 June 1874, p. 3.

58. *Hawick Advertiser*, 12 June 1875, p. 3.

59. *Hawick Express*, 26 May 1893, p. 3.

60. *Ibid*, 4 June 1872, p. 3.

61. Edgar, J., *Hawick Common Riding* (Hawick, 1886), p. 12

62. *Hawick Advertiser*, 19 June 1858, p. 3.

63. *Ibid*, 14 June 1862, p. 3.

64. *Border Advertiser*, 16 June 1865, p. 3.

65. *Ibid*, 16 June 1848, p. 3.

66. *Ibid*. See also Edgar, J., 'Common Riding Finances 85 Years Ago: The Festival of 1846', *THAS* (1932), pp. 1-7.

67. *Ibid*, 23 June 1848, p. 3.

68. *Hawick Advertiser*, 13 June 1857, p. 3.

69. *Hawick Express*, 24 February 1877, p. 4.

70. *Hawick Advertiser*, 16 May 1857, p. 3.

71. *NSAS*, vol. iii, p. 399.

72. *Hawick Advertiser*, 13 June 1857, p. 3.

73. *Ibid*, 19 June 1858, p. 4.

74. Wilson, R., *The History of Hawick*, 2nd edition, (Hawick, 1841), p. 39.

75. *Hawick Advertiser*, 19 June 1858, p. 4

76. *Hawick Express*, 10 June 1876, p. 3.

77. Edgar, J., 'Hawick's Prominent Men in Victorian Times', *THAS* (1941), p. 13.

78. Beattie, D., *Lang Syne in Eskdale* (Carlisle, 1950), p. 143. In July 2003, the *Hawick News* reported that John Elliot was to retire from the position of Fair Cryer at Langholm Common Riding after thirty years service. His eldest son Iain was ready to take over the role. *Hawick News*, 11 July 2003, p. 3.

79. Mason, J., *The Border Tour* (Edinburgh, 1826), p. 163.

80. Wilson, *History of Hawick*, p. 181. *The Scotsman* commented on the publication of Wilson's *History* that: 'We have not seen so resolute and fearless a thinker start from the ranks of the Scottish peasantry since the time of Burns.' Quoted in *ibid*, p. 400.

81. This statistic compares the Old and New Statistical Accounts. See Harvie C., and Walker, G., 'Community and Culture', *People and Society in Scotland*, vol. 2: 1830-1914, eds Fraser, W.H. and Morris, R.J. (Edinburgh, 1990), p. 350.

82. *The Southern Counties Register and Directory* (Kelso, 1866), pp. 300-26.

83. Paton, 'Drink and Temperance', p. 390.

84. MacDougall, I. (ed.), *Labour in Scotland* (Edinburgh, 1985), p. 84. Wilson, A., *The Chartist Movement in Scotland* (Manchester, 1970), p. 127.

85. *Hawick Advertiser*, 13 June 1863, p. 3.

86. *Hawick News*, 16 June 1883, p. 4.

87. *Hawick Express*, 10 June 1876, p. 4.

88. *Ibid*, 24 February 1877, p. 4.

89. *Ibid*, 16 June 1877, p. 4.

90. *Ibid*, 2 June 1893, p. 3.

91. *Hawick Advertiser*, 7 June 1890, p. 2.

92. *Hawick News*, 15 June 1906, p. 4.

93. *Hawick Advertiser*, 4 May 1900, p. 6.

94. *Ibid*, 18 May 1900, p. 5.

95. *Ibid*.

96. *Ibid*, 21 June 1890, p. 3.

97. *Hawick Express*, 2 June 1893, p. 3.

98. *Hawick Advertiser*, 14 June 1895, p. 5.

Chapter Six

1. Hunter, J.Y., 'Follow the Flag!', *Hawick in Song and Poetry* (Hawick, 1945), p. 42.

2. Harold Perkin has written that between 1780 and 1850, England (and presumably Scotland) underwent a 'Moral Revolution' and 'ceased to be one of the most aggressive, brutal, rowdy, outspoken, riotous, cruel and bloodthirsty nations in the world and became one of the most inhibited, polite, orderly, tender-minded, prudish and hypocritical.' Perkin, H., *The Origins of Modern English Society 1780-1880* (London, 1969), p. 280.

3. *Official Guide to Lanark* (Cheltenham, 1910), p. 26.

4. *Hawick Express*, 14 June 1890, p. 2.

5. *Ibid*, 5 June 1891, p. 3.

6. *Ibid*.

7. Galbraith, J.K., *The World Economy Since the Wars* (London, 1994), p. 2.

8. Bruce, J., Duncan, W. and Robertson, J., *The Riding of the Landymyrs of the City of Aberdeen* (Aberdeen, 1840), p. 5.

9. *The Scotsman*, 9 June 1899, p. 5. 'The comic element, too, was not forgotten. A mounted troop of the Lanarkshire Yeomanry made a striking appearance as Lord Kitchener and the Khalifa and his followers. The representative of the hero of Omdurman was enthusiastically received and the followers of Mahdism, whose faces were blackened, and who wore black hose and the flowing robes of the Soudan, were subjected to much good-humoured banter.'

10. *Musselburgh Riding the Marches. Official Programme*, (Musselburgh, 1995), p. 14.

11. Kerr, W., *Peebles Beltane Festival Jubilee Book 1899-1949* (Peebles, 1949), p. 17.

12. *Hawick Express*, 8 May 1891, p. 3.

13. *Southern Reporter*, 16 May 1946, p. 7.

14. 'DOT', *The Riding of the Marches* (Aberdeen, 1889), pp. 13-14. This is a humorous skit on

the Aberdeen Riding, especially at the expense of the Aberdeen town council.

15. Keith, A., *A Thousand Years of Aberdeen* (Aberdeen, 1972), p. 431.

16. *Hawick News*, 18 June 1897, p. 2.

17. Conan Doyle's election candidature was not successful. *Memories and Adventures* (London, 1924), pp. 205-6. In the early 1960s, a young Parliamentary hopeful called David Steel, 'made a point of joining in these festivities, though I was far from an accomplished horseman. It was an easy, informal way of meeting people and the local press reported my completion of those longer rides.' David Steel was elected MP for Roxburgh, Selkirk and Peebles in a famous by-election win in March 1965. Steel, D., *Against Goliath* (London, 1989), p. 162.

18. *Hawick Monthly Advertiser*, 1 September 1855, p. 3.

19. *Hawick News*, 1 June 1906, p. 6.

20. *Hawick Express*, 12 June 1875, p. 3.

21. *Hawick Advertiser*, 24 June 1898, p. 5.

22. Lynch, M., *Scotland. A New History* (London, 1991), pp. 358-9.

23. *The Border Magazine*, vol. xix, no. 223 (July 1914), p. 145.

24. *Hawick Express*, 18 June 1897, p. 4.

25. *Ibid*, 5 June 1914, p. 4.

26. Girouard, M., *The Return to Camelot. Chivalry and the English Gentleman* (London and New Haven, 1981).

27. 'In 1834 John Mackay Wilson at the age of twenty-eight published the first of his *Tales of the Borders* in the *Berwick Advertiser*. He died within a year of the first weekly copy, but had the satisfaction of seeing the circulation rise from 2,000 to 16,000 – a phenomenal figure in those days. The *Tales* were then published in book form in 1840, edited by Alexander Leighton, and went into numerous editions, the last of which was published in the mid-1930s. They sold remarkably well all around the world.' Brander, M., *Tales of the Borders* (Edinburgh, 1991), p. 9.

28. *Selkirk and Flodden. Quater-Centenary of Flodden 1513-1913* (Selkirk, 1913), p. 4.

29. Quoted in Coltman, M.H., *Lest We Forget. Tom Scott RSA* (Hawick, 1991), p. 9.

30. Dyer, G., *The Missing of the Somme* (London, 1994), p. 18.

31. *Hawick Express*, 7 June 1901, p. 3.

32. Details of the Hawick Callants' Club are taken from Park, W., *The First Fifty Years of the Hawick Callants' Club. A Short History* (Hawick, 1954).

33. For information on Adam Laing, see *The Border Magazine*, vol. xxiv, no. 283 (July 1919), pp. 99-101; on Robert Craig, *In Borderland. Border and Other Verses*, 2nd edition (Hawick, 1922), introduction; and on Thomas Craig-Brown, *The Border Magazine*, vol. iv, no. 42 (July 1899), pp. 121-5.

34. Craig-Brown, *History of Selkirkshire*, vol. i, preface.

35. Russell, D., *Popular Music in England 1840-1914. A Social History* (Manchester, 1987), preface.

36. *Ibid*, p. 13.

37. *Ibid*, p. 1.

38. Thompson, F.M.L., *The Rise of Respectable Society. A Social History of Victorian Britain 1830-1900* (London, 1988), p. 194.

39. The Saxhorn Band was named after a valve instrument of the bugle type devised by Adolphe Sax, a Paris-based instrument-maker. For details of the Hawick Saxhorn Band, see Connelly, O., *Seven Score Years. Hawick Saxhorn Band 1855-1995* (Hawick, 1995).

40. Quoted in *Ibid*, p. 5.

41. *Ibid*, p. 9.

42. Checkland, S. and O., *Industry and Ethos. Scotland 1832-1914* (London, 1984), p. 184.

43. Bell, I., *Robert Louis Stevenson. Dreams of Exile* (Edinburgh, 1992), p. 14.

44. *The Border Magazine*, vol. iii, no. 29 (June 1898), p. 110.

45. *Hawick Monthly Advertiser*, 7 October 1854, p. 3.

46. *Hawick Express*, 2 July 1915, p. 4.

47. Neville, G.K., *The Mother Town* (New York, 1994), *passim*.

48. *Hawick Quater-Centenary Souvenir Programme* (Hawick, 1914), p. 54.

49. Turnbull, J., *Hawick in Olden Times* (Hawick, 1927), p. 18.

50. *Border Advertiser*, 15 June 1881, p. 3.

51. Edgar, J., *Hawick in the Early Sixties* (Hawick, 1913), p. 113.

52. Brown, J.L. and Lawson, I.C., *History of Peebles 1850-1990* (Edinburgh, 1990), pp. 269-70.

53. *Hawick News*, 12 June 1903, p. 3.

54. *Ibid*, 14 June 1901, p. 3.

55. *Hawick Advertiser*, 13 June 1863, p. 3.

56. Hobsbawm, E. and Ranger, T. (eds), *The Invention of Tradition* (Cambridge, 1984).

57. Hobsbawm, E., 'Mass-Producing Traditions: Europe 1870-1914', *Ibid*, p. 282.

58. *The Scotsman*, 23 June 1897, p. 11.

59. Frazer, J., *The Golden Bough*, abr. edition (London, 1959), pp. 632-6. In April 1901, the *Hawick News* reported that 'one hundred years ago' an annual 'boon-fyr' and Beltane fires had been burned on local hill-tops. Competition existed between people on opposing banks of the River Slitrig to build the largest bonfire. *Hawick News*, 19 April 1901, p. 3.

60. Quoted in Brown and Lawson, *History of Peebles*, p. 277.

61. 'R. W.' 'Lines Written on the Occasion of the Ancient Custom of Riding the Marches Being Revived to Celebrate the Diamond Jubilee of Queen Victoria'. Quoted in Kerr, *Peebles Beltane Festival*, p. 14.

62. These details are from Anderson, J.A., *The Cleikum. Being Interesting Reminiscences of Innerleithen* (Galashiels, 1933).

63. *Riding the Marches Official Programme. 5 July 1947*, (Annan, 1947), p. 7. *The Border Magazine*, vol. xviii, no. 215 (November 1913), p. 253.

64. *Hawick Express*, 12 June 1914, p. 4.

65. *Hawick Express*, 22 October 1915, p. 4.

66. *The Border Magazine*, vol. xxi, no. 244 (April 1916), p. 77.

67. *Hawick Express*, 15 March 1915, p. 3.

68. Later in the month, Peebles chose a Beltane Queen and organised children's sports, but did not elect a Cornet or stage a riding. Kerr, *Peebles Beltane Festival*, pp. 17-19.

69. *Hawick Express*, 25 June 1915, p. 4.

70. 'Song of Joy for the Selkirk Souters', *Ibid*, 4 June 1915, p. 4.

71. *Ibid*, 23 June 1916, p. 4.

72. *Ibid*, 10 May 1918, p. 3.

73. Craig, R.S., *In Borderland*, pp. 32-3.

74. Buchan, J., *The History of the Royal Scots Fusiliers 1678-1918* (London, 1925), p. 334.

75. For more details on Gallipoli, see Richardson, G., *For King and Country and Scottish Borders* (Galashiels, 1987). The commemorative service for 12 July 1915 became a significant annual event in the Borders. In the 1920s and 1930s, hundreds of First World War veterans attended the special service. The service survives under the auspices of the Hawick Callants' Club, who every year organise the placing of a wreath at the 1514 Memorial and also on the Hawick war memorial. Gradually, the service has become a more general commemoration of the First and Second World Wars.

76. *Hawick Express*, 10 January 1919, p. 4.

77. For details of the first Braw Lads' Gathering, see Brown, I. *et al.*, *Galashiels. A Modern History* (Galashiels, 1983), pp. 134-7.

78. *The Scotsman*, 30 June 1930, p. 9.

79. Morton, H.V., *In Search of Scotland* (London, 1929), p. 29.

80. *Southern Reporter*, 20 June 1946, p. 3.

81. *Hawick Express*, 5 June 1946, p. 5.

82. *Ibid*, 12 June 1946, p. 5

83. *Southern Reporter*, 16 May 1946, p. 3.

84. *Ibid*, 20 June 1946, p. 3.

85. *Ibid*.

86. *Edinburgh Evening News*, 8 June 1946, p. 5.

87. *Ibid*, 17 July 1947, p. 3.

88. Thomson, W.P.L., 'Riding the Marches of Kirkwall', *The Orcadian*, 17 July 1986, p. 6.

89. Hyslop, R., (ed.), *Echoes from the Border Hills* (Sunderland, 1912), p. 230.

90. *Ibid*, p. 231.

91. McNeill, F.M., *The Silver Bough Volume 4. The Local Festivals of Scotland* (Glasgow, 1968), p. 136.

92. Quoted in Bold, A., *MacDiarmid. Christopher Murray Grieve. A Critical Biography* (London, 1988), p. 429.

93. The story is also given in Bold A., (ed.), *The Thistle Rises. An Anthology of Poetry and Prose by Hugh MacDiarmid* (London, 1984), pp. 345-51.

94. *Ibid*, p. 346.

95. *Ibid*, p. 347.

96. *Ibid*, p. 348.

97. Bold, *MacDiarmid*, p. 435.

98. In his autobiography, MacDiarmid wrote: 'Another thing about Langholm. There is an annual Common-riding, and amongst the emblems that are carried in procession through the streets in the blue twilight of so long ago – in addition to the Crown of Roses – an eight-foot thistle and a barley bannock with a salt herring nailed to it, with a twelvepenny nail, and all the children carry heather besoms. In the same way I was always

determined that in whatever work I might do, the emblems of my nationality would figure second to none.' *Lucky Poet* (London, 1943), p. 222.

99. MacDiarmid, H., *Complete Poems*, vol. 1, eds Grieve, M. and Aitken, W.R. (Manchester, 1993), p. 97.

100. *Ibid*, vol. 2, p. 1429.

Final Canter

1. Landles, I.W., *Safeway* (Hawick, 1993).

2. Neville, G.K., *The Mother Town* (New York, 1994), p. 37.

3. McIntyre, I., 'The Flowers of the Forest', *The Listener*, vol. 84, no.2164 (1970), p.370.

Bibliography

Manuscript Sources

Hawick Town Hall
Hawick Records: Hawick Town Council Minute Books 1640-1968.

National Library of Scotland
Notebooks of Thomas Wilkie. Adv. Ms. 121-3.
Macfarlane, W. (ed.), 'Geographical Collections Relating to Scotland Containing a Particular Description of Shires, Parishes, Burroughs, etc.' Adv. Ms. 35.3.12.
Treasurer's Book of the Linlithgow Shoemakers 1825-1912. Ms. 19292-3.

Scottish Borders Council Library Service, St Mary's Mill, Selkirk
Scroll Book of Selkirk Common Riding 1907-1911. SC/S/12/6/1.

National Archives of Scotland
Linlithgow Court Books 1581-1809. B48/8/1-28.
Linlithgow Records: Linlithgow Town Council Minute Books 1620-1904. B48/9/1-23.
Linlithgow Treasurer's Vouchers 1563-1911. B48/14/1-170.
Peebles Minute Books: Peebles Town Council Minute Books 1604-1799. B58/13/1-8.
Accounts Books of the Souters of Selkirk 1788-1830. GD1/13/5.
Minute Book of the Incorporation of Selkirk 1717-1824. B68/8/1.

Printed Primary Sources

Chambers, W. and Renwick, R., (eds), *Peebles Records: Extracts from the Records of the Burgh of Peebles*, 2 vols, (Scottish Burgh Records Society, Edinburgh and Glasgow, 1872-1910).
Dickinson, W.C. (ed.), *Early Records of the Burgh of Aberdeen 1317, 1398-1407*, (Scottish History Society, Edinburgh, 1957).
Dundee Records: Charters, Writs and Public Documents of the Royal Burgh of Dundee 1292-1880 (Dundee, 1880).
Imrie, J., Rae, T.I. and Ritchie, W.D. (eds), *Selkirk Burgh Court Book: The Burgh Court Book of Selkirk 1503-45*, 2 vols, (Scottish Record Society, Edinburgh, 1960-9).
Marwick, J.D. (ed.), *Edinburgh Records: Extracts from the Records of the Burgh of Edinburgh*, 4 vols, (Scottish Burgh Records Society, Edinburgh, 1869-82).

Marwick, J.D. (ed.), *Glasgow Records: Extracts from the Records of Glasgow 1573-1642*, (Scottish Burgh Records Society, Glasgow, 1876).

Renwick, R. (ed.), *Lanark Records: Extracts from the Records of the Royal Burgh of Lanark 1150-1722*, (Scottish Burgh Records Society, Glasgow, 1893).

Renwick, R. (ed.), *Stirling Records: Extracts from the Records of the Royal Burgh of Stirling*, 2 vols, (Glasgow, 1887-9).

Stuart, J. (ed.), *Aberdeen Records: Extracts from the Council Register of the Burgh of Aberdeen*, 2 vols, (Spalding Club, Aberdeen, 1844-8).

Stuart, J. (ed.), *Extracts from the Council Registers of Aberdeen 1643-1747*, (Scottish Burgh Records Society, Edinburgh, 1872).

Newspapers and Magazines

Border Advertiser; *The Border Magazine*; *Border Telegraph*; *Hawick Advertiser*; *Hawick Express*; *Hawick News*; *The Herald and the Glasgow Herald*; *The Scots Magazine*; *The Scotsman*; *Southern Reporter*.

Local Studies

Aberdeen, *The Rydin' o' the Landimyres. 12 October 1851. By the Auldest Inhabitant* (Aberdeen, 1851).

Anderson, J.A., *The Cleikum. Being Interesting Reminiscences of Innerleithen* (Galashiels, 1933).

Annan, *Riding the Marches Official Programme. 5 July 1947* (Annan, 1947).

Bayard, J., *Selkirk After Flodden* (Selkirk, 1913).

Beattie, D.J., *Lang Syne in Eskdale* (Carlisle, 1950).

Brown, I. et al., *Galashiels. A Modern History* (Galashiels, 1983).

Brown, J.L. and Lawson, I.C., *History of Peebles 1850-1990* (Edinburgh, 1990).

Bruce, J., Duncan, W. and Robertson, J., *The Riding of the Landymyrs of the City of Aberdeen on the Seventh day of September 1840* (Aberdeen, 1840).

Craig, R.S. and Laing, A., *The Hawick Tradition of 1514: The Town's Common, Flag and Seal* (Hawick, 1898).

Craig-Brown, T., *The History of Selkirkshire or Chronicles of Ettrick Forest*, 2 vols (Edinburgh, 1886).

Davidson, W., *History of Lanark* (Lanark, 1828).

'DOT', *The Riding of the Marches* (Aberdeen, 1889).

Edgar, J., *Hawick in the Early Sixties* (Hawick, 1913).

Finlayson, J., *The Marches Day. A Dramatic Entertainment of Three Acts* (Edinburgh, 1771).

Gilbert, J.M. (ed.), *Flower of the Forest. Selkirk: A New History* (Galashiels, 1985).

Hendrie, W.F., *Linlithgow. Six Hundred Years of a Royal Burgh* (Edinburgh, 1989).

Hyslop, J. and R., *Langholm As It Was* (Langholm, 1902).

Hyslop, R., *Echoes From the Border Hills* (Sunderland, 1912).

Keith, A., *A Thousand Years of Aberdeen* (Aberdeen, 1982).

Kerr, W., *Peebles Beltane Festival Jubilee Book 1899-1949* (Peebles, 1949).

Linlithgow, *Linlithgow Marches* (Linlithgow, 1981).

Maxwell, A., *The History of Old Dundee* (Dundee and Edinburgh, 1884).

McDowall, W., *History of Dumfries* (Edinburgh, 1867).

Musselburgh Fair: The Grand Procession of Musselburgh Fair or Marches Riding: Delineated in a Poem by a Member of One of the Incorporations (Place of publication not given [Musselburgh?], 1766).

Paterson, J., *History of the Regality of Musselburgh* (Musselburgh, 1857).

Peebles March Riding and Beltane Queen Festival 1899-1974 (Peebles, 1974).

Reid, T., *Lanimer Day 1570 to 1913*, 2nd edition (Lanark, 1921).

Robertson, A.D., *Lanark. The Burgh and its Councils 1469-1880* (Lanark, 1974).

Robson, W.S., *The Story of Hawick*, 2nd edition (Hawick, 1947).

Scott, R.E., *Companion to Hawick and District*, rev. edition (Hawick, 1981).

Selkirk and Flodden. Quater-Centenary of Flodden 1513-1913 (Selkirk, 1913).

Thomson, A., *Lauder and Lauderdale* (Galashiels, 1903).

Ure, D., *The History of Rutherglen and East Kilbride* (Glasgow, 1793).

Waldie, G., *Linlithgow. A History of the Town and Palace*, 3rd edition (Linlithgow, 1879).

Wilkie, J., *Historic Musselburgh* (Edinburgh and London, 1919).

Wilson, J., *Hawick and Its Old Memories* (Edinburgh, 1858).

Wilson, R., *The History of Hawick*, 2nd edition (Hawick, 1841).

Wright, D. (ed.), *Peebles March Riding and Beltane Queen Festival Centenary 1899-1999* (Peebles, 1999).

General works

Adams, I.H., *The Making of Urban Scotland* (London, 1978).

Barclay, H.B., *The Role of the Horse in Man's Culture* (London and New York, 1980).

Barr, N., *Flodden 1513. The Scottish Invasion of Henry VIII's England* (Stroud, 2001).

Bennett, M., *Scottish Customs from Cradle to Grave* (Edinburgh, 1992).

Billington, S., *Mock Kings in Medieval Society and Renaissance Drama* (Oxford, 1991).

Brand, J., *Observations on Popular Antiquities. Chiefly Illustrating the Origin of Our Vulgar Customs, Ceremonies and Superstitions*, 2 vols, 2nd edition, rev. Ellis, H. (London, 1813).

Burke, P., *Popular Culture in Early Modern Europe* (London, 1979).

Bushaway, B.W., *By Rite. Custom, Ceremony and Community in England 1700-1880* (London, 1982).

Cameron, D.K., *The English Fair* (Stroud, 1998).

Chase, M. and Shaw, C. *The Imagined Past. History and Nostalgia* (Manchester, 1989).

Cohen, A.P., *The Symbolic Construction of Community* (Chichester and London, 1985).

Colley, B.L., *Britons. Forging the Nation 1707-1837* (London, 1992).

Cunningham, H., *Leisure in the Industrial Revolution 1780-1880* (London, 1980).

Dallas, D., *The Travelling People* (London, 1991).

Edwards, E.H., *Horses. Their Role in the History of Man* (London, 1987).

Elias, N., *The Civilising Process* (Oxford, 1978).

Elliot, F.W., *The Battle of Flodden Field and the Raids of 1513* (Edinburgh, 1911).

Ewan, E., *Townlife in Fourteenth-Century Scotland* (Edinburgh, 1990).

Fairfax-Blakeborough, J., *Northern Turf History*, 4 vols (London, 1973).

Girouard, M., *The Return to Camelot. Chivalry and the English Gentleman* (London, 1981).

Gulvin, C., *The Scottish Hosiery and Knitwear Industry 1680-1980* (Edinburgh, 1984).

Guthrie, D.J., *Old Scottish Customs. Local and General* (London, 1885).

Henderson, W., *Notes on the Folklore of the Northern Counties of England and the Borders* (London, 1866).

Hobsbawm, E.J. and Ranger, T. (eds), *The Invention of Tradition* (Cambridge, 1984).

Holt, J.C., *Robin Hood* (London, 1982).

Holt, R., *Sport and the British. A Modern History* (Oxford, 1989).

Hutton, R., *The Stations of the Sun. A History of the Ritual Year in Britain* (Oxford, 1996).

Knightly, C., *The Customs and Ceremonies of Britain. An Encyclopedia of Living Traditions* (London, 1981).

Lynch, M., Spearman, M. and Stell, G. (eds), *The Scottish Medieval Town* (Edinburgh, 1988).

Malcolmson, R.W., *Popular Recreations in English Society 1700-1850* (Cambridge, 1979).

Mason, J., *The Border Tour* (Edinburgh, 1826).

McNeil, F.M., *The Silver Bough*, 4 vols (Glasgow, 1956-68).

Mill, A.J., *Medieval Plays in Scotland* (Edinburgh, 1927).

Neville, G.K., *The Mother Town* (New York, 1994).

NSAS: New Statistical Account of Scotland, 15 vols (Edinburgh and London, 1845).

Ormand, D. (ed.), *The Borders Book* (Edinburgh, 1995).

Russell, D., *Popular Music in England 1840-1914. A Social History* (Manchester, 1987).

Sinclair, J. (ed.), *OSAS: The Statistical Account of Scotland*, 21 vols, (London, 1791-9).

Storch, R.D. (ed.), *Popular Culture and Custom in Nineteenth-Century England* (London, 1981).

Thompson, F.M.L., *The Rise of Respectable Society. A Social History of Victorian Britain 1830-1900* (London, 1988).

TSAS: Third Statistical Account of Scotland, 31 Vols (Edinburgh, 1951-92).

Vamplew, W., *The Turf. A Social and Economic History of Horse Racing* (London, 1976).

Articles and Book Chapters

Borsay, P., '"All the Town's a Stage": Urban Ritual and Ceremony 1660-1800', *The Transformation of English Provincial Towns 1600-1800*, ed. Clarke, P. (London, 1984), pp. 228-58.

Bryce, W.M., 'The Burgh Muir of Edinburgh', *Book of the Old Edinburgh Club*, vol. x (1918), pp. 2-278.

Bushaway, R.W., 'Grovely, Grovely and all Grovely. Custom, Crime and Conflict in the English Woodland', *History Today*, vol. xxxi (May 1981), pp. 37-43.

Cannadine, D., 'The Transformation of Civic Ritual in Modern Britain: the Colchester Oyster Festival', *Past and Present*, no. 94 (1982), pp. 107-130.

Cowan, E.J., 'From the Southern Uplands to Southern Ontario: Nineteenth-Century 'Emigration from the Scottish Borders', *Scottish Emigration and Scottish Society*, Devine, T.M. (ed.), (Edinburgh, 1992), pp. 61-83.

Cunningham, H., 'The Metropolitan Fairs: A Case Study in the Social Control of Leisure', *Social Control in Nineteenth-Century Britain*, Donajgrodizki, A.P. (ed.), (London, 1977), pp. 163-84.

Davies, N.Z., 'The Reasons of Misrule: Youth Groups and Charivaris in Sixteenth-Century France', *Past and Present*, no. 50 (1971), pp. 41-78.

Flodden: 'A Contemporary Account of the Battle of Flodden' ['Trewe Encounter'], *Proceedings of the Society of Antiquaries of Scotland*, vii (1866-7), pp. 141-52.

James, M., 'Ritual, Drama and Social Body in the Later Medieval English Town', *Past and Present*, no. 98 (1983), pp. 3-29.

Lamond, R., 'The Scottish Craft Guild as a Religious Fraternity', *Scottish Historical Review*, vol. 16 (1919), pp. 191-211.

Mackie, I.D., 'The English Army at Flodden', *Miscellany of the Scottish History Society*, vol. viii (Edinburgh, 1951), pp. 33-85.

Phythian-Adams, C., 'Ceremony and the Citizen: The Communal Year at Coventry 1450-1550', *Crisis and Order in English Towns 1500-1700*, Clark, P. and Slack, P. (eds), (London, 1972), pp. 57-85.

Reid, D., 'The Decline of St Monday 1766-1876', *Past and Present*, no. 71 (1976), pp. 76-101.

Woolf, D.R., '"The Common Voice": History, Folklore and Oral Tradition in Early Modern England', *Past and Present*, no. 20 (1988), pp. 26-52.

Unpublished Theses and Dissertations

Bottomley, R.P., 'The Battle of Flodden 1513', M.A. thesis, University of Keele, 1988.

Cardew, A., 'A Study of Society in the Anglo-Scottish Borders 1455-1502', Ph.D thesis, University of St Andrews, 1974.

Park, H., '"There is no one quite like us": History, Identity and Ritual in Siena', Ph.D thesis, University of Cambridge, 1990.

Paton, D.C., 'Drink and the Temperence Movement in Nineteenth-Century Scotland', Ph.D thesis, University of Edinburgh, 1977.

Sexton, R.D., 'Travelling People in Britain', Ph.D thesis, University of Southampton, 1989.

Symms, P., 'Social Control in a Sixteenth Century Burgh: A Study of the Burgh Court Book of Selkirk 1503-1545', Ph.D thesis, University of Edinburgh, 1986.

Index

Figures in bold indicate illustrations

If you are interested in purchasing
other books published by Tempus, or in case you have
difficulty finding any Tempus books in your local bookshop,
you can also place orders directly through our website

www.tempus-publishing.com